0149314

065813

55

a AVK
Jil)

This book is due for return on or before the last date shown below.

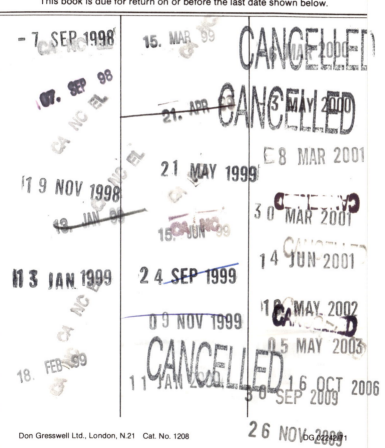

- 7 SEP 1998   15. MAR 99   CANCELLED

07. SEP 98   21. APR   CANCELLED 3 MAY 2000

19 NOV 1998   21 MAY 1999   E 8 MAR 2001

13 JAN 1999   15. JUN 99   3 0 MAR 2001

                 2 4 SEP 1999   14 JUN 2001

                 0 9 NOV 1999   18 MAY 2002

18. FEB 99   CANCELLED   05 MAY 2003

                 11 JAN   CANCELLED 16 OCT 2006
                             3 0 SEP 2009

26 NOV 2009

1863734864

Other books by this author

The sociological quest: *an introduction to the study of social life* (1993)

Medical dominance: *the division of labour in Australian health care* (1983, revised edition 1989)

Technology and the labour process: *Australasian case studies* (1988)

ILLNESS AND SOCIAL RELATIONS

Issues in the Sociology of Health Care

Evan Willis

ALLEN & UNWIN

For Johanna

First published 1994
Allen & Unwin Pty Ltd
9 Atchison Street, St Leonards, NSW 2065 Australia

National Library of Australia
Cataloguing-in-Publication entry:

Willis, Evan, 1952– .
   Illness and social relations.

   Bibliography.
   Includes index.
   ISBN 1 86373 486 4.

   1. Medical technology—Social aspects. I. Title.

306.461

Set in 10/11pt Times by DOCUPRO, Sydney
Printed by Chong Moh Offset Printing, Singapore

Contents

Preface   vi

1 Introduction   1

Part 1: THE HEALTH WORKFORCE

2 Who does what to whom?: The social structure of health
  care delivery   9
3 Sister Elizabeth Kenny and the evolution
  of the occupational division of labour in health care   26
4 Medical dominance and the politics of nursing skills   44
5 Complementary healers   54

Part 2: TECHNOLOGY AND HEALTH CARE

6 Technological innovation and the labour process
  in health care   77
7 The social relations of medical technology:
  the case of echocardiography   96
8 The changing social relations of condom
  technology in the AIDS era   114

Part 3: ILL HEALTH AS SOCIAL PROCESS

9 RSI as a social process   133
10 The industrial relations of occupational health and safety:
   a labour process approach   151
11 Hierarchies, bureaucracies and professions:
   the Medicare review (part 2)   169

Appendix   189
Bibliography   191
Index   203

Preface

This book brings together essays I have written, either alone or jointly, over the previous decade or so, in the field of the sociology of health and illness. Some minor editorial adjustments have been made to the individual chapters to avoid too much repetition, modify the expression or to enhance the clarity of the original essays. At the end of each chapter a postscript has been appended to reflect on developments in that area since the original essay was published.

No intellectual endeavour takes place in isolation and I have been privileged to benefit from the collegiality of a number of people. Johanna Wyn is foremost amongst these. To my colleagues from the Health Sociology Research Group at La Trobe University, in particular Jeanne Daly and Allan Kellehear, I owe ongoing gratitude. The ideas contained in this book have also been formed, developed and modified through contact with a variety of colleagues in the wider academic community. Locally these include Neville Hicks, Glenda Koutroulis, Jake Najman, Ian McDonald, Michael Quinlan, Eveleen Richards, Bryan Turner, and Kevin White. Internationally they include David Coburn, Ian Coulter, Karl Figlio, Eliot Freidson (whom I have never had the benefit of meeting), Jerry Larkin, John McKinlay, and David Silverman.

The chapters of this book are reproduced with appropriate permission kindly given by original publishers as follows. Chapter 1 was written for this volume. Chapter 2 was originally published in A. Kellehear et al. *Sociology of Health Care*, Deakin University teaching materials, 1989. Chapter 3 appeared in *The Australian and*

New Zealand Journal of Sociology, vol. 15, no. 3, pp. 30–9, 1979. Chapter 4 appeared in L. Pittman (ed.) *Shaping Nursing Theory and Practice*, La Trobe University, 1988, Nursing monograph no. 1, pp. 68–78. Chapter 5 appeared in J. Najman and G. Lupton (eds) *The Sociology of Health and Illness*, 1989, pp. 259–79, and is reprinted with permission of the publishers, Macmillan. Chapter 6, written with Jeanne Daly, appeared in *Social Science and Medicine*, 1989, vol. 28, no. 11, pp. 1149–583. Chapter 7, written with Jeanne Daly and Ian McDonald, appeared in M. McNeil, I. Varcoe and S. Yearly (eds) *Deciphering Science and Technology*, 1990, pp. 227–46 and is reprinted with permission of the publisher, Macmillan. Chapter 8 is previously unpublished. Two chapters originally appeared in *Community Health Studies*, and are reproduced with permission of the editor. Chapter 9 on RSI appeared in 1986, in vol. 10, no. 2, pp. 210–19; and chapter 11 on the Medicare inquiry appeared in 1990, in vol. 16, no. 2, pp. 97–107. Chapter 10 appeared in *Labour and Industry*, 1989, vol. 2, no. 2, pp. 317–33 and is reprinted with permission of the editor.

1 Introduction

She stood in front of the full length mirror, viewing her six-year-old body, after the bath. 'Dad,' she said, frowning, 'I'm going to have to go on a diet, I'm too fat!'

It had been a long and tiring afternoon in the spinal injuries ward. The patient was tense, angry and frustrated in coming to terms with his recently acquired quadriplegia. The doctor, who had patiently tolerated the angst being directed at the world in general but him in particular, finally cracked and snapped. 'Look mate,' he said in exasperation, 'to me you're just a head on a pillow.' The patient fell silent.

At its most basic, sociology is concerned with the relationship between the individual and society. As a disciplined approach to the study of social life, it seeks to elucidate the relationship between individuals and the social groups of which they form a part. The field of the sociology of health and illness seeks to do that in relation to the inescapable inevitability of morbidity and ultimately mortality of individuals that comprise a society. The classic representation of this study in sociology generally is that of C. Wright Mills (1959) who characterises it as the study of the relationship between personal troubles and public issues; to understand the experience of individuals in their social context. It is to study the relationship between individual biography and social history; to relate personal troubles— two of which are represented anecdotally above—concerned with individuals and their bodies, to the social organisation of the society as a whole.

1

To exercise a sociological imagination involves asking: 'What is it about the way our society is organised that leads to this or that phenomenon?'. What is it about the way our society is organised for instance, that can lead six-year-olds to feel the effects of social pressure to conform to some culturally accepted body shape; the consequences of which for some may be pathological in the form of eating disorders such as self-starvation?

In the field of sociology that has previously been known as medical sociology but is now more commonly known as the sociology of health and illness, the focus is upon how the phenomenon which we have come to call illness, and its corollary health, mediate the relationship between the individual and society. This specialism of the discipline of sociology therefore involves particular consideration of a basic relationship: that of the relationship between the physical and biological world ('nature') on one hand and the social world on the other ('culture'). Traditionally, health and illness have been viewed primarily from a biomedical perspective as biophysiological processes, perhaps with some social elements. The aim of a sociological account by contrast, is to articulate the complex manner in which these phenomena are constituted much more as social processes albeit with biophysiological foundations. It is often assumed that many of the objects of study in this field derive mostly from 'nature'. On closer examination however using sociological and other methodologies, social and cultural arrangements turn out to be as, if not more, important.

The threat and the actuality of physical impairment of various sorts acts as a powerful means by which the relationship between the individual and society is mediated in the sense of being modified, structured, and influenced. Mediation implies the social process of negotiation; much of this negotiation is over the relationship between the social and the biomedical world. Indeed the study of how this occurs is the basic contribution of this field of sociology to the parent discipline in general.

Such an insight formed the basis of the (lasting) contribution of Talcott Parsons (see Parsons, 1964, 1968), the sociologist usually credited with having been responsible for opening up this field of sociological study. Parsons' basic insight was that ill health could be understood as a social process as much as a biological one, and could be analysed as a form of deviance which constituted a threat to the social order of a society. The societal response that developed was the health system, which sought to contain that threat. Although much modified and developed in a variety of directions, the wisdom of that basic insight remains and continues to unify the sociological study of health and illness.

Without accepting the theoretical and ideological baggage that

Parsonian structural functionalism brings, the view originating from Parsons that illness is a form of conditionally legitimated release from role expectations is an important one. In this manner, illness, and the threat of it mediates social relations in all spheres of life. Take the example of AIDS; the threat to the health of every person in society is (slowly) changing the accepted expression of intimacy, in particular the way in which sexual relationships are established and conducted. Many of our social relationships are conducted in the context of unequal power to influence social outcomes; from decisions about whether or not to use a condom at the private level, to organisation of employment relationships in the work sphere. Ill health and its threat, mediates the expression of power in these relationships.

Illness mediates social relations in all areas of society; the essays contained in this book aim to spell out how that occurs. In many respects they collectively represent the working out of the intellectual agenda set by the study conducted for my doctoral dissertation subsequently published as the book *Medical Dominance*, (rev. edn 1989a). In spite of two editions and a couple of reprintings, the program of specifying how, under what circumstances and with what effects the social structure of health care delivery operates has been a considerable one and much still remains to be done. My original interest in this field emerged from a concern with the sociology of occupations and professions, and later the sociology of work and technology. I started out in the vein of the Frankfurt school, in particular Habermas, being interested in the role of technology in social life. The medical arena is a particularly interesting field in which to examine those processes, particularly in articulating the relationship between nature and culture. Later as the work of Michel Foucault became known in the English language, this became more focused on the power–knowledge relationship, particularly around the use of the instruments of congealed knowledge in the form of technology.

Much of the work is opposing what has come to be known as technological determinism in the health field, and which operates as a convenient ideology for legitimating the social structure of health care delivery. Such an approach I argue, and several papers in this volume attempt to argue in detail, divorces the actual material component of the technology from its social relations. At its most basic, I argue, it sets the boundary between nature and culture too much on the nature side. Conventional explanations for the shape of the health system rely too much on explanations concerning medical knowledge and medical technology as independent of social processes.

The essays chosen for this book reflect an explicit concern with a sociological sense of problem. A number of them were written specifically for teaching purposes; that is, to attempt to explain to students relatively inexperienced in their study of the discipline what sociological analyses could offer to an understanding of health and illness. As a result most are not highly theoretical in approach; the theoretical frameworks largely underlie the analysis being made. I have generally attempted to write at a level between that of the abstracted empiricism which regrettably remains common (and unfortunately now appears in qualitative as well as quantitative guise), and highly theoretical accounts divorced from the practical problems of service provision etc. Attempting to write in the level between, I have generally had in mind a more general social medicine/public health audience than a solely sociological one. As a result, on the policy level I have frequently concentrated on the question, central to a sociological imagination, 'How could it be otherwise?'.

A criticism sometimes levelled at the sociological specialty of the study of health and illness, and potentially at this book of essays as well, is that of theoretical impoverishment in sociological terms and a failure to relate findings to the broader concerns of sociology, mainly because of the practical rather than sociological concerns which had traditionally informed such research. As a result, the sociology of health and illness is sometimes seen as having contributed little to the discipline as a whole. This issue is an important one to explore as I have done elsewhere in more detail (Willis, 1982, 1990).

Certainly, the sociological study of health and illness has traditionally been one of the most practical and applied fields of sociology, frequently taking its sense of research problem directly from the practical concerns of the pain and suffering which is the human condition. As a result, researchers in this field have more frequently addressed themselves to practical problems rather than to explicitly theoretical issues. At the same time though, there is awareness of the central issues of the discipline and central traditions of sociological theory. As a result (as Turner (1987) has shown for instance), the sociology of health and illness should be considered a mainstream part of the discipline as a whole. Recent theoretical developments in the discipline of sociology as a whole are being utilised in the health field. Social constructionism in general and the work of Michel Foucault in particular has made a significant impact on this area of study as the long-term significance of his work both to this field and to sociology in general, is debated. Health is a major theme developed in his work and is used to illustrate his theories of the relationship between power and knowledge. His view of ill health, not as a biological reality but as a social and cultural construction is being actively debated; particularly as it is the conceptual approach most removed from the medical (and indeed commonsense) worldview. Health is a substantive terrain on which this debate is being pursued as the question is resolved of whether this approach will be a passing phenomenon or become an integral part of social science analysis. The emerging field of the sociology of the body is another example of this debate.

The invoking of a sociological imagination, I have argued elsewhere (Willis, 1993) involves paying attention to four crucial sensitivities or elements in analysis: historical, cultural, structural and critical. To invoke a critical sensitivity involves the search for alternative futures. Asking, 'How could it be otherwise?' carries with it an implied critique of the existing social order. In the health arena, the central sociological feature of health service provision is of course medical dominance; a shorthand concept for a long historical process of creating and defending the pre-eminent position of the medical profession in all things to do with health and illness. When sociologists of health and illness, invoking the sociological imagination, turn their collective gaze to the social order of health care provision, the charge of 'doctor-bashing' frequently rings out. This has certainly been a charge that I have worn on many occasions, although in fact, as one or two commentators have noted, the *Medical Dominance* project can be read as a history of how the doctors won!

In the sense that sociology is concerned with reflexively studying and critiquing the existing social order, this charge is probably an inevitable one and contributes to the somewhat controversial character of the discipline in general. Yet there is much more to it than that. Part of the exercising of the social imagination is a structural sensibility; to seek to understand the activities of individuals in the wider social context of the social structure of society. If one reflects on the quadriplegia anecdote at the beginning of this introduction and applies a structural sensitivity, the sense of outrage that the doctor's response probably generates on first being told this incident is not the whole story. A structural component would analyse both the way in which much of the patient's understandable anger and frustration is focused on the doctor, and the goaded doctor's understandable though still inappropriate response.

To analyse what occurs in the health system only in terms of interaction between patients and practitioners in other words, does not go far enough. In McKinlay's (1977) terms it gives only a locker-room view of the medical game. Also important is the wider structural context involving consideration of other levels of analysis in the wider context of society as a whole, especially economic interests and the democratic capitalist State. To return to the original

Parsonian insights, the corollary of understanding illness as deviance, is to analyse medicine as an institution of social control, and doctors as agents in this process. Medicine has always been important in social control in societies; the consequence of modernism has been to separate the social control institutions of medicine and the law whereas previously and in tribal societies the two had been fused in the institution of the medicine man. Asking the, 'How could it be otherwise?' question involves considering the question of whether that social control is benign or repressive. The answer has to be that it varies, sometimes more benign, sometimes repressive. Doctors are agents of social control ultimately on behalf of the State[1] and this State patronage for the medical profession has had many advantages. But it also often places doctors in difficult positions. 'Does this patient have RSI?', for instance. If the doctor is examining the patient on behalf of an employer or insurance company, the outcome may well be different than if the patient is attending their local general practitioner. The decision taken will have the effect of setting in train a series of complex social consequences involving the mediation of social relations by illness.

This book of essays is set out in several parts. The first deals with the health workforce. Chapter 2 analyses the social structure of health care delivery in general but focuses especially on the division of labour surrounding the taking of X-rays. The next two chapters deal with the place of nursing in this social structure; chapter 3 with an important historical 'moment' in the subordination of nurses and chapter 4 on the issue of nursing skill in general terms. Chapter 5 analyses the role of complementary or alternative healers in the Australian health system.

The second part analyses the social relations of medical technology, attempting to set out a sociological framework for analysing different sorts of medical technologies; in general in chapter 6, the 'high-tech' example of echocardiography in chapter 7 and the 'low-tech' example of condoms in chapter 8.

The third part focuses on the broader concerns of ill health as social process. Chapter 9 analyses the occupational health and safety condition known as RSI, while chapter 10 considers the industrial relations of occupational health and safety more broadly. The final chapter is a health policy analysis of an inquiry into Medicare which reviewed the existing social structure of health care delivery.

Part 1
THE HEALTH WORKFORCE

2   Who does what to whom?: The social structure of health care delivery

Sooner or later all of us have some symptoms of ill health which must be responded to. In turning to that part of our society that is called the health industry we are likely to come in contact with people from a whole lot of different occupations. About six per cent of Australians in paid work receive their livelihoods from dealing with the human sickness which is our lot. That's some 450 000 people, organised into a vast array of different occupations, some 105 in all according the most recent *Handbook on Health Manpower* produced by the Commonwealth Department of Community Services and Health (1980). These occupations relate together not in a haphazard way, but in a complex structured fashion known as the *division of labour.*

The aim of this chapter is to analyse that division of labour from a sociological point of view by considering the following questions:

- On what basis is it organised? (*Organisation*)
- How did it get to be like that? (*Evolution*)
- How is it justified? (*Legitimation*)

In outlining and discussing these questions, I will spell out these broad themes that I have been writing about for some years and which are contained in my book *Medical Dominance: The Division of Labour in Australian Health Care*, (rev. ed, 1989a).

THE SOCIOLOGICAL DEBATE

First, however, it is necessary to consider how the subject of this essay relates to some general sociological issues, in particular to an important theoretical debate. The division of labour is one of the central concepts of the discipline of sociology. In its most general sense it refers to the social organisation of tasks and can take a number of forms: sexual; ethnic; international; or, as primarily used here, *occupational* division of labour.

The increasingly complex division of labour has been observed to be a particular feature of the general process of modernity since the earliest days of sociology. For both Emile Durkheim and Karl Marx for instance, increasing division of labour was a feature of the development of society. They differed sharply though in their assessment of it. Durkheim (1947) saw it as a positive moral phenomenon in promoting interdependence and helping to regulate and integrate societies undergoing the process of modernisation. In particular it helped to prevent the onset of *anomie* (the breakdown of behavioural expectations or norms that serve to regulate social interaction) which he was concerned would be a consequence of the process of modernity.

Marx (1963) however (writing in the nineteenth century) saw increasing division of labour as a more negative economic phenomenon and responsible for *alienation* under modern capitalist societies—perhaps epitomised by car assembly work requiring the performance of a small mundane task over and over. Alienation was a concept used by Marx to analyse the effect upon individuals of working in a society characterised by capitalism. The difference between Marx's and Durkheim's approaches revolves around whether there was a relationship between an increasing division of labour and the emergence of a stratified class system in a particular society. Marx saw a close link; specialisation and increasing division of labour could only be understood in the context of the emergence of an increasingly polarised class system in capitalist societies. Whereas for Durkheim, increasing division of labour was not related to class but instead to a more general process of modernisation.

For our purposes here, a distinction is necessary between what will be called the *technical* division of labour and the *social* division of labour. The former refers to the division of labour that exists in the workplace itself, in this case by occupation within health settings. So there is a technical division of labour between, for instance, obstetricians and midwives in childbirth. The midwife makes observations of the condition of the mother and baby (pulse, blood pressure etc.), while the doctor arrives usually when the actual delivery is imminent.

The social division of labour by contrast refers to the wider society; that is, to the usual sources of social variation that sociologists deal with all the time. Class, gender, ethnicity, and age are the most important ones. The sexual division of labour is a part of this more broad social division of labour. In the case of the division of labour surrounding childbirth for instance, the doctor is usually male while the midwife is almost always female.

When dealing with the issue of how the work of healing as a whole is organised (that is, the labour process in health care), we need to consider the relationship between the technical and social division of labour. In other words the labour process in health care is carried out by a wide array of health workers belonging to a wide range of occupations each performing a specialised range of tasks which together make up the labour process.

In considering who does what and to whom as part of this labour process, the empirical question is: 'Is this pattern of work tasks more the result of the technical than the social division of labour?'. Later this question will be considered in some detail in relation to the taking of X-rays.

ORGANISATION: UNDERSTANDING THE PHENOMENON

Before discussing the division of labour in health care in general, there are a couple of things to bear in mind. Firstly, it should be remembered that what is being discussed here is mainly the *formal* division of labour; that is, what goes on within hospitals, community health centres, doctors' surgeries and the like. Also important in terms of health services is the *informal* division of labour, pertaining to those health services provided outside the formal health care industry. It is probably true to say that most health services in this country of this informal type are provided in the home, overwhelmingly by women—giving medications, applying sticking plasters and administering TLC 'to make it better' as part of the general domestic labour.

Secondly, drawing on the insights from the theoretical tradition of interactionism originating with the work of Max Weber, it is also necessary to make the distinction between the division of labour as a *negotiated* or *imposed* phenomenon. What the rules (imposed) say about 'who shall do what to whom under what circumstances' is all very well in a big teaching hospital in metropolitan Melbourne, but in Bourke hospital, in the middle of the night, or in an emergency, these rules will frequently be modified to cope with the situation on hand (that is, negotiated). It is often reported by nurses who have worked in 'the bush' and then returned to the metropolitan area that they are 'not allowed' to do a number of things in the city that they were used to doing—suturing or putting in intravenous lines being examples. Having said all that, the focus in the rest of this chapter will be upon the division of labour in health care in the formal, imposed sense. The two are obviously related however. Over time, negotiation may lead to a task being more formally incorporated into the work domain of that occupation. What at first may be done only in an emergency, during times of staff shortage or in the middle of the night, may eventually come to be a routine part of the task domain.

Thirdly, it should be noted that the division of labour has evolved in the health industry somewhat differently than in the manufacturing workforce. Elsewhere a major feature of the development of the workforce has been the process of mechanisation, the substitution of capital for labour as jobs have become less labour intensive and more capital intensive. In the health area, however, this has only rarely occurred. There may be a few areas where technological innovation has reduced the demand for labour, but for the most part, health care has become both more labour intensive and more capital intensive. To take as an example the invention and innovation of X-ray machines into the health arena late last and early this century, this technological innovation led to the formation of two new occupations which had not previously existed (medically qualified radiologists and also radiographers) without any labour being displaced.

Hierarchy and dominance

The division of labour in health care has two major features: its hierarchical nature; and its dominance by one occupation, the medical profession. Occupations are organised into an hierarchical structure entailing huge disparities in power, status and ultimately rewards for their labours. This can be referred to as the social structure of health care. At the apex of this structure stands the medical profession which dominates the division of labour in this field of human endeavour in a fashion unparalleled in other areas of the workforce. This phenomenon has come to be known as medical dominance and is the key feature of the delivery of health services in Australia and most other countries.

Medical dominance over the health division of labour is sustained at three related levels. *Autonomy* is the first; that is, at the level of doctors' own work. The medical profession is not subject to the direction and control of any other occupation, they have self-direction of their work. *Authority* is the second level: doctors have the authority to direct the work of almost all other health occupations. This authority can either be direct, through supervising the work of others, such as nurses; or it can be indirect through doctors' involvement in the supervising organisations of other health occupations. The third level is called *medical sovereignty*: doctors are the institutionalised experts on all matters relating to health in the wider society. Whenever an opinion is called for in the media or elsewhere on a health matter, it is invariably doctors who are called upon to give it. Medical dominance is thus the term used to describe the division of labour in health care as it exists today. Health occupations work in a complex hierarchical social structure, dominated by the medical profession.

EVOLUTION: HOW DID IT GET TO BE LIKE THIS?

To describe the social structure of health care as characterised by medical dominance is of course a shorthand way of referring to a long historical process by which this division of labour has evolved. What we have now is the outcome or end point of an historical process. To describe it as medical dominance does not mean that it has always been like this, or that it always will be. In order to understand how health care is delivered it is salutory to analyse how it got to be like this. In other words, it is necessary to consider the historical process by which medical dominance emerged (how it was produced) and also how it is being defended against encroachment (reproduced).

What has happened over time is that the health workforce has gradually become more numerous but also more specialised into more and more occupations. In the 1871 Australian census for instance, doctors constituted 33 per cent of the total health workforce, whereas by the 1986 census they constituted only about 12 per cent. The census of 1911 officially recognised only 13 categories of health worker; by the 1933 census, 33 were recognised; as mentioned previously, by 1981, 105 were officially recognised. While the *number* of doctors has been steadily increasing, they have been decreasing as a *proportion* of the health workforce as the number of different health occupations has been increasing. Doctors, in other words, have managed to stay on top of the pile as the size of the pile has grown enormously beneath them.

The actual process of specialisation and differentiation by which the division of labour has evolved, is two-fold: horizontal and vertical. *Horizontal* specialisation occurs within an occupation, that is to say *intra-occupational* division of labour. The medical profession is a good example: horizontal specialisation within medicine is the result of two complementary processes. One is *segmentation* where over time there is an increasing refinement of specialties. ENT specialists (that is, doctors specialising in diseases of the ear, nose and throat) emerged from a previous specialty of eye, ear, nose and throat. Within the specialty of diseases of the eye, now called ophthalmology, there is further specialty into diseases of only the retina, etc. The other way horizontal specialisation occurs is by *accretion*, where previously parts of other specialties combine to form a new specialty. An example is paediatrics which emerged from those general practitioners interested in the diseases of children, combining with specialist physicians also interested in children's diseases (see Rosen, 1944).

Of greater importance to the overall shape of the division of labour however is *vertical* specialisation, that is the *inter-occupational* division of labour. This process operates by means of the phenomenon of 'pass-the-task'. All occupations have as part of their work some aspects that are the more mundane, more routine and less challenging. Over time there has been a tendency in those occupations that are able to do so, to pass off those tasks to lower-order occupations, often specially created for that purpose. This process has been important to the way in which the division of labour has evolved in the health arena. It has happened at two levels. Firstly, doctors have passed off to nurses (RNs) many of the more mundane aspects of medical practice, while nurses have in turn passed off some of their less demanding and less satisfying tasks to SENs (State-enrolled nurses). Take the measurement of blood pressure (with a sphygmomanometer) for instance. Initially this task was performed only by doctors, partially because it involved the use of a stethoscope. Gradually however, nurses came to measure blood pressure and in the last few years, particularly associated with the technological innovation of automated digital machines, it has become increasingly common for SENs to perform this task as well.

In other words, it is an issue about occupational territory or task domains. On the occupational territory of which health occupation does measuring blood pressure lie? Initially, it was part of the occupational territory of medicine, then also RNs, now also SENs. This is how the negotiated aspect of the division of labour (outlined above) is represented historically. Over time, what begins as an occasional task done in an emergency, or to relieve pressure of work may become gradually accepted and redefined as part of the occupational territory of another occupation. An example is what seems to be an emerging (technical) division of labour surrounding ECG (electrocardiograph) machines. It appears to be becoming common for nurses to actually take the ECG, leaving it to the doctor to interpret it.

How this process of 'pass-the-task' occurs is important. While there are some instances where the process is a consensual one (everybody agrees it's a good idea), for the most part, social interaction in the health arena is stabilised not on the basis of consensus but only through conflict and coercion. Negotiation is permissible under certain circumstances, but heaven help anyone who steps too far out of line! Anyone who is inclined to believe that demarcation disputes happen only in the trade union context need only examine the history of relations between some health occupations to be put right on that score. Hardly anywhere in the health division of labour is there an agreed-upon occupational territory, indeed there are enormous areas of overlap. An example is the giving of dietary advice: many occupations—among them doctors, dietitians, naturopaths, some chiropractors—give it and, generally speaking, each claims to be the best at it. Should antenatal classes be taken by physiotherapists or midwives? Is it better to go to an optometrist or an ophthalmologist to have your eyes tested? To whom should you take your bad back: doctors, physiotherapists or chiropractors? Who will be most likely be able to help you give up smoking: doctors, acupuncturists, clinical psychologists, or hypnotherapists? Furthermore, attempts by some health occupations to improve their relative position in the hierarchy have at times met with a swift and hostile response. Recent attempts by medical laboratory scientists to move towards a more independent status within the division of labour, met with no success (see Gardner & McCoppin, 1988).

From this point of view, differentiation in the division of labour in health care has evolved as part of a process of conflict and struggle, over appropriate occupational territories for particular occupations. Medical dominance has resulted from the success of the medical profession in establishing and then maintaining itself in a position of pre-eminence. The historical process by which the occupational division of labour in health care has evolved has been an ongoing struggle for control of occupational territories as the different occupations have sought to defend and extend their task domains.

What resources are available to an occupation in this struggle? What sanctions exist to attempt to legitimate its view of what its occupational territory is or should be? Ultimately the social structure of health care delivery rests upon State patronage. To achieve medical dominance of the division of labour in health care, the medical profession has managed to convince the State that it is deserved, both in its achievement and also in its maintenance. The State here refers to a set of institutions (legislative, executive, judiciary, bureaucratic, police, armed forces etc.) which acts as the institutionalised framework of political domination in a capitalist society and also, importantly, has a monopoly on the legitimate use of force.

The State in other words underwrites the dominance of the medical profession in a number of ways but especially through legislation. In this regard statutory registration or licensing legislation is of great importance. What this type of legislation does is to formally establish in law the occupational territory of health occupations; thus legislation specifies whom may call themselves by the occupational title and what those practitioners may do. The struggle for and over the content of statutory registration legislation has been a major part, historically, of the evolution of the division of labour, while statutory registration has been a much sought-after goal of health occupations. As Bucher and Strauss (1961) have argued, licensing laws are the historical deposits of the exercise of power and authority.

As the division of labour has evolved, different health occupations have come to occupy a variety of positions in relation to medical dominance. Many are *subordinated*: that is, they have their work ordered directly by doctors. All occupations that work in hospitals experience this mode of domination, including nurses. For other occupations however, the relationship is one of *limitation*: that is, their area of expertise is limited to one part of the body only and they do not 'compete' with the medical profession in the core areas of its occupational territory. Dentists, optometrists, podiatrists and pharmacists are examples of occupations that experience this mode of domination. Others experience *exclusion*: those usually known as 'alternative' health occupations, such as naturopathy, and homeopathy. Others still have experienced *incorporation* as they have been incorporated into the medical profession itself. Homeopathy is the best example in this country of an occupation that was absorbed into medicine although homeopathy as a treatment modality has again emerged as a separate occupation. In the United States, osteopaths are an occupational group that now form part of the medical profession in many states.

Over time, some occupations have managed or are managing to change their relative position, either with or without medical approval. Chiropractic is an example, now having statutory registration in all states of the Commonwealth and gradually moving towards a position more of limitation; that is limitation to the treatment of musculoskeletal conditions. Physiotherapy appears to be pursuing a long-term strategy of incorporation.

LEGITIMATION OF MEDICAL DOMINANCE

Having considered how the division of labour in health care is organised around medical dominance, and secondly how this developed, I will now turn to its legitimation—how it is justified—and some of the problems with that justification, before turning finally to some of the social policy implications. By justification is meant a political process by which medical dominance has been accepted and underwritten by the State. It is important to note that, following the assumption of coercion or conflict rather than consensus as the basis for social order, I am not arguing that 'everyone agrees' that it is appropriate that the medical profession dominates the health division of labour. Rather, while the dominance may have become accepted in some circles, it is more the case that control is established and maintained by ideological processes of coercion. What that means is that a powerful ideology operates to sustain medical dominance at all three levels outlined above: autonomy, authority and sovereignty. This ideology has two related parts: one the ideology of professionalism and the other the ideology of technological determinism. Together they provide the hegemonic 'cement' by which medical dominance is legitimated.

The ideology of professionalism

Briefly, the term profession as analysed here, does not denote a special sort of occupation but rather a *claim* to a certain sort of occupational control which will allow self-direction or autonomy. Professionalism then refers to an occupational ideology seeking to legitimate autonomy ('we don't need to be controlled from outside because we can take care of ourselves, and besides it is in the public interest for it to occur in this way').

Professionalism has quite explicit class and gender elements. Those occupations that are able to successfully espouse professionalism are those which are in powerful positions already and seek to maintain those positions, such as doctors. For others seeking to espouse professionalism as a means for collective self-advancement, especially those occupations lower in the hierarchy which are not able to call upon resources based on class and gender from the wider social division of labour, there are considerable problems with the effectiveness of espousing professionalism to gain advancement.

Nurses are a good example; for many years they pursued a strategy for collective self-advancement based upon emulating doctors in espousing professionalism. In the nursing context, very important to their occupational ideology has been the notion of 'dedication'. Within a division of labour dominated by another occupation to whom nursing is formally subordinated however, pursuit of professionalism has met with little success—as the bumper stickers say 'dedication doesn't pay the rent'. Recognition of this has led to nurses gradually abandoning professionalism as a strategy for collective self-advancement and opting instead for direct action through trade unionism. Not that the two should be seen as too different, both professional associations and trade unions are strategies directed at the same ends, the difference is in the techniques used to achieve those ends. Whereas professional associations promote themselves through ideological means ('we really do have the best interests of the public at heart'), trade unions tend to rely more on the threat of collective action through strikes to achieve their ends.

Besides the claim to the public interest, professionalism has a number of other elements as well. Most important for our purposes here is what Habermas (1970: 81) calls 'the ideology of expertise': that only those who have expert knowledge are competent to judge on the many decisions involved in the conduct of the health industry, and therefore because doctors have the most expert knowledge, it is appropriate that they are in a position of dominance. In other words, medical dominance is legitimate.

The expertise or skill here of course relates to, on one hand, the knowledge held about how the body works and what can go wrong with it; and on the other hand, to knowledge of what to do about illness to restore or at least ameliorate the effects of the condition. The basis for the claim that medical dominance is legitimate is that the medical profession knows better than any other health occupation and therefore should control the division of labour in health care.

Technological determinism

The second ideology important in legitimating medical dominance is technological determinism. According to this view, the division of labour is related to the different amounts of knowledge that different occupations have. That knowledge is put into practice in the treatment of ill health by technological means; in other words it is knowledge about medical science and medical technology. From a technological determinist viewpoint, it has been the development of medical science and medical technology that has led to the division of labour evolving in the fashion that it did. The development of new medical technology led to specialisation of occupational tasks and the emergence of new health occupations to cope with that technology. A 'technological imperative' has existed; the invention of new technology has led to the progressive differentiation of the division of labour; the technology in other words has determined the societal response to occur in the way it has in the form of an increasingly differentiated division of labour. Medical dominance, from this point of view, is explained and legitimated ('it is right and proper that . . .') by this technological development. The nature of the technology determined the division of labour to cope with that technology in the most efficient way. 'Most efficient' in this context has meant that doctors should be in control because they are the only health occupation trained to make the necessary complex decisions to get the most out of the technology for the alleviation of human suffering. Thus, according to this argument, it has been the technology that has created the hierarchy which today constitutes the social structure of health care delivery characterised by medical dominance.

Take X-ray machines as an example to illustrate this point of view. When they were invented and diffused into medical practice, the nature of the technology (the X-ray machine) determined the societal response to it: it was most 'efficient' to introduce it in a particular way. With the assumption of consensus, this approach argues that its invention necessitated the creation of two new occupations to cope with that technology in the most efficient way: radiographer-technicians on one hand and radiologists (medical specialists) on the other. In other words, it has been the requirements of the new medical technology itself, which have imposed limits upon the types of social organisation possible (how to best cope with the technology), and have been the determining force in the development of modern health care. Technology has determined the division of labour; the position of the various occupations that collectively make up the division of labour in health care is related to the different amounts of knowledge of medical technology that different health occupations have. Medical control of that division of labour is justified furthermore because medical practitioners have the most knowledge about how that technology works.

Having outlined in some detail what the ideology of technological determinism is, I now propose to attempt to show the ideological nature of this position as a justification for medical dominance. Firstly, though we need to have a definition of technology itself that is not too narrow, it is necessary to include in that definition both a *material* component (the tools and machines), and a *social* component (the social relations that go with those machines). The social component should not just be seen as *derivative* of the material component (as technological determinism sees it), but as an *essential* component, since there are often a variety of social arrangements which are possible (radiographers could be taught as part of their curriculum to interpret X-ray plates for instance). Frequently, the social arrangements are engineered into the machine itself, such as in industrial settings where new machines may have engineered into them a capacity to measure the absences of the operator from the machine and to trigger a red light in the office of the supervisor if the absence exceeds a certain length of time.

Secondly, technological determinism conflates (that is to say, merges together inappropriately) the technical with the social division of labour. As outlined earlier in this essay, the technical division of labour refers to the specialisation of tasks on-the-job, by occupation. Technological determinism assumes the primacy of the technical over the social division of labour. The latter occurs in the wider society as a whole: a divison of labour based on factors such as class, gender, ethnicity and age. Let's examine this point in some detail in relation to the X-ray technology example mentioned earlier.

When you go for an X-ray, and experience the labour process surrounding this procedure, you encounter both a technical and a social division of labour. That labour process consists of two main steps: firstly, you have the X-ray image taken by a radiographer; then you see or hear from a radiologist to be told the result ('yes—you do have a broken leg'). The radiologist and the radiographer co-exist in a technical division of labour: one takes the image, the other interprets it. As outlined above, taking a technological determinist position, one would argue that this division of labour is necessary in order to utilise this particular technology in the most 'efficient' manner. However when we consider the social relations of the imaging technology, it is apparent that the social relationships are a microcosm of the wider society. The radiographer will almost always be female and the radiologist usually male. Furthermore they will hail from quite different class backgrounds.

Let's explore this more. In 1980, together with a group of advanced level undergraduate students, I did a study comparing the social profiles of students training in ten different health occupations (Willis, 1980), amongst them radiography and medical students (some of whom subsequently go on to train as radiologists). A number of social characteristics were surveyed, including the class background from which the students originated. First, in table 2.1 we surveyed the occupational background of the students.

Some explanation about how this table was constructed will help here. We considered the type of work done by the family of the student. To do this, we asked questions about the work done by both the mothers and fathers of the respondents. To arrive at an assessment of the family as a whole, it should be noted that we 'coded up': in cases where both the mother and father were in paid

Table 2.1   Family type by occupation

Occupation	Managerial–professional (%)	White collar (%)	Blue collar (%)	Total (%)	Number in sample
State-enrolled nurse	11	23	66	100	47
Chiropractor	23	27	50	100	48
Radiographer	30	26	44	100	43
Naturopath	33	25	42	100	40
Registered nurse	38	26	36	100	42
Social worker	50	9	41	100	34
Dentist	55	20	25	100	40
Physiotherapist	58	18	24	100	50
Prosthetist\orthotist	69	8	23	100	26
Medical practitioner	83	4	13	100	48

employment we coded to the 'higher' of the categories. For example, where the father worked in a blue-collar occupation and the mother in a white-collar occupation, then the family was entered in the white-collar category. In most cases, this meant that the father's work type decided the final category. As a result, it should be noted that the results are slightly biased 'upwards', but this was considered preferable to ignoring the work of women which many other stratification type studies have done. White-collar work was separated from professional/managerial on the basis both of educational qualifications and also a question about whether parents supervised the work of others as part of their normal work duties. As table 2.1 indicates, medical students had by far the greatest proportion with families in professional/managerial type occupations and also the lowest proportion who worked in blue-collar occupations.

Secondly, we constructed a measure of class background of the students training in the various health occupations, using neo-Marxist categories in which we took into consideration the class position of both the father and the mother. The results are given in table 2.2.

It is useful to examine how this table has been constructed. An elaborate explanation of the schema used is beyond this chapter, but can be briefly outlined. Economic factors are the primary source of differentiation. The ruling class was arbitrarily defined as those who were themselves self-employed and employed more than five employees. It also included those who control and supervise the labour of others—managing directors and factory managers. The working class were defined as wage earners who were not self-employed and did not supervise the work of others. Under this classification, the middle class was divided into two classes. The old or traditional middle class were those who were self-employed

Table 2.2   Class position by occupation

Occupation	Ruling class (%)	New middle class (%)	Old middle class (%)	Working class (%)	Total (%)	Number in sample
State-enrolled nurse	4	35	23	38	100	48
Chiropractor	12	31	26	31	100	49
Radiographer	9	50	14	27	100	44
Naturopath	19	28	32	21	100	43
Registered nurse	12	49	30	9	100	43
Social worker	17	46	17	20	100	35
Dentist	7	64	22	7	100	41
Physiotherapist	14	58	20	8	100	50
Prosthetist\orthotist	7	70	19	4	100	27
Medical practitioner	2	81	8	8	100	48

with less than five employees. The new middle class consisted mainly of the professions, those who were not self-employed and who did supervise the work of others.

As Table 2.2 illustrates, medical students again came from the most advantaged social class backgrounds. Radiography students had one of the highest proportions of working-class backgrounds of the occupations surveyed.

Now, there is nothing inherent in the X-ray technology itself that requires one occupation to be female and from a class background lower in the class hierarchy than the other; that is to say, there are no technological imperatives associated with the technology itself. What the data on social background of students shows in relation to the technical and social division of labour surrounding imaging technology, is that the social division of labour is more important in establishing the social organisation of healing tasks in this area, than are the technical requirements of the machines themselves.

Let's look further still. The division of labour can be differentiated on a number of bases; one important one is income. The starting wage for a radiographer (or a medical imaging technologist, as they now prefer to be known) in a public hospital, according to the 'Wageline' telephone advice service in November 1989, was approximately $22 000 per annum. For a radiologist by contrast, according to the personnel department of one of our large public hospitals, it is nearly $60 000 per annum on commencement. But that is by no means the whole story. In the 1980s in Victoria, there was perceived to be a shortage of radiologists in public hospitals. The Economic and Budget Review Committee of the Victorian Parliament (1986) established an inquiry into this shortage and assessed it to be the result of radiologists leaving the public hospital system for the greener pastures of private practice. The committee found that few were keen to stay for long in the public system when incomes of between $200 000 and $400 000 were not uncommon for private radiologists in 1986, an income substantially above that earned by even most other medical specialties. In their defence, the radiologists pointed to the very high level of practice expenses to be paid out of that income, claimed to be as high as 80 per cent. While there may be some validity in this argument, the fact that the committee reported an advertisement which had appeared in the local press at the time of the inquiry which offered a *salary* of $150 000 plus fringe benefits including a car, is a measure of the rewards of radiological practice. They also made the point in their report that the advertisement ran for over six months (Economic and Budget Review Committee, 1986: 31).

Nor should it be assumed that this division of labour has been arrived at by consensual means. Rather, it is the result of the imposition of control by radiologists over radiographers. The current division of labour has evolved from a process of struggle—occupational, class and gender based. Medical dominance in the field of imaging technology has been the result of and, indeed, in this area is enshrined, in legislation; that is, it has the backing of the State. When you have an image taken by a radiographer, he or usually she is not allowed by law to interpret it for you. To tell you that your leg was indeed broken would technically constitute an offence. The most you will be able to get from the radiographer, prior to seeing the radiologist to have the image interpreted is what is called 'the radiographer's whisper' ('well, I don't think you'll be playing sport again for a few months!').

This phenomenon is often referred to as 'secondary deskilling'. It is apparent when one considers the length of training undergone, the usual way (incidentally) the income disparities between radiographers and radiologists is rationalised and legitimated. Radiographers train for four years, whereas radiologists undertake specialist training after basic medical training, as much as ten years in all. However, secondary deskilling takes place when the content of the curriculum undertaken by students training to be radiographers is influenced by radiologists. It would be quite possible to train radiographers to interpret the simpler images, indeed the government committee examining ways of alleviating the shortage of radiologists in private practice considered the option of training and allowing radiographers to do some of the interpretations of the X-rays. Yet the financial basis for remuneration requires the position of the radiologist to be maintained statutorily as having to interpret all the images taken.

The argument being made here then ('what came first, the technology or the hierarchy?'), contrary to a technologist determinist position, is that hierarchy precedes technology, not vice versa. We need to consider the way that technology interacts with society, rather than how technology determines societal response. Although medical dominance is usually explained as being the result of differing amounts of knowledge and control over technology, this fails to take adequate account of the way in which the technical division of labour is the result, not so much of the technological imperatives internal to the labour process, but more so of the way in which the social relations of the technology are a microcosm of the social division of labour in the wider society—a society stratified along class, gender and other lines not related to the technology in question. In other words, advances in medical technology have been incorporated into an already existing hierarchy.

CONCLUSION

What I have done in this essay is to explore the issue, from a sociological viewpoint, of 'who does what to whom, in health care settings, under what circumstances?'. I have outlined how the division of labour operates as well as a number of sociological issues relating to it. I have tried to show how the rather complex organisation of healing tasks performed by occupations who work in the health industry, has developed and can be explained in sociological terms. Students training to take up a place in that division of labour will confront this hierarchical arrangement throughout their working lives, not as some static rigid structure, but as a phenomenon which changes over time.

POSTSCRIPT

This paper was written for the external teaching material for students at Deakin University. It originally included additional reading materials, some of which were papers of mine contained elsewhere in this book. As a whole, the paper was an attempt to summarise and provide a contemporary example of my work which appeared originally as the book *Medical Dominance* (1989a). The paper went on to draw on a survey conducted with a group of advanced undergraduate students into the relationship between class background and health training in various health occupations around Melbourne. Further, it went on to develop a contemporary example based on 'what happens when you go for an X-ray?'.

This relatively simple instance of diagnostic technology reveals nicely the social structure of health care delivery in our society. The act of having an X-ray exposes the individual to both a technical as well as a social division of labour. In this as in other cases it is backed up by the law. Another example of this is the pharmacist conducting a pregnancy test. By law, the pharmacist is not allowed to tell you whether or not you are pregnant. Such an act constitutes diagnosis, the legal preserve of the medical profession. Instead he or she are able to tell you only that 'the test is positive or negative'. This theme is returned to in later chapters.

NOTES

1 Throughout this book, I have observed the convention of referring to individual geographic *states* (such as New South Wales and South Australia), and the democratic capitalist *State*.

3 Sister Elizabeth Kenny and the evolution of the occupational division of labour in health care

The division of labour has long been recognised as a central issue in the study of society. Its effect, however, has been the subject of considerable disagreement since early in the development of sociology. However, while its importance is stressed, the concept has received less attention than the continual references to it in the works of the founders would have foreshadowed. The concept has been studied in several different ways. In focusing on it in a sociological mode (rather than an economic or ecological one), it is useful to define the division of labour as involving not only specialisation of productive labour (its common empirical referent) but also, more generally, the social organisation of tasks or work activities in society by either individuals or groups of individuals. This social organisation of tasks occurs both at the level of the society in general, and also within the different parts of society.

In this paper the emphasis is upon the latter: the interrelation of occupational groups in a division of labour which has evolved within one part of society, the health sector. This division of labour involves the social organisation of different health occupations involved in the allocation of tasks associated with the treatment of illness. My argument is that the division of labour in health must be studied historically and in terms of a continuing political struggle over appropriate 'occupational territories' or 'task domains' for each occupation. By 'occupational territories' is meant the area of treatment over which an occupation makes an effective claim to competence. I argue that the creation of boundaries between these occupational territories cannot be adequately explained by technical factors associated with the development of medical knowledge nor by factors internal to the health system. Rather, it is necessary to locate the explanation in the political economy of the society of which the health sector is a part. The argument is illustrated by a particular historical instance of this struggle over occupational territory, involving doctors and nurses and concerning the treatment of poliomyelitis, occurring in Australia during the 1930s.

THE HEALTH DIVISION OF LABOUR[1]

The major feature of the health division of labour in capitalist societies is its hierarchical organisation and domination by one occupation over all others. Eliot Freidson (1970a, 1970b), the major writer in this field, argues that the division of labour in the health field is organised by the principle of what he calls 'professional dominance' which is: 'the legally or otherwise formally created position of the profession—a position granted a monopoly over a set of services and the accessories they require' (Freidson, 1970a: 127). This, Freidson argues, is a result of the exclusive right granted to doctors to penetrate the body, physically by surgery and chemically by drugs. It is dominant furthermore because: 'it has the authority to direct and evaluate the work of others, without in turn being subject to formal direction and evaluation by them' (1970a: 135). Even those occupations that work outside the specifically *medical* division of labour, while not liable to direct evaluation and thence control by doctors (such as optometrists, etc.) are nonetheless likely to be indirectly controlled by the involvement of doctors in the formal organisation of their work, such as sitting on their registration boards.

The central issue, as with all occupations, is control over the performance of work. Achieving control over work requires the defining of a distinct occupational territory or task domain. Freidson in fact defines a profession (structurally) as a position of dominance within a division of labour, and on this basis is to be differentiated from mere occupations. The claim is to autonomy (the right to deny legitimacy to outside evaluation) in the performance of work, and is sustained for doctors by the dominance of that profession's expertise in the health division of labour. In any hierarchical division of labour, however, there can only be one 'profession' as such, since to be autonomous, an occupational group must be able to control the production and application of knowledge in the performance of its work, without having that knowledge criticised by others. By being unable to defend their occupational territory from evaluation by doctors, other health occupations are effectively subordinated to them. In focusing on the health sector, the crucial question then becomes: 'How does the medical profession control its work and its competitors?'.

Negotiated and imposed division of labour

When we come to actually describe the occupational allocation of work tasks in the everyday world of health work, there are two aspects to consider. The actual task allocation is the result both of informal negotiation between the parties involved, and of a legal or otherwise formal division which is imposed on the work situation. That negotiation in the allocation of tasks is possible and common has been documented by a number of researchers, in a number of institutional settings (see, for example, Goldie, 1977). My own study of general practice (Willis, 1976) found a variety of tasks fulfilled by practice nurses, beyond what would be expected from the formal division of labour. As Freidson (1976: 311) comments, the division of labour in health must be seen at least partially, as:

> a process of social interaction in the course of which participants are continually engaged in attempting to define, establish, maintain and renew the tasks they perform and the relationships with others which their tasks presuppose . . . [since] most of the time the limits to interaction posed by consensual conceptions of 'scientific' necessity and legal propriety are sufficiently broad and permissive that a variety of bargains is possible for the participants.

While acknowledging that negotiation is common, Freidson (1976: 311) recognises that: 'there are boundaries set on what will be considered legitimate to negotiate, how the negotiations will take place and what bargains can be struck'. My concern in this paper is with this imposed division of labour, the formal task differentiation, and how that has evolved. The two undoubtedly are related however; the everyday world of work, taken historically, is one of the factors that has influenced the formal framework.

Explaining doctor dominance

When we come to explain this doctor dominance, it is necessary to consider the historical process by which that dominance has evolved and been sustained. That such an approach is uncommon within the sociology of health, especially in Australia, reflects upon the current state of that discipline. There have appeared over the last couple of years, (1977–78) a spate of articles in the specialist journals, reviewing the current state of the sociology of health (e.g., Stacey, 1978; Murcott, 1977). Almost without exception, these articles have lamented the 'medicocentric' bias which the discipline displays. The consequences of this bias are many: in terms of the problems investigated (which are not usually historical problems), the ahistorical approaches usually taken, the consequent relatively meagre contribution to sociology generally; indeed even in the terminology by which sociologists interested in health operate (for example, mental illness, alternative medicine, lay referral networks, marginal professions, even medical sociology). As Murcott (1977: 157) comments: 'the object of investigation remains things medical, in that categories, albeit understandable in the lay as well as the professionally medical world, are yet acknowledged in each as having to do with doctors, illness and medicine'. The consequence of this medicocentricity however, when we come to consider the evolution of the division of labour in health, is the overwhelming preponderance (with rare exceptions) of 'official' histories in which the evolution is either not seen as problematic, or else as a gentlemanly process by which it was 'obvious' that doctors should control health care provision.

By contrast, I propose to consider aspects of the evolution of the division of labour as a political process, a power struggle, and one furthermore which can be considered independently of the nature, or effectiveness of the technical factors or health knowledge involved. Viewed this way, doctor dominance is achieved by control and domination of other health occupations whose occupational territory overlaps. Different health occupations have historically been dominated in different ways and it is possible to isolate a number of modes of domination to describe the relationship of various other health occupations to doctors. The first of these is *exclusion*, where the occupation is denied official legitimacy as a health occupation, prevented from having registration Acts, is not allowed to use hospitals, and so on. As a result, these occupations are mostly known as 'alternative' medicine; for example, naturopathy, acupuncture, chiropractic, etc. *Subordination*, the second mode, has occurred with those occupations which now work within the 'medical' division of labour; nursing being the prime example, but also including technicians of various sorts, nurse aides, etc. All these occupations have their work largely directed by doctors. *Limitation*, the third mode, involves occupations whose occupational territory is legally limited, for example, optometrists, chiropodists, dentists etc. While officially legitimated, their area of expertise is generally limited to one part of the body. *Incorporation* has also occurred where occupations are absorbed into the medical profession and lose their separate identity; homeopathy being the best example in the Australian context, while osteopathy is currently undergoing this process in many parts of the United States.

The case study presented in this paper is an instance in the reinforcement of the subordination of nurses in Australia. One important caveat should be laid down first, however. There is a tendency within the social sciences to focus upon the behaviour and motivation of individuals and groups of individuals as determining how conflict between these groups is resolved, and thus viewing the nature of the political process in this way. The concern in this paper is rather to argue *structurally*, to move beyond the level of the actors involved such as doctors, to consider their activities in relation to the more basic structural processes which impinge upon them. I am also aware of the considerable cleavages which exist within the medical profession as well as those between it and other health occupations. The focus here is rather with the political mechanisms which have created the occupational territory in which individual medical practitioners exist and which sustain their autonomy in practice.

SISTER KENNY AND THE TREATMENT OF POLIOMYELITIS

Australia suffered a severe epidemic of poliomyelitis in the 1930s and a controversy developed over how this disease should be treated.[2] The figure at the centre of the controversy was a nursing sister, Sister Elizabeth Kenny, who conducted a small backyard clinic at Townsville in Queensland in the early 1930s. The clinic was concerned with the after-care and rehabilitation of adults and children with longstanding physical disabilities including victims of paralysis following poliomyelitis. Her particular interest was in attempting to rehabilitate children who had been declared beyond hope by members of the medical profession. Public interest arising from her claims of success in this rehabilitation was such that a second clinic was established in Brisbane following at least one favourable report from an official medical observer appointed by the state government to observe the Townsville clinic.[3]

Her method of treatment was considerably different from the accepted medical treatment at the time, however. She stressed the importance of psychotherapy in treatment, insisting children had to be 'willed' to move paralysed limbs. As well, she believed graduated exercises especially in water were important. This contrasted with the prolonged rest and permanent splinting, often involving massive plaster casts, which constituted the accepted medical treatment at the time. Sister Kenny was strongly opposed to these methods, which she believed militated against the eventual return of muscular control.

The interest in her methods was felt in all eastern states. In

Queensland, the government asked Dr Raphael Cilento of the Commonwealth Health Department to investigate her methods and the possibility of making them the standard treatment for polio victims. His reports in 1933 and 1934 were at first broadly favourable (though nonplussed at her methods) though later highly unfavourable, reporting only minor improvements and criticising her lack of technical knowledge of anatomy and specifically poliomyelitis which he alleged led her to make serious errors in treatment. In particular, he was opposed to the removal of splints for frequent exercise. Cilento opposed any expansion of her clinics and advocated medical supervision and control of her work, in the form of a register of all paralysed cases, his (Cilento's) approval being necessary before any case could attend the Kenny clinic. The issue, however, soon gained wider political significance.

> By 1935, Cilento, now Sir Raphael, was Director General of Health in Queensland and Kenny had become a pawn in the Labor government's internal squabbles over deputy leadership . . . the government decided to support Kenny and Cilento was advised by E. M. Hanlon, the new minister for Health 'not to hamper government business', and to 'have nothing further of any kind to do with the Kenny clinic'. (Thame, 1974: 353)

In October 1935 a Royal Commission was appointed in Queensland to inquire into the different methods of treatment of infantile paralysis. The commission was comprised entirely of doctors. An investigation of her methods was also begun at Royal North Shore Hospital in Sydney following her request to the Commonwealth Government for a proper investigation of her work. In Victoria, the State Poliomyelitis Consultative Committee and Dr Jean McNamara, the acknowledged medical expert on the disease in Australia, were strongly opposed to the removal of splints and to the Kenny clinics generally. As Thame comments: 'they were almost universally backed by both the public and private sections of the medical profession, which now closed ranks to discredit the non-medical rival' (1974: 354). A letter from the (then) Victorian Branch of the British Medical Association to the Victorian premier clearly pressed for the retention of the orthodox methods:

> We feel that instead of indulging in experimental methods, it should be expanded in the best interests of the children by the use of trained teams of workers now available and we are not able to support any but the proved methods founded on anatomical and physiological principles and the knowledge gained by the experience of the world's best orthopaedic surgeons. This is not the time for experimentation. (*Age*, 16/11/37)

Public interest was by now at a high level. Doctor-politicians warned in Parliament about quackery (*Argus*, 11/11/37) and many articles and letters appeared in the press.[4] One Melbourne newspaper in a now rather quaint-sounding editorial commented: ' "Truth" comes out into the open, takes off the gloves and asks the brutal question; "what are our doctors up to?" ' (*Truth*, 13/11/37).

The reports to the various medical investigative committees reflected the medical profession's opposition to her. The Royal North Shore clinic admitted some improvement, but claimed (without presenting any evidence of the efficacy of their own methods) that no better results were achieved than could have been obtained by orthopaedic specialists if the necessary funds had been provided to set up a specialist hospital for crippled children. The report opposed the extension of the Kenny method, recommending instead setting up a medically controlled system of treatment, staffed by orthopaedic surgeons and resident medical officers. On the provision of nurses and masseuses it recommended: 'in this department the personnel already trained by Sister Kenny can be absorbed, although in future it would be preferable that the hospital trains its own staff and thus produce a continuity of ideas and practice' (New South Wales Parliamentary Papers, 1937–38: 1074). What they advocated was training a general nurse, specialising in muscle reduction, trained in the orthopaedic ward of a general hospital rather than in a Kenny clinic.

The report of the Queensland Royal Commission published in 1938 was also unfavourable to Sister Kenny's methods. It claimed that cases that had improved would have done so anyway under orthodox treatment, 'given the facilities, the time and the financial aid' (*Medical Journal of Australia (MJA)*,[5] 29/1/38: 205). It also claimed that Sister Kenny had modified her treatment to bring it more in line with orthodox treatment in all areas, except the removal of splints. The report was extremely critical of this technique, believing immobilisation to be of crucial importance, and the lack of it dangerous.

The report argued that her success (such as it was) was the result of a 'placebo' type effect:

> this commission in view of its own observations considers that the opinions expressed by those personally interested in the welfare of the patients attending the Elizabeth Kenny clinic are so influenced by the psychological effects of faith and hope that they are not a true reflex of the practical benefits bestowed by the Kenny clinic and therefore must be discounted. (*MJA*, 29/1/38: 214)

In a passage sounding almost identical to Balint's (1964) discussion of the 'apostolic function' so important in a doctor's therapeutic repertoire, the commission states that the improvement in cases examined:

> is attributable to Miss Kenny's strong personality, her own conviction of technical competence and to improvement in patients treated by her, all of which combined to inspire the patients and relatives with great hope and especially with unshakeable loyalty to Miss Kenny. (*MJA*, 29/1/38: 219)

The Queensland Royal Commission recommended that the Kenny method should *not* be generally adopted, as no better results were achieved than under the orthodox system. However, having 'two-bob each way', the commission also recommended:

> if the government takes the responsibility of rejecting the advice implied in this report and decides to allow the Kenny clinics to remain, the commission strongly urges that they be placed under the control of a competent orthopaedic surgeon or surgeons with the object of rejecting obviously hopeless cases, of avoiding the cruelty of disappointed hopes, of saving public money, and in general of getting a *sane and balanced view* of the patients' possibilities [*emphasis added*]. (*MJA*, 29/1/38: 219)

Not surprisingly, Sister Kenny openly attacked this report (especially the imputations contained in it) and threatened to stop her entire treatment program in Queensland unless the commission retracted its comments on several specific examples, on which she claimed she had been falsely represented. Her position in the ongoing debate was strengthened furthermore by growing international acclamation of her methods especially in the United States and United Kingdom. Her 1937 visit to the United Kingdom resulted in the establishment of her fifth clinic at Queen Mary's Hospital for Children at Carshalton in England.

The long controversy continued and gradually the various state governments established clinics, despite the widespread opposition of most doctors. In New South Wales, the Royal North Shore Hospital Clinic, with a waiting list of 400 by late 1937, was expanded. In Victoria, after considerable public pressure, a ward at the Hampton Convalescent Clinic, a part of the Melbourne Children's Hospital Clinic, was set up early in 1938 as a Kenny clinic. Active obstruction from the Children's Hospital administration and medical staff occurred, but the report of this Hampton ward, issued in early 1939, was generally favourable to the Kenny methods, and concluded that she had made a definite contribution to the treatment of poliomyelitis. In particular, it claimed that immobilisation after the initial stages of the disease militated against rehabilitation, and that both pain and stiffness and the tendency to deformity, in cases treated without permanent splinting, were less than similar cases treated by orthodox methods in the same hospitals. An ideal scheme, it suggested, could be formulated by using the best of both the Kenny and orthodox methods.

In fact, Thame argues (1974: 355) that by this time the most successful of the Kenny methods had been gradually taken over and incorporated into orthodox treatment, and thus the difference between doctors' success rates and her own was narrowed. Furthermore, this was done without acknowledgment being given to Sister Kenny: 'for it was not the procedures themselves, so much as the threat of non-medical interference which so distressed the majority of the profession' (Thame, 1974: 355).

The development of new methods for the rehabilitation of polio victims represented a threat to the autonomy of doctors in this area of treatment, especially if the proposal to establish Kenny clinics had eventuated. By gradually taking over her ideas and implementing them in their own practice, doctors were able to ensure that after-care would continue to be carried out in existing hospital clinics *over which they had direct control*. The establishment of Kenny-style public clinics, run by government departments, would have led to the development of an alternative method of after-care, less controlled by doctors. Incorporating this method of treatment within their own practice and subordinating its practitioners (the Kenny nurses and 'technicians'[6]) within the medical division of labour effectively dealt with the threat of competition by another occupation claiming to have an overlapping occupational territory. The autonomy of doctors was thus preserved, their occupational territory defended and the division of labour sustained. As Thame (1974: 355) concludes: 'the medical profession had been shown to be wrong in this controversy, but by a judicious and unacknowledged change of direction, it ultimately emerged in a position of strength'. This appears to have been in large measure the result of the greater access of doctors to the legal and political processes, relative to Sister Kenny. The inquiries were carried out entirely by doctors, for example. By denying Sister Kenny's expertise, and the effectiveness of her methods, the profession was able to politically sustain the dominance of its own expertise in the division of labour.[7]

STRATEGIES IN THE CONTROL OF COMPETITORS

By analysing the Kenny controversy in some detail we are able to shed light on the process by which the occupational division of labour in health care has evolved and been sustained. The strategies employed in this particular instance are not specific to the Kenny controversy, nor are they atypical. Indeed they bear a striking similarity to those analysed by Andrew Scull (1975) in his work on the capture of the area of treatment we now call (as a result) mental illness in England, during the early nineteenth century. Very briefly there developed through the Quaker Church what came to be called 'moral' treatment, practised by non-medically qualified personnel. The development of this treatment undermined the claim of the medical profession to expertise and special competence in the treatment of insanity. The orthodox medical treatment at the time involved purging, vomiting, bleeding and chaining; whereas advocates of moral treatment stressed quiet, counselling, gentleness etc. By arguing that insanity was a disease (on metaphysical grounds, rather than demonstrably), doctors gradually through the 1830s and 1840s gained control over the treatment of insanity. Once having achieved control, they incorporated many of the methods of moral treatment into their own.

ON TECHNOLOGICAL DETERMINISM

What explanations have been proposed to account for this development of a hierarchical doctor-controlled division of labour in health? The most common, and one I wish to argue against here concerns developments in the technology of medicine both in the form of better knowledge of aetiological factors in disease, and also improvements in the techniques for treating illness. Two varieties of this argument are common. In its crudest form (the 'progress of science' explanation), the argument is that this technological development 'caused' the division of labour to evolve; that the hierarchical division of labour which emerged was 'necessary' for coping with improvements in medical knowledge and techniques of practice. However, as Scull (1975: 221) argues in regard to psychiatry:

> as ideology, an account of the establishment of a medical monopoly over the treatment of insanity in these simplistic terms has obvious value, creating a myth with powerful protective functions for the profession of psychiatry. As explanation however, its adequacy is distinctly more dubious in that it ignores the social processes involved in the transformation of perspectives.

The second and more developed variation of this argument is that proposed by theorists within a broadly Weberian framework, such as Illich (1975). The development of technology is seen as a consequence of the general process of industrialism, which all modern societies are undergoing. Different positions within the hierarchical division of labour are associated with different amounts of control over the technology and knowledge used—in this case, in the provision of health services. The development of this division of labour furthermore leads to the growth of bureaucracies which Illich, like Weber, sees as a dominant feature of modern life.

Contrary to this, I would argue that it is necessary to differentiate between the technology itself and the social relations that evolve in the application of that technology. The social relations which are of particular importance are those resulting from a hierarchically organised social structure organised along class, race and gender lines within the health sector, the health sector being in turn a microcosm of the wider societal social structure. These social relations dictate patterns of control within the health sector, reinforced and legitimated by the ideology of professionalism. These social relations dictate what technology is used and also how it is used in health care. As Navarro argues: 'the responsibilities that the different members of the team have, are primarily due to their class backgrounds and sex roles and only secondarily, very secondarily to their technological knowledge' (1976: 116).

From the Kenny case, it can be argued that changes in the technology associated with the treatment of poliomyelitis did not lead to a further refinement of the health division of labour in the development of a nurse practitioner type occupation. Instead, as a result of the political processes described, this instance of technological change effectively reinforced an already existing hierarchical division of labour. Changes in the technique of treating polio occurred, but only within the constraints of maintaining the existing hierarchical control, as the Kenny methods became absorbed into the practice of doctors. As Braverman (1974) has shown in the development of the division of labour in general, the existence of a hierarchy preceded the development of 'scientific management'. Thus I would agree with Navarro (1976: 206), and I think the Kenny case confirms that 'both hierarchy and technology develop in a dialectical fashion, i.e. each one has influence on the other. But in that dialectical relationship hierarchy based on class comes first and takes precedence over the other' (Navarro, 1976: 206).

THE IDEOLOGY OF PROFESSIONALISM

In the analysis of the social and political processes by which the division of labour in the health system evolved as doctors gained control over their work and competitors, consideration must also be given to the role of professionalism as a strategy in this process. As already indicated, professions can be located structurally by their dominant position within a particular division of labour. The occupational ideology ('professionalism') generated to legitimate this dominance, is extremely important and is integrally related to the claim for autonomy in the performance of work. Autonomy, however, as we have seen, involves being able to deny the legitimacy of evaluation of an occupation's work by others. Sister Kenny and her methods challenged this autonomy and in the political process involving her subordination, some of the classic elements of the ideology of professionalism are found.

Firstly, doctors criticised her lack of understanding of the anatomy and physiology of the disease: 'an anterior horn cell might have been on the head of a buffalo for all she knew' (*MJA*, 5/9/70: 473). Because of this claimed lack of technical knowledge on her part they opposed her method of treatment. Yet concessions about the state of current *medical* knowledge are also found in the same article:

> because poliomyelitis is a relatively rare disease and because moreover its acute manifestations are seen only in epidemics at irregular intervals, there is no question that the education of the average medical man has been unsatisfactory and of necessity theoretical rather than practical.

Furthermore, despite claims early in the debate about the extent to which her treatment was at variance with those recommended by leading orthopaedic surgeons, the report of the Victorian inquiry published in 1939 conceded: 'orthodoxy is not capable of precise description. Orthopaedists vary very much among themselves in one country and from country to country in detail and even principle' (cited in *MJA*, 25/2/39: 323). Yet despite all this, the British Medical Association could still recommend to the Victorian premier that it was not the time for experimentation in methods of treating poliomyelitis. Especially it seems they were opposed when that experimentation came from outside the medical profession.

The second element of the ideology of professionalism is the assumption that 'effective' health care can only come from doctors. The report of the New South Wales committee of inquiry argued that the Kenny methods were: 'not in the best interests of the patient, as there does not exist the close and continuous contact between patient and orthopaedic surgeon, *which is essential for a full understanding* of the progress of each case' (*MJA*, 29/1/38: 328, [*emphasis added*]). This ideological stress on the primacy of the *doctor*–patient relationship for health care has been reproduced, largely uncritically, in much of the sociology of health as well.

Thus I believe the ideology of professionalism to have been an important strategy in the development of doctor dominance, and one that is frequently neglected in analyses of the division of health

labour, including that of Navarro (1976). So successful has the
medical profession been in controlling its work and competitors in
fact, that it has become the archetypical profession and a model for
professionalisation on which other occupations are modelling themselves. Professionalism thus legitimates an hierarchical division of
labour in the health sector, a division of labour which is stratified
on the class, gender and race lines of the broader society. It
legitimates an upper-middle-class, largely male, white, domination
of lucrative healing tasks.[8] Professionalism must be seen therefore
as a mystification of what is basically a class interest. Segall (1977)
comments: 'professionalism is an ideological justification for the
purveyor of commodities based upon knowledge and skills to promote their economic and social interests in a market economy.
Among health workers it is the highest expression of the distortion
of their social consciousness'.

STATE PATRONAGE AND DEPENDENCE

The discussion so far has been mainly concerned with how doctors
came to dominate the health division of labour. The related issue,
of crucial importance, is why they have been able to do so. What
is the source of their political and economic power? Why in the
Kenny case study did they have greater access to the legal and
political processes than did Sister Kenny? As I have already argued,
it was not the case that they had better knowledge, and so the
question can be asked independently of the effectiveness of the
knowledge concerned. The argument proposed by Illich (1975) and
others, that this power comes from power over knowledge, I have
already discussed and would argue is inadequate. Rather, it is
necessary to consider the political economy of the society in which
the health sector exists, in particular to analyse the role of the State
in granting and supporting the dominance of doctors in the division
of labour.

Freidson (1970a: 23) provides an explanation of doctor dominance at two levels of analysis. Firstly in terms of the State:

> The foundation of medicine's control over work is thus clearly
> political in character, involving the aid of the state [State] in
> establishing and maintaining the profession's pre-eminence . . . the
> most strategic and treasured characteristic of the profession—its
> autonomy is therefore owed to its relationship to the sovereign state
> [State] from which it is not ultimately autonomous.

Its power in other words derives from State patronage in the form
of a legally based monopoly over practice. Freidson (1970a: 72)

also identifies the pre-eminence of doctors with certain groups in societies:

> a profession attains and maintains its position by virtue of the protection and patronage of some strategic élite segment in society, which has been persuaded that there is some special value in its work. Its position is thus secured by the political and economic influence of the élite which sponsors it—an influence that drives competing occupations out of the same area of work and that requires still others to be subordinated to the profession.

As McKinlay (1977) indicates, there are certain problems with Freidson's analysis as he shifts from one level of analysis to another, but there are also questions raised which he does not answer. Who are these strategic élites? What is their relationship to the State? And what special value does the work of doctors have for this group?

The answer to these questions, raised but not answered by Freidson, lies in the analysis of the class structures as it emerges out of the productive order of a society. Following Frankenberg (1974), I would argue it is more useful to see the élites which Freidson mentions, as a class—the ruling class of the society in this case. By being able to then locate the professions in general, and doctors in particular, in the class structure relative to the ruling class, we can examine ways in which the division of labour is conditioned by the wider politico-economic context in which it occurs, in particular by the processes of financial and industrial capital.

Two factors are important in explaining State and ruling-class patronage for doctors. The first of these is the class origins of doctors which have always been important in the selection of medical students, thus assuring a community of outlook with legislators, businessmen, inter alia. Navarro (1976) has shown for the United States, how despite the increase in the proportion of women and minorities entering medical school, the proportion of students from working-class homes has largely remained unchanged. Recent studies in Australia by both Pensabene (1978) and Fett (1975) document the superior class backgrounds from which medical students have traditionally been recruited.

The second explanatory factor is the structural compatibility between the knowledge over which doctors have control and the needs of the economic system. As Berliner (1975) has argued, 'scientific' medicine serves a social and ideological function that has been and is convenient to the dominant class. This ideology saw disease as individual and biological, rather than social and political; in other words disease was conceived as a dysfunction of the body that had to be controlled or eliminated by therapeutic intervention aimed at the individual. It was therefore compatible with capitalist ideology. Johnson (1977) locates this compatibility in class terms following Carchedi (1977):

> core work activities (of professionals) fulfil the global functions of capital with respect to control and surveillance, including the specific functions of the reproduction of labour power. The professionalism of medicine—those institutions sustaining its autonomy—is directly related to its monopolisation of official definitions of illness and health. The doctor's certificate defines and legitimates the withdrawal of labour. (Johnson 1977: 106)

An example from the Kenny controversy will illustrate this point. As Johnson indicates, in capitalist (and State capitalist) societies, health is institutionally defined as the ability to take part in the productive process, that is, to go to work (see Kelman, 1975). One of the grounds upon which Cilento argued against the Kenny methods in his 1934 report was that: 'the benefit she gives them is not of economic but of sentimental value' (cited in *MJA*, 29/1/38: 190). That the patients may have had a better quality of life following treatment by the Kenny method was not important. The object of medical treatment was to return the patient's ability to work and so contribute to capital accumulation:

> it must not be overlooked that the objective of treatment is the saving of the country from the burden of pension commitment by the restoration to the patient of function adequate to permitting his normal life as a citizen earning a living. Short of such a result it is doubtful whether it is worthwhile either to the patient or the public to transform a low grade potential pensioner, into a physically high grade pensioner, none the less dependent. (*MJA*, 29/1/38: 189)

It appears then that doctors could only achieve professionalism—as a form of work control which gives them dominance within the health division of labour—when the political and economic conditions necessary to sustain it coincide with the requirements of capital. As Johnson (1977: 107) argues, doctors act as agents on behalf of collective capital and as a result: 'stand at the apex of an occupational hierarchy within which divisions are based not on levels of expertise alone, but on differences in production relationships and potentially social class location'. It also follows that if the political and economic conditions required to sustain doctor dominance do not coincide with the requirements of capital, then doctor dominance is likely to be undermined. In other words, while doctors are important in shaping what occurs within the health sector, they are not the ultimate determinants. That committees of inquiry and extensions of Kenny treatment facilities were established even in the face of medical opposition is evidence of that. More important is the role of financial and industrial capital which a number of commentators have argued is transforming medical care (see McKinlay, 1977; Rodberg & Stevenson, 1977) and even beginning to challenge doctor dominance.

CONCLUSION

In this paper I have attempted to indicate some useful directions to follow in order to explain adequately the division of labour in health. Drawing on an historical case study in the evolution of this division of labour, the focus has been on the social and political processes involved, which it is claimed are more important than technical factors. Developments in the techniques of treating poliomyelitis reinforced an already existing hierarchical division of labour based primarily on class and sex roles. An explanation of how doctors gained control over their work and competitors and came to dominate health care requires a consideration of the politico-economic context in which the health sector occurs. In particular, it requires a consideration of how the hierarchical division of labour is conditioned by the processes of capital and legitimated by the ideology of professionalism. Both of these are necessary for an adequate explanation of the role of the medical profession in a capitalist society.

POSTSCRIPT

This paper, which originally appeared in the *Australian and New Zealand Journal of Sociology*, was written in the early stages of my Ph.D. project. It seemed a nice microcosm of the processes that I was examining in the larger study and was also an opportunity to work out some of the theoretical framework for use there. The historical research mainly involved secondary sources of data, and I am grateful to Tasmanian nurse–historian John Wilson, who has made a detailed study of primary sources, for pointing out some minor points of historical detail that have been incorporated here.

By all accounts, Elizabeth Kenny was a remarkable woman— feisty, flamboyant and imperious. The contemporary question for Australian nursing is her relevance as a role-model in a profession where the benefits of role-models in the person of Florence Nightingale have been exploited for all they are worth to form the basis of the professional ideology. Might Elizabeth Kenny not provide a more suitable role-model for Australian nursing; resistant to medical dominance rather than submissive to it?

My own view is that she deserves her ranking in the pantheon of nursing heroines, though it is now apparent there are some aspects of her biography which might be considered to disqualify her. It appears that she was never registered as a nurse; she made her own uniform with material purchased from a mail-order outlet. Her training consisted of being apprenticed for a period of two months to a Nurse Sutherland in Tamworth in country New South Wales whereupon she began calling herself Sister Kenny (John Wilson, peronal communication). Perhaps we should not judge this too harshly by our contemporary standards, after all an apprenticeship type of training was common in the professions last century and there were also many 'irregular' medical practitioners plying their trade on the local populace especially in more remote communities, often with great success. Even Florence Nightingale never formally trained as a nurse.

On balance though, my view is that nurses should study this historical moment in the evolution of the occupational division of labour in health care in their training rather more than is the case at present.

NOTES

1   Needless confusion has arisen in this area because of the imprecision with which terms such as 'health' and 'medicine' are used. The 'health' division of labour here will refer to all health occupations including the so-called 'alternative' practitioners such as chiropractors, naturopaths, acupuncturists etc. The 'medical' division of labour on the other hand refers more specifically to the social organisation of 'official' illness-treating occupations, effectively those that work, or can work in hospitals.

2   I am indebted to the analysis of the Kenny controversy carried out by Thame (1974), whose work I have drawn upon substantially here. Originally sources are only indicated where I have gone beyond her analysis.

3   The former premier of the state of Queensland, Sir Joh Bjelke-Petersen was among those treated by Sister Kenny's methods (allegedly successfully).

4   A collection of these newspaper reports are held in the Dame Jean McNamara collection, Australian National Library, Canberra.

5   Henceforth referred to as MJA.

6   Not all Kenny practitioners were nurses. Some were physiotherapists, others had no prior training before undertaking the two-year training course at the 'Sr Elizabeth Kenny Institute' in Minneapolis, USA.

7   An afterword is found in Dame Jean McNamara's obituary '. . .

actually a lot of good came from that era, for early splinting and inadequate kind nursing made the lot of the paralysed poliomyelitis victim very painful until a more liberal staff was available for the "Kenny trial" and was always available subsequently for orthodox management' (MJA, 5/9/70: 473).

8 Empirical documentation of this is provided in Australia by Fett (1975: 131–7) and in the USA by Navarro (1976; 136–45).

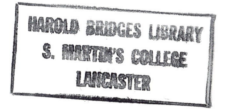

4 Medical dominance and the politics of nursing skills

The theme of this chapter is the issue of the politics of nursing skills, discussed in order to consider the theme of medical dominance. What do we mean by the politics of nursing skills? By politics, first of all, is meant politics with a small 'p'; not party politics but politics in the sense that it involves an expression of power. Skill is a very difficult concept to define. I don't want to deal with it as an absolute notion of the precisely defined knowledge, formulas and rules, but as a relativist concept. That is to say it is socially constructed at different periods. Skill as a concept varies historically: there is not much demand today for the skill of wheelwrights and coachbuilders. It also varies culturally: in mainstream Australian society there is not a lot of demand or market advantage to be gained by the holders of traditional Aboriginal skills, especially their skills in living off the land. It depends very much on *who* defines what skills are considered to be appropriate. In the definition of skill then, power is involved; skill is a political issue. What skills are recognised and how they are recognised is a highly political process and changes over time.

In the health arena, the politics of skill are organised around the phenomenon of medical dominance, which is of course the major feature of health service delivery in this society. Medical dominance is a phenomenon which has State backing and is enshrined in Medicare. A large number of the submissions made to the Layton inquiry [1986] reviewing Medicare (see Chapter 11), to which I was an adviser, commented on the assumption of universal competence or skill on the part of members of the medical profession. This was reflected in the fact that whatever went on in the consultation between a doctor and a patient could be claimed for on Medicare. Yet I think it is possible to make a good argument that in some contexts practitioners other than doctors are in fact more skilled. It is possible, for instance, to make a good argument that midwives are more skilled than general practitioners or obstetricians at uncomplicated deliveries; that chiropractors are better at fixing bad backs than most general practitioners are; that dietitians are better at providing nutritional advice than most general practitioners; that 'lay' acupuncturists are more skilled at providing acupuncture than many members of the medical profession who have done very short courses in acupuncture, some as short as four weeks as against often seven years' study that the 'lay' acupuncturists have done. Yet only medicine receives State support through Medicare rebates in the form of subsidy, and other health occupations do not (optometry is the only exception). Skill, in other words, is defined in relative terms and what is recognised as skill at various times, is a highly political issue. Medical dominance in the health arena means that we largely have medical definitions of what constitutes skill, including the skill of all other health workers, including nurses.

Why is this important? Skill levels are of course the basis in society for rewards, incomes, prestige, occupational status and many other benefits. It is the basis for the amount of remuneration for which people get and is enshrined in the wages system through the Industrial Relations Commission. The basis for arguing for increases in remuneration is through work value cases, by which an occupation must show 'changes in the nature of work, skill and responsibility required, or in the conditions under which work is performed' and to sustain a work value case, occupations or professions must show 'a significant net addition to work demands'.

Skill is important not only in monetary terms but in a whole lot of other areas as well that have to do with the sort of livelihood which the occupation provides. Things like work satisfaction, parking, childcare arrangements, and occupational health and safety are all related to it. I have recently been trying to assess whether the extent of medical dominance that existed in the Australian health system in the late 1970s still holds true nearly a decade later (Willis, 1989b). One of the things that members of the medical profession cited to me as evidence in their minds of a loss of medical dominance was the case of one large city hospital in Melbourne where doctors had lost their privileged parking positions and had to take their chances along with the rest of the health workforce in getting parking spots.

What then is nursing skill? What do nurses offer that is unique and able to be identified as tied to nursing, especially that which might provide a basis for a secure task domain or occupational territory? Furthermore, what might a sociologist contribute to this discussion? I would argue that one contribution is analysing the politics of nursing skills as a social and historical process; to look at the questions of how skill is currently defined in terms of the historical process and how it is changing. I would like to outline and then discuss four issues in the politics of skill as it affects nursing.

THE GENDER BASIS OF NURSING

Although males have become more involved in nursing, it is still largely a female occupation. The 1981 census showed that 93 per cent of the nursing workforce were still female. This is an historical issue which has been important since the earliest days of nursing, expressed through the Florence Nightingale tradition. This tradition has been a contradictory one for nursing, in that it has had both positive and quite negative consequences for the way that nursing has developed. As a result, it is possible today to say that this tradition represents at the same time both nursing's greatest strength and greatest obstacle. Historically, nursing has been viewed as women's work, and traditionally the skill that nurses applied has been defined in feminine terms. While nurses themselves have moved well beyond this, I think there still is a fairly widespread community perception along these lines. The traditional skill definitions are largely held to be biologically based ones, 'natural' feminine nurturing ones if you like. To patients, nurses have traditionally been seen as a mother surrogate, the nurse–patient relationship understood in the same way as the mother–child relationship. This skill was thought to flow naturally from the nurse's female qualities.

To doctors, nurses were defined in the role of handmaiden; obedient, unquestioning, and uncritical. Skill in this context was defined as the ability to carry out doctors' orders. The caring and nurturing side was tied up inevitably with submissiveness and 'feminine' attributes, and it was widely thought by doctors and others that what nurses mainly applied was TLC (tender loving care). Such a view has some currency still; a lament written by a retiring doctor, Dr Feelgood, (*Australian Hospital*, May 1986), in the 'Doctor's Diary' section, was headed 'Nurses knew their places in the good old days'. As he said, 'In those days [the good old days], a nurse knew her place, obedience was a religion and the doctor's word was final. You may call me old-fashioned, but I believe a good nurse is an obedient nurse, she should follow her instructions to the letter and should never question or challenge a doctor'.

Such a view, and the difficulties expressed in defining skill in other than feminine terms, are aptly demonstrated by the failure of the comparable worth case in the (then) Arbitration Commission which in effect clearly showed that male work was inherently more valued than women's work. This was effectively demonstrated by the failure of the work value case attempting to establish comparable worth between the work of ambulance officers and nurses (see Short, 1986).

A MEDICALLY DEFINED TASK DOMAIN

What nurses do is still defined to a considerable extent by doctors as a consequence of medical dominance. Their task domain has evolved largely from those tasks considered beneath, or not important enough to be done by doctors, being passed off to nurses to perform. Historically, as detailed earlier in this text, this process is called 'pass-the-task'. As one of the doctors interviewed for the professional issues inquiry, published as the SPIN report (Committee for the Study of Professional Issues in Nursing, 1988), established as part of the settlement of the landmark 1986 nurses' strike in Victoria commented, 'Nurses have picked up those tasks dropped by doctors'. The more routine, the more mundane aspects of an occupation's work have been passed on to subordinated occupations often expressly created for that purpose. This is of course a process that happens not only in health care but throughout the workforce as a whole. Nurses have also been involved in the process; there have been a number of tasks passed to SENs with task redefinitions as a result.

How is the situation of medically defined task domains maintained? Largely by control over what nurses do and what they are told they are not allowed to tell patients. It has been achieved to a large extent by control over nursing knowledge and this is one of the areas which is changing. Nurses have traditionally been fed a sanitised version of medical knowledge. The texts were often written by medical doctors and there was a fairly superficial discussion of what a good, that is a skilled, nurse needed to know, such as 'how to greet a doctor respectfully'. As Colliere (1986: 107) has argued, based on a wide review of nursing textbooks,

> nurses are fed a literature especially adjusted for them as if they possessed a smaller brain. The publishers favoured the addition of

manuals especially written for nurses. This enforces the distillation of ready made principles and norms ready to apply without questioning. It does not encourage the development of a literature which could be a source of extended knowledge.

This state of affairs has been the situation until recently. There has also been control over training; one of the effects of bedside or hospital training has been that the relations of domination and subordination have been built into the technical training of nurses. The medical opposition to the tertiary training of nurses and the length of time taken to achieve it, appears to be the result, in part at least, of an awareness of the implications for the independence of nurses as well as the dangers of nurses being exposed to the subversive and dangerous ideas of people like medical sociologists!

SEGMENTATION

This has existed within nursing since the Nightingale days. Nursing is not a homogeneous profession, but, generalising very broadly, there are two groups that make up nursing, differentiated on a whole lot of grounds, class origins being one of the most important. The lady nurses, as they were known, of middle-class origins, often doctors' daughters and wives, tended to be less interested in career-type issues. Insofar as they thought it was important to have representation, they saw professional associations as the best way to achieve that. For others however, of working-class origin, nursing was a means of social mobility and one of the few which existed until relatively recently. To these women, the notion of career was important, and they perceived their interest to be best collectively pursued through trade union involvement. Now this form of seg-mentation is, of course, not unique by any means to nursing; it exists within all professional associations, including the Australian Medical Association (AMA).

Whereas one segment tends to stress subordination, the other stresses independence. Whereas one stresses traditional values and norms, the other tends to stress open and critical attitudes. While one stresses professional goals such as status, the other stresses industrial goals such as pay and working conditions; and while one pursues professional models of development, the other tends to be more sceptical of that as an approach.

Since the days of these traditional definitions of nursing skills, there have developed different strategies such as professionalisation and unionisation. These strategies have been developed to move away from traditional notions of nursing skills. Within the professionalisation strategy, two different directions can be identified as having occurred. One has been specialisation into clinical areas; the other one moving into administration of one sort or another with an associated tendency towards bureaucratisation. Conflicts between the two segments have had two ongoing effects. On one hand these conflicts have prevented a unified response occurring, and on the other hand the potential exists for nurses to be dealt with at the political level by 'divide and rule'.

CHANGES IN THE NATURE OF NURSING

It is difficult to define nursing skills precisely, because what nurses are expected to do is undergoing quite rapid changes, especially associated with the technological transformation of nursing work. The professional issues inquiry (Committee for the Study of Professional Issues in Nursing, 1988) made clear that there was quite considerable disquiet amongst nurses about how technology is introduced and what its effects are. Elsewhere in the workforce, technology is often introduced in such a way as to deskill some areas of the workforce; printers are a good example, with their skills now largely redundant. In health care, however, while there is some evidence of this, such as with digital blood pressure measurers, there has also been *enskilling*. One area which I thought was interesting in submissions to the professional issues inquiry was that made by midwives claiming that they thought that their traditional skills of knowing on the basis of their clinical judgment, interpreting many of the signs and symptoms involved in the process of giving birth, were being subverted by an insistence from outside that they rely upon readings from instruments rather than their own judgments from non-technological means about what was occurring. Instead of using a simple technology like an obstetrical stethoscope to monitor the progress of the mother and baby, they were being required to rely on technologies such as foetal heart monitors where they felt their own skill input was less and their midwifery skills in danger of being redundant. It is possible to argue that the extent of enskilling in this particular instance, by which midwives are required to know how to operate, maintain, and teach by new technologies, was very little.

DISCUSSION

Having outlined each of these four major issues I would now like to comment briefly on each of them. First of all the gender specificity. It is very clear that the history of nursing is tied to the history of women, and that women will continue to make up the majority of the nursing workforce despite increasing numbers of males becoming nurses. Social change in regard to women in society as a whole is affecting nursing and it is very clear that feminist ideas are having a substantial impact in the health care sector. As well, a re-evaluation is occurring on what the taken-for-granted role of the mother surrogate actually means.

There has also been a re-evaluation of what health care is and a growing recognition that medical science has absorbed many male ideas and is in many ways a male construct with all the drawbacks such as dehumanisation, depersonalisation, and so on, which go with it. The re-evaluation and reorientation raises the potential for improving health care as a whole, with other ways of doing things being developed. I am reminded here of the feminist slogan which goes: 'women who want to be like men lack ambition'. Applied to the health area this might be modified to: 'nurses who want to be like doctors lack ambition'. In other words, the possibility is to make the feminine basis of nursing into a strength and male nurses would benefit from this as well.

The second issue outlined was the medically defined task domain. Medical dominance continues I think, but it has become a bit more fuzzy around the edges and is a bit more covert than was the case ten years ago. The implication of this though is that nursing theory cannot be worked out in isolation from the medical profession, who need to be persuaded by whatever means nurses have at their disposal of the value of what nurses have to say. There certainly has been a move towards a more independent stance, a recognition of the importance of tertiary training, a move away from the sanitised version of medical knowledge which nurses received, and the growing stress on the importance of nursing research. When I did a review of teaching, research and publications in the field of the sociology of health and illness in the early 1980s (Willis, 1982), I was struck by the fact that published sociological research on nursing was almost conspicuous by its absence at that time compared to lots of other areas. In the time since then the situation has been somewhat rectified.

The third issue identified was that of segmentation. The issue here is how to manage the segmentation that exists and make it into a strength. It is important to recognise that both the strategies of professionalism and trade unionism are strategies directed towards the same ends; that professional associations and trade unions are the same strategies in some ways, and while it is common to discuss their differences, we should also focus on their similarities. The well-known medical sociologist, Eliot Freidson has commented that professional associations and trade unions differ only in their degree of sanctimoniousness about what they are actually doing. From his point of view professionalism can be analysed as a strategy to convince the powerful that their profession deserves special concessions, such as autonomy. A comparable example from the medical profession of how they have dealt with the issue of segmentation is to build in a division of labour between the colleges on one hand, who pursue the scientific and educational bases, and the AMA on the other who pursue the industrial aspects. They operate very much a sort of iron-fist-in-the-velvet-glove strategy and have done this very successfully over a very long period of time. I think there is something that might be learnt here.

It should also be said that there are some dangers that might be associated with professionalism as a strategy, particularly its reliance upon the ideology of expertise which has come into so much criticism in the medical area. The debate is also well represented in the education field. The assumption is that you can't really understand what nursing is about and where it is going unless you happen to be a nurse. I feel this is a misplaced focus and not one that is likely to be very fruitful in the future.

The fourth issue in the politics of skill concerned the rapid change in the nature of nursing, especially concerning technological innovation and how this is different from the rest of the workforce. Whereas elsewhere technology is introduced in a way which usually displaces labour, in the health area technological innovation has largely meant that health areas have become both more capital- and more labour-intensive rather than just more capital-intensive. What has to be guarded against here is what is called technological determinism, the view which says 'but we have no choice' but to introduce this technology in this way. The view is of technology as being like a great boulder, which has implications for everything in its path. It is important to realise that technology involves not only the tools and machines, but the social relationships that go with them. You can't separate the material component—the tools and machines—from the social component, which is the way that it is dealt with in the social relations of the technology concerned.

An example comes from the study by Brewer (1983) of the failure of a communications technology known as the patient–nurse monitor system. The technological innovation failed because the social relations of the technology were ignored. The patients found it embarrassing giving private information into private microphones in the ceiling, and the idea on the part of the health administrators to have a non-nurse operator, a communication technician to staff the switchboard that operated the microphones. It would effectively create the situation of non-nurses giving orders to nurses to 'take

Mrs Smith a bedpan' and this was an intolerable situation to nurses. Rapid changes of course provide opportunities to advance the position of nursing and the professional issues inquiry (Committee for the Study of Professional Issues in Nursing, 1988) had a lot of recommendations about what can be done here and which are very positive.

CONCLUSION

By way of summing up then, where we are now is a part of the process of historical development in which the politics of skill are being renegotiated all the time. There is rapid change in that new skills are being developed. There is also a renegotiation of the gender aspect and a re-evaluation of what women's work is. There is a widespread recognition, I think, in which the Marles professional issues inquiry is important, that women are no longer trapped in nursing as they once were, in the sense of that there used to be only a fairly limited range of other career opportunities available. Now there is a wider range of opportunities available, nurses are not prepared to tolerate the fairly appalling working conditions that had existed in the past. There is a renegotiation of skill levels around the issue of what the market demand for nursing skills is. The shortage of nurses has had a substantial impact on pay increases, on career and on a number of other things, helped along by industrial action which has meant that the community has been persuaded to place more value on the skill of nurses! In conclusion then, I think the politics of skill are a key issue for nursing. They have always been, and are likely to remain so in the future.

POSTSCRIPT

This chapter was originally given as a spoken address to a nursing conference and subsequently published in the conference proceedings. Since the time the paper appeared, the politics of nursing skills have remained important in the nursing labour process. Changes in the industrial relations climate associated with the gradual infiltration of economic rationalist policies in society as a whole have, and are, resulting in a new phase of the politics of nursing skills. Abolition of awards, termination of penalty rates for weekend and night work have resulted in nurses being affected probably as much as any group of workers. In other areas of the economy (such as building and construction), changes in established industrial procedures have resulted in a decline of payment of financial margins for skills possessed. Whether this will occur in nursing remains to be seen, but there appears no doubt that both the State, and private employers of nurses will seek to avail themselves of the opportunity presented by the new legislation to reduce the costs of nursing labour.

The process of secondary deskilling which is present in other areas of the workforce, by which some of the tasks traditionally done by nurses may be passed off to lower-paid health occupations such as State-enrolled nurses, ward assistants or personal care attendants, is being experienced in this area. The nursing career hierarchy through the various grades—a hard won industrial gain— is being compressed in the name of cost savings to employers. Likewise, the expansion of a secondary labour market in society as a whole (characterised by part-time, insecure, unsuperannuated jobs) and the reduction of the primary labour market (characterised by permanent, full-time jobs) is being reflected in nursing as well with the growth of agency nursing where the relationship between nurse and employer is mediated through a third party of a contract labour organisation. Such developments in the politics of nursing skills have considerable implications for the quality of patient care.

There are also some signs of countervailing trends in the other direction, of increasing the recognition of nursing skills, with the recent announcement that the Federal Government is considering provision of a legislative basis for nurses to expand their occu-pational territories in areas of rural and remote Australia at least. The scarcity of medical practitioners in these areas is the justifica-tion for consideration being given to providing an independent financial basis for nurse practitioners, by permitting them to claim reimbursement through Medicare and being allowed to perform some tasks hitherto restricted to doctors. The politics of nursing skills will remain important in deciding what it means to profess the occupation of nurse in the late twentieth century.

5 Complementary healers

Developing a sociological awareness about the society in which we live involves a willingness to question the beliefs and assumptions that people have and make in the course of their daily lives. This critical awareness involves investigating and demystifying 'commonsense'; the sort of taken-for-granted beliefs that people have about how our society operates. In considering these issues in relation to people's health and the illness care they receive, a 'taken-for-granted' assumption is that sick people will seek help from a doctor, that is from a member of the medical profession. Such 'commonsense', it should be noted, has also permeated some of the sociological study of health and illness. In the classic formulation of the sick role developed by Talcott Parsons (1964), one of the responsibilities of patients who enter the sick role is to seek 'competent' help, for Parsons undoubtedly, meaning help from a medical practitioner.

Yet there are many others besides the medical profession to whom individuals routinely turn when illness strikes. For this reason, no account of the social aspects of health and illness in general, and the providers of health services in particular, can be complete without an analysis of what has been variously called alternative, unorthodox, fringe, marginal or what, for reasons outlined below, I shall call complementary health practitioners. It is clear that large numbers of people seek assistance with maintaining or restoring their health from practitioners other than medical doctors. These complementary health providers are organised into modalities comprising a body, or more particularly a *paradigm* of knowledge about health and illness, together with a set of therapeutic techniques based on it.

The aim of this chapter is to analyse sociologically this complex area of the provision of health services, an important component of the overall system of health care in this country. The technical issues are complex and a huge debate exists over the relative merits of the services of different modalities and no attempt is made to do that here. Health care, however, is primarily a social process albeit with important biophysiological foundations and the sociological analysis here aims to unravel the complexities involved. The particular tools for making this sociological analysis are the concepts of commensurability and legitimacy. Commensurability for our purposes here refers to the extent to which the paradigms fit together or are compatible (see Chalmers, 1976).

The concept of legitimacy derives from the work of the founding father of sociology, Max Weber (1968) but has been importantly developed more recently by Habermas (1976). Legitimacy is a politico-legal process whereby a set of practices is accepted as authoritative and becomes dominant through the political process of justification. The practices in this case are a set of diagnostic and therapeutic techniques based upon a paradigm of knowledge, which an occupation utilises in the routine performance of its services. Growing public acceptance of a modality, for instance, is one indication of increasing legitimacy. The advantage of the concept of legitimation is that it avoids the thorny issue outlined by Habermas (1976) of whether one paradigm has greater truth value than the other. Legitimacy is not related to a single 'truth' standard, even if such a standard could be decided on the basis of criteria other than those internal to the paradigm itself.

This chapter takes as its sociological problem for analysis and investigation the curious phenomenon of the survival and indeed blossoming of this component of health care, in the face of continued opposition and indeed hostility from the medical profession on one hand, together with a continuation of the situation where the efficacy of the therapeutic techniques of these modalities remains for the most part unestablished according to the canons of scientific evidence on the other hand. The argument to be made is that this growing legitimacy is to be explained by two factors: firstly convergence or declining incommensurability between the paradigms of health knowledge of what is usually called 'orthodox' and 'alternative' medicine, and related to that, secondly, a decline in the importance of the issue of the commensurability of 'alternative' paradigms of health care knowledge with conventional ones. Instead the issue of clinical effectiveness has replaced commensurability as the basis for legitimacy in health care provision.

In making the analysis, the focus is primarily upon what can be regarded as the three major complementary modalities: chiropractic and osteopathy (the manipulative ones); the natural therapies, principally vitamin and mineral therapy, botanic medicine and homeopathy; and traditional Chinese medicine (acupuncture and other techniques). One other point to note is that the critical analysis and demystifying approach to understanding the social world which is characteristic of a sociological analysis, must be applied equally to the complementary modalities themselves. In making the analysis, two particular sources of evidence are drawn upon, the two most recent in a long tradition of inquiries into complementary modalities: one the inquiry conducted by the Medicare Benefits Review Committee (Second Report) under the chairpersonship of Judge Robyn Layton in 1985–86 (henceforth MBRC, 1986); the other the inquiry by the Social Development Committee of the Victorian Parliament, under the chairpersonship of Judith Dixon, MLC, into alternative medicine and the health food industry also 1985–86 (henceforth VSDC, 1986, vols 1 & 2). The latter inquiry commissioned excellent survey research into the significance of alternative medicine in Victoria.

HISTORICAL ASPECTS

The place to begin a sociological analysis of a social phenomenon such as complementary health care is historically; to trace briefly the emergence of the situation as it exists today. The search for relief from illness is as old as civilisation itself. When attempts at self-treatment failed, others were consulted and the role of healer gradually developed. Different healers used different treatments which drew upon different paradigms of health knowledge and the healers who shared these paradigms and the diagnosis and treatment techniques based upon them gradually became occupationally organised into different modalities. Social class was a major means of differentiating both the clientele and the practitioners of different modalities.

The pattern until the nineteenth century was for different modalities to wax and wane in popularity and many fell by the wayside. From about the mid-nineteenth century, however, one of these modalities—known at the time as allopathy—gradually rose to a position of dominance. It did this by hitching its destiny to the rising star of science as a new form of authority, and abandoning much of the allopathic paradigm in the process. Gradually its practitioners, the emerging medical profession were able, through State patronage to have their paradigm accepted as the paradigm of health knowledge.

In the process, other modalities came to be excluded and increasingly marginalised. Homeopathy is a good example; political restrictions on the immigration of homoeopathic practitioners in the state of Victoria from the early twentieth century eventually led to the takeover of the Melbourne Homoeopathic Hospital and its renaming as Prince Henry's Hospital in the mid-1930s (see Templeton, 1969). Since the establishment of medical dominance in the 1930s, complementary modalities have largely struggled to maintain sufficient demand for their services to generate a sufficient livelihood for their practitioners to survive. Some (such as phrenology) which have been unable to do so, have ceased to be practised to any great extent. Others (such as homeopathy) have been incorporated into the broader practices of natural therapists as one of several submodalities which they utilise.

Over the last two decades, a gradual increase in demand for, utilisation of and availability of the services of the complementary health practitioners under consideration here, is discernible. Analysis of the listings of acupuncturists, herbalists and homoeopaths in the Melbourne telephone directory *Yellow Pages* between 1970 and 1986 showed an exponential growth. The number trebled between 1975 and 1980 and did so again between 1980 and 1986. The biggest growth was for natural therapists and acupuncturists (VSDC, 1986, 1:25). By the time of the 1983 Australian health survey conducted by the Australian Bureau of Statistics, almost 2 per cent of the population had visited a chiropractor, osteopath, naturopath, herbalist or acupuncturist in the two weeks prior to the survey. In all, a total of 301 700 consultations took place. During the same period in addition, vitamins or minerals were consumed by almost 19 per cent of the population (MBRC, 1986: 76). Research conducted for the VSDC found that in the previous year nearly 400 000 Victorian adults had used the services of natural therapists alone (as defined in this chapter) which together with evidence of broad community support and acceptance led to the unanimous conclusion of the all-party inquiry 'that alternative medicine plays a very significant part in the life of many Victorians' (VSDC, 1986, 1: XV).

THE PRINCIPAL MODALITIES

Before proceeding to examine issues of commensurability and legitimacy in detail, it is appropriate to briefly consider the principal modalities involved. Of course the term complementary modalities needs to be applied, as the MBRC did, not only to so called 'alternative' modalities but also to what are often called 'paramedical' or 'ancillary' services as well. These would include such modalities as physiotherapy, speech therapy, occupational therapy and nursing. Furthermore, within the field of what is often called 'alternative' medicine there is a huge range of health care modalities. A recent handbook of alternative medicine lists 51 such modalities (Drury, 1981). Besides the ones analysed here, others include aromatherapy, phrenology, reflexology, hydrotherapy, rolfing and yoga.

Indeed, the modalities may be thought of as occurring along a continuum of legitimacy with chiropractic and osteopathy, natural therapy and traditional Chinese medicine at one end, shading off into more esoteric and spiritual modalities of healing at the other end of the continuum. For the purposes of this chapter, however, the following modalities are the main focus.

Chiropractic specialises in manipulation of the spine for preserving and restoring health. While spinal manipulation is an ancient therapeutic practice, chiropractic itself originated in the United States in the late nineteenth century, with D. D. Palmer and was subsequently developed by his son B. J. Palmer. Chiropractic was first practised in Australia after the First World War and has grown substantially since then to the point where, according to the 1983 health survey conducted by the Australian Bureau of Statistics, chiropractic ranks fourth in demand as the most frequently consulted health modality after orthodox medicine, dentistry and pharmacy.

Chiropractors have statutory registration in all states and territories, and training within the tertiary education system in Melbourne. Chiropractic's paradigm of health knowledge is based upon the notion of 'subluxations' which can be identified by chiropractors from X-ray photographs of the spine. A subluxation is a misalignment of one of the spine's vertebra which causes impaired nerve impulses to be sent out through the spine resulting in a wide variety of disorders. Various inquiries into chiropractic have found it useful to distinguish between two sorts of disorders which chiropractors treat by detection and correction of these subluxations through adjustments: *Type 'M'* or musculoskeletal conditions such as bad backs and the headaches etc. which may result from such condition; and *Type 'O'*—organic or visceral disorders such as ulcers, hypertension and diabetes.

This 'scope of practice' issue has been important in these inquiries as will be discussed later. Two modes of chiropractic practice are evident, though perhaps the distinction is less important than has been the case historically: the practice of *straight* spinal manipulation as the only therapeutic technique; and the practice of *mixers* who combine manipulation with other complementary techniques such as dietary advice (for a more detailed account see Willis, 1989a). In 1984 there were 1475 chiropractors and, as the most popular complementary modality, they gave an estimated 9.7 million treatments in Australia in 1985, a demand, according to the 1983 health survey which was 22 per cent higher than for physiotherapists (MBRC: 1986).

Osteopathy was established in 1874 in the United States by Andrew Taylor Still. In the United States osteopathy has largely been incorporated within orthodox medicine but in Australia, where osteopaths have practised for almost 60 years, it remains a complementary modality, closely aligned with chiropractic. Both utilise spinal manipulation as their primary therapeutic technique, but osteopaths' theory of disease causation differs from chiropractors'. Arterial obstruction, brought about by vertebral displacement (the 'osteopathic lesion') is the cause of the disease, solved by correction of spinal alignment. There were estimated to be between 250 and 300 osteopaths in Australia in 1986, with statutory registration in all states and territories except Western Australia and Tasmania, often under the same act as chiropractic. To a considerable extent osteopathy 'has ridden on the coat tails' of chiropractic and owes much of its success to that relationship. The 1983 health survey found quite low levels of utilisation of osteopathic services; demand was only 10 per cent of that for chiropractic and 40 per cent of that for natural therapies (see MBRC, 1986: 295–305).

Natural therapies is the term that now tends to be preferred to that of naturopathy. As summarised by the VSDC (1986, 1: 62) its paradigm of knowledge is based on the theory that 'ill health is the result of a departure from living in accordance with nature's laws'. Therapy is based upon assisting the body to re-establish its homoeostatic equilibrium, its self-regulating and self-healing capacity. Therapy consists of 'the clinical application of various stimuli which are designed to activate the natural health restoring and health sustaining properties of the body'. A philosophy of an inherent 'vital force' basic to human life is important to this paradigm. In practical terms, as the MBRC (1986: 258) found, 'natural therapies' is an umbrella term used for all treatments that are drugless and non-invasive. Differences in philosophy and preferred treatment are reflected in a lack of unity amongst natural therapists, with several competing occupational organisations claiming to represent their collective interests. The 1983 health survey found significant community demand for naturopathic services, with an estimated annual usage rate of 1.2 million services. A wide range of conditions are claimed to benefit from naturopathic treatment. These include the following conditions: nervous, catarrhal, rheumatic and arthritic, circulatory, gastrointestinal, and urogenital (MBRC, 1986: 262).

The main modalities utilised by a natural therapist are:

- *Nutrition*, including vitamin and mineral therapy.
- *Botanic medicine* or herbalism, an ancient therapy and the basis of some of the treatments of orthodox medicine. Herbs are used to adjust and restore the homeostatic balance of the body.
- *Homeopathy*, developed by a German doctor, Samuel Hahnemann, at the turn of the nineteenth century, is based on the principle of 'like cures like'; that a substance which produces symptoms of disease in a healthy person cures those symptoms in the sick. Its technique consists of diluting therapeutic substances for administration to patients which, far from diminishing its treatment potency, according to homoeopathic theory actually increases it, acting on the sick to restore health. This is a situation for which, almost all parties agree, there is no satisfactory theoretical explanation (see Coulter, 1984: 57–9).
- *Iridology* or iris diagnosis, is a diagnostic technique whereby the iris of the eye is examined to assess the condition of all body organs and thus enable diagnosis of past and present disease. It is a diagnostic technique used by most natural therapists in conjunction with more conventional investigations such as case histories (see VSDC 1986, 1: 73–4).

Traditional Chinese medicine (TCM) has been introduced into Australia on a large scale only in the last twenty years, though of course it is many centuries old. The paradigm of health knowledge is based on the philosophies of Confucianism and Taoism and was fully evolved as early as 600 BC. The paradigm is 'first and foremost a holistic one in which health is understood as the cooperative functioning of parts within a context' (Chow, 1984: 115). The treatment techniques outlined below are based on the principles of yin and yang (the polarities or opposites and their interplay), the five phases (the sequence of relationships), and the chi (the flow of vital energy).

The main modalities utilised by a practitioner of traditional Chinese medicine are:

- *Acupuncture* which is the best-known treatment technique and involves the insertion of fine needles into surface points on the skin. The needle is manipulated to disperse or reactivate the chi. The surface points, of which 700 are well known, are connected in a network of meridians which make internal organs accessible to treatment of a wide variety of conditions. Acupuncture can also be used as an analgesic in performing operations.

- *Acupressure* treatment uses the same points of the body as acupuncture but fingertips rather than needles apply pressure. It is particularly used for pain relief.
- *Moxibustion* is frequently used to complement acupuncture. The remedial effect comes from heating the skin by burning moxa sticks over energy points.
- *Remedial massage* involves a complex set of hand movements on specific areas of the body.
- *Cupping* involves placing heated jars over points of the body, sometimes containing herbs, to disperse congestion.
- *Chinese herbal medicine, respiratory exercise*, and *physical exercise* (tai chi) are also important as therapies (see Chow, 1984).

Acupuncture is the most commonly utilised of these modalities, though often in conjunction with other therapies. It is difficult to assess how many practitioners perform acupuncture. On the orthodox medicine side, practitioners have varying amounts of training in TCM in addition to training in orthodox medicine. They range from highly trained practitioners who perform acupuncture solely or mainly in varying combinations with other TCM techniques, to others with relatively minimal amounts of training who might occasionally attempt acupuncture when conventional treatments fail. Then there are also a large number of 'lay' (that is, non-medically qualified) practitioners of TCM also with variable amounts of training. Again these also vary from those who solely use TCM therapies, to others, particularly natural therapists who occasionally use them. One estimate given to the MBRC (1986: 101) was that there were approximately 730 non-medical practitioners describing themselves as acupuncturists.

THE CASE FOR CONVERGENCE

Here it is argued that the term complementary is to be preferred to that of 'alternative' medicine, not merely for semantic reasons but because of decreasing incommensurability. Either is a fairly loose umbrella term which does only partial justice to the complexities of the issues involved as well as the differences not only between the different modalities but also within them. Natural therapists, for instance, have quite considerable differences in orientation represented by several different and mutually hostile occupational organisations.

The two governmental inquiries being reviewed in this paper, differed in their approach to this question. The narrower Victorian inquiry was constrained by its terms of reference to examine only what is referred to in this paper (more or less) as natural therapies (naturopathy, homeopathy, herbalism, iridology and orthomolecular medicine). The broader Commonwealth MBRC by contrast preferred 'complementary health services' as its focus, arguing it to be a more neutral term 'in the sense of those [modalities] which complement the services of the medical profession without implying any relationship of superiority or inferiority' (1986: 72).

The issue hinges on the extent of commensurability between the paradigms of health knowledge of conventional western scientific medicine and those of complementary modalities such as chiropractic, homeopathy or traditional Chinese medicine. While it has been traditional to view the paradigms of knowledge upon which treatments were based as entirely different 'alternatives', a careful reading of submissions made to the various inquiries into complementary health care supports an argument of convergence at least amongst the more widely accepted complementary modalities analysed here. Several points can be made in support of this argument of convergence.

Firstly, practitioners of these modalities have gradually and now commonly include as components of at least their process of diagnosis, techniques common in conventional medical treatment. Research conducted amongst natural therapists for the VSDC (1986, 1: 85–6) found that 94 per cent of the 278 who responded utilised patient histories, 83 per cent measured blood pressure and 81 per cent conducted physical examinations. Significant proportions also did pathology tests of various sorts. The only diagnostic technique widely used by natural therapists which has little or no place in conventional medical diagnostic techniques was iris diagnosis (73 per cent). In addition, many patients seen by these practitioners had already consulted orthodox practitioners, often had had their conditions diagnosed and had turned to complementary modalities when orthodox treatment failed.

Secondly, a trend has become evident of practitioners of complementary modalities assuming greater responsibility for recognition of their limitations and a growing willingness to refer patients in whom serious illness is detected or suspected, for conventional medical treatment. Amongst natural therapists surveyed for the VSDC (1986, 2: 107–8) 94 per cent sent patients to orthodox medical practitioners, most commonly for problems they were legally not allowed (84 per cent) or not trained to treat (78 per cent) or for pathology tests (73 per cent). Interestingly 68 per cent of those natural therapists surveyed, claimed that referrals were reciprocal, that they had patients referred to them by orthodox medical practitioners.

With this growing responsibility there has been a considerable (though by no means total) abandonment of some of the claims to provide a complete and total system of health care. This has been based upon a growing recognition, at least amongst major segments of these modalities and their occupational associations in particular, that this is essential in order to secure increased legitimacy represented on one hand by the development of a secure niche in the division of labour in health care in Australia, and State patronage in the form of registration, State subsidised education through the tertiary education system, and even entry into State health schemes such as Medicare on the other. Chiropractic is a good example, where there is considerable recognition that its safest ground and most secure occupational territory is in the treatment of musculo-skeletal conditions (Type 'M') such as back problems (the bulk of services provided) and that the process of growing legitimacy it has enjoyed will be enhanced by de-emphasising its ability to treat organic or visceral conditions (Type 'O'). The Medicare inquiry, for example, qualified its acceptance of the effectiveness of chiropractic as follows

> sufficient material was placed before us to satisfy us that the services provided by chiropractic in relation to musculo-skeletal conditions, are effective . . . For the other services namely the Type O treatments . . . there is insufficient material for us to determine their effectiveness. (MBRC, 1986: 150–1)

They went on to conclude:

> the continued claim by chiropractors to be able to treat 'Type O' conditions is a major obstacle to us making any recommendations for public funding for chiropractic services in general. . . . Because administratively it is impossible to perform only part of the work performed by a practitioner of any modality we do not feel able to recommend such public funding while the issue of scope of practice in relation to 'Type O' conditions remain unresolved. (MBRC, 1986: 159)

The third argument in favour of convergence arises out of the apparent paradox that all the treatment techniques provided by these complementary practitioners are also provided by at least some members of the medical profession. Manipulation, acupuncture, vitamin and mineral therapy and herbal remedies are all available from medical practitioners as well as from other complementary practitioners traditionally considered orthodox. Perhaps only iridology is an exception. In other words, the question is not so much the techniques or indeed the paradigms of knowledge themselves, but who should perform them. Indeed it is arguable that in some cases complementary practitioners are much better trained in these services than medical doctors. 'Lay' acupuncturists (that is, non-medically trained) are a good example; they are trained in many cases for up to seven years, compared to short courses of training offered to existing medical practitioners, and with considerable justification, regard the training undertaken by medical practitioners as akin to first-aid training in the modality. The extent of incommensurability has therefore tended to be overemphasised, often for political reasons on both sides.

The fourth argument for convergence is the trend towards the decline in the importance of the issue of commensurability or incommensurability as the basis for legitimacy. Here it is necessary to draw on a distinction made elsewhere (Willis, 1989a) between scientific legitimacy on one hand and clinical legitimacy on the other as different bases for politico-legal legitimacy. Such politico-legal legitimacy is achieved by an occupation through the education of its practitioners (for example, medical practitioners) into a paradigm of occupational knowledge (for example, western scientific medicine) culminating in the attainment of a recognised degree or degrees (MB, BS for medical practitioners) as the basis for occupational registration, certifying the acquisition of role knowledge necessary to practise that occupation. Science is of course an important source of legitimacy in modern capitalist societies, and is claimed by the medical profession as the basis for its politico-legal legitimacy and the denial of such legitimacy to the complementary modalities under consideration here. *Scientific* legitimacy however is not the only basis for politico-legal legitimation, also important is *clinical* legitimacy; that is to say, that in order to survive and flourish over time any health occupation must continue to be patronised by clients. In other words it must be legitimated on-the-job, in the day-to-day routine performance of its work in the practical solving or alleviation of the health problems its patients present.

The argument to be made here is that clinical legitimacy has become increasingly important as the basis of politico-legal legitimation and has come to assume greater importance than scientific legitimacy such as to make the overall issue of the extent of incommensurability less central in assessing politico-legal legitimacy.

The traditional basis of opposition from the medical profession to the complementary modalities under consideration here is their unscientific basis, that is to say that there is little or no evidence of a scientific nature to support the paradigms of knowledge that these practitioners use. These modalities have been labelled 'cults' or 'philosophies' as a result of their alleged lack of scientific legitimacy and the politico-legal legitimacy denied them. While orthodox medicine has always had difficulty claiming to be more successful in treating many of the conditions also treated by the complementary modalities considered here, it has always been able to claim that it was more scientific. The VSDC (1986, 1: 95) summed up the view of orthodox medicine that:

> many of the procedures and associated beliefs of alternative medicine are incompatible with the corpus of scientific knowledge and must be rejected by anyone who accepts the general validity of the latter . . . Scientific methodology is accepted as an integral part of Western society and as the most widely acceptable basis for evaluation of therapies and remedies employed in medicine.

Whereas 'alternative medicine' provided evidence based upon anecdotes, testimonials and single case studies, orthodox medicine lays firm emphasis on observation, measurement, reproducibility of findings, peer review and publishing of results in professional journals (VSDC, 1986, 1: 95–97).

There are a number of problems with this commonly expressed claim that the complementary modalities are unscientific, such that it must be considered part of the political process of exclusion which has operated historically and is only recently being eroded. Firstly, there has been very little research done on the basic science aspects of these complementary modalities. Most of their limited funds have been directed to survival, and medical dominance of research funding has ensured no support for research of this nature. Even very specific recommendations from official inquiries have remained unanswered; as was the case with the specific recommendation from the Webb inquiry (1977: 207) that $200 000 be made available annually for research into chiropractic. In other words, the scientific basis of their modalities remains neither proven nor disproven, but unproven one way or the other.

Secondly, if, as is often claimed by the medical profession, much of the success of these complementary modalities is due to the placebo effect, then the same argument must apply to many conventional medical treatments. Thirdly, there is the paradox outlined above that a lack of an established scientific basis has not prevented some sections of the medical profession utilising therapeutic techniques which are clinically similar to those used by the complementary practitioners. In other words, what the theories say may be different to what actually happens in practice. Fourthly, the emphasis has changed from an emphasis on researching the *basic* science aspects (do subluxations exist?) to *applied* considerations of whether the treatments work, especially utilising the methodology of randomised control trials. Here again there are difficulties, not only of getting funding but of a methodological nature. There are difficulties for instance in measuring 'improvement', which necessarily has a subjective component (what the patient tells you).

Various trials have been conducted into aspects of these complementary modalities, both in Australia and overseas. Most have been conducted in the area of chiropractic treatment with varying thoroughness and sophistication (Kane et al., 1974; Doran & Newell, 1975; Breen, 1971; Parker & Tupling, 1976; Fisk, 1980). The best that can be said of them is that they are inconclusive and don't really allow specific conclusions to be drawn either way as to the efficacy of spinal manipulative therapy.

In the case of traditional Chinese medicine such as acupuncture, the outcomes of trials have also been equivocal, though in cases of chronic pain up to 70 per cent of cases experienced a useful effect in reducing pain. For other conditions such as obesity and smoking cessation, acupuncture was about as effective as other common methods (Moore & Berk, 1976; Fox & Melzack, 1976; Mendelson et al., 1983).

In the case of natural therapies which have more recently begun to be evaluated by this method, some promising results have been shown. Strictly vegetarian 'vegan' dietary regimes have been shown to have some effectiveness in reducing hypertension (Lindahl et al., 1984); the use of the herb valeriana has been shown to be effective in sleeplessness (Leatherwood et al., 1982) and most recently homeopathic treatment has been shown to be effective in the treatment of hayfever (Reilly et al., 1986). This last trial, conducted on a randomised, double blind, placebo-controlled basis, is worth commenting on further. Patients with active hayfever (rhinitis) treated with a homoeopathic preparation showed a significant improvement in their symptoms compared with those treated with a placebo. Since the preparation of homoeopathic treatments involved diluting the chemical substance to the point where in theory none of the original active ingredient remains, the result makes no sense at all when viewed from the perspective of the medical profession. As the authors conclude, the findings 'are a contemporary restatement of an empirical puzzle now in its second century and represent a confusing challenge to orthodox scientific models' (Reilly et al., 1986: 885). With all these complementary modalities, the appearance of a few relatively successful swallows in the form of trials, don't make a summer of effectiveness but certainly provide a basis for pursuing more research of this nature.

The growing emphasis on the outcome of treatment rather than the underlying theory of ill health and treatment, however, marks a change from the basic science aspects to the applied aspects and makes less relevant the question of the underlying commensurability of the paradigms of knowledge. As the New Zealand report on chiropractic (1979: 45) concluded on this issue, 'the efficacy of the treatment becomes the important issue in the inquiry, rather than the adequacy of the explanations so far advanced in an attempt to account for chiropractic's apparent success'.

From this point of view, the lack of scientific legitimacy becomes less important as the emphasis has shifted towards clinical legitimacy as the basis for politico-legal legitimation. Indeed medicine's opposition to chiropractic on the grounds of it being a 'philosophy' rather than a 'science' is labelled a 'red herring' by the New Zealand report (1979: 45).

The increasing utilisation of the complementary modalities discussed here, and high levels of satisfaction reported by many patients, leave little doubt as to clinical legitimacy. Research conducted for the Webb inquiry estimated that a quarter of a million new patients visit these complementary practitioners with high levels of satisfaction reported by many (Boven et al., 1977). Research conducted for the VSDC (1986, 2: 65) on levels of satisfaction with the assistance received from natural therapists found that 85 per cent of the 497 users of these services surveyed were either very satisfied (56 per cent) or quite satisfied (29 per cent).

But while there is considerable evidence of the clinical success of these complementary modalities, explanations of *why* this occurs are less than adequate. As the New Zealand report (1979: 45) concluded of chiropractic, 'indeed it is probably true to say that chiropractic is a form of treatment still in search of an explanation for its effectiveness'. In other words, there has emerged a significant disjunction between scientific legitimacy on one hand which still remains largely unestablished, and clinical legitimacy on the other which arguably is well established. In the face of this disjunction, a trend is discernible whereby practitioners of these complementary modalities, more secure in their clinical success, have become less dogmatic and openly oppositional in relation to their underlying paradigm of health knowledge vis-à-vis the medical profession. In this context, greater openness and less emphasis on incommensurability have promoted convergence.

How then is the clinical success of these modalities (as indicated by high levels of patient satisfaction) to be explained? Apart from the obvious answers that they may actually work or may be substantially due to a placebo effect, a number of different explanations have been advanced. A major one is to stress the psychosocial aspects of treatment, that the complementary practitioner may be more interpersonally skilled in the sense of being more attuned to the total needs of the patient than doctors are. Parker and Tupling

(1976: 61) summarise this view based upon their study of the psychosocial aspects of chiropractic treatment.

> It may be that chiropractors have successfully combined a physiologically effective therapy with an elaborate healing ritual in such a way that they can help more people by spinal manipulation than would respond to a doctor or physiotherapist performing the same manipulation without the trimmings.

A recent analysis of the growth in popularity of these modalities in the last twenty years by Maddocks (1985: 550), written for a medical audience, concluded:

> Reasons for the success of alternative medicine should therefore be sought in its preparedness to enter areas of human discomfort which conventional medicine tends to ignore as trivial or beyond hope, in its reputed rapidity of benefits, its intimate and touching style and its congruence with social aspirations for holism and balanced ecology. It also constitutes a criticism of some features of current medical practice.

The last point Maddocks makes is particularly significant. It reflects the implied critique of conventional medicine; in other words the clinical success of these complementary modalities may be effective because of the failure of conventional medicine to provide the sort of care that people need, rather than their excellence *per se*. The direction in which scientific medicine has developed identified by Salmon (1984) is important in this. He cites trends such as the separation of the theoretical unity of mental, emotional and spiritual aspects of healing with the physical or somatic aspects, the increasing emphasis on technological intervention rather than human mediation of illness (see also Berliner, 1984) and the requirement of passivity on the part of patients as they are increasingly separated from their own social histories. As Salmon (1984: 5) comments, 'the fact remains that while healing is undeniably a social process, scientific medicine has generally downplayed the connections of its social aspects to the practical content of therapeutics'.

One note of caution to be entered here in assessing these arguments proposed for the clinical success of the complementary modalities, is that the modalities differ substantially in the extent to which they espouse the holistic orientation which is often seen as one of their unifying features. Chiropractic for example, particularly as practised as '*straight*' spinal manipulation rather than that technique *mixed* with other therapeutic techniques such as dietary advice, would rank low in terms of holism.

In an overall sense though, to summarise this section, if the argument made here about convergence has validity, then the use-fulness of the term 'alternative' must be called into question. On the basis of this argument, a distinction must be made between those modalities analysed here—chiropractic and osteopathy, natural therapies, and traditional Chinese medicine—and all the other modalities usually lumped together under the umbrella term 'alternative medicine'. The modalities focused upon constitute a legitimate part of the health services of this country and must be considered as complementing rather than being in opposition to orthodox medicine. Continuing to lump these modalities with all others serves no one's interest except perhaps that of the medical profession in tarring all with the same brush in a rearguard action opposing the growing politico-legal legitimacy of the modalities under consideration here, and justifying their continued exclusion from State patronage, the focus of the next section of this paper.

SOCIAL POLICY ASPECTS

If large numbers of Australians are increasingly consulting practitioners of these complementary modalities with considerable success, to the point where these modalities constitute an important component of the health services of the nation, then the crucial social policy question that has had and is increasingly having to be addressed is: 'How can the provision of these complementary services be organised so as to benefit in the maximum possible way the greatest number of the populace?'. Answering this question is furthermore complicated by the fact that the same services (such as acupuncture) are provided by both conventional and complementary practitioners.

The answer provided by the medical profession to this question has been relatively consistent: that these services should be provided only by practitioners qualified in western scientific medicine first and foremost, and then subsequently trained in these modalities. In other words, incorporation of the best of these complementary modalities into conventional medicine would remove the need and the rationale for separate health occupations. Homeopathy in the United States is a good example of a modality that has been incorporated into mainstream medicine (see Maddocks, 1985: 550).

The medical profession's solution to the social policy question in this country has met with very limited favour. One reason is that the number of medical practitioners who utilise some of the techniques (such as spinal manipulation) has remained small, despite repeated requests from a vocal section of the profession to expand its use and thus remove the justification for, in this case, chiropractors.

Another reason is that the complementary modalities themselves have struggled long and hard to prevent this occurring, demonstrating at different times both their potential strength and, through contracted research, the extent of their clinical legitimacy. In 1981 for instance, a proposal from the National Health and Medical Research Council to limit the administration of vitamin and mineral supplements to being supervised by medical practitioners led to an estimated 120 000 letters being sent to members of parliament and a government decision was made not to proceed.

This controversy has been the basis for the long struggle between conventional and alternative medicine. The rewards in terms of income, prestige and control of economic resources are enormous. These complementary modalities are of course no different in this respect. Their striving for legitimacy and a secure niche in the division of labour in Australian health care is in considerable part an attempt to improve their share of health rewards. Indeed, the debate is characterised by a certain coyness about its competitive aspects from both sides; much is heard about what is in the best interests of the patient but demarcation issues remain central.

The arena for this struggle has always been the State. Politico-legal legitimacy ultimately rests upon State patronage. This patronage takes several forms: subsidised training in the occupation through the tertiary education system; statutory registration of practitioners to provide a legal basis to occupational territory; receiving of research funds; and more recently entry into State health insurance schemes such as Medibank and Medicare. All these forms require the allocation of public funding of varying proportions. Historically these complementary modalities under consideration here have sought State patronage as outlined above. While some have achieved the provision of rebates for their services through private health insurance companies, this does not itself constitute State patronage even though it confers some, though nothing like, the legitimacy that State patronage would confer. A decision by a private health insurance company to offer rebates for these complementary services is a purely commercial decision of assessed profitability.

Their search for State patronage has been continually opposed at all levels, however, by the medical profession. The phenomenon of medical dominance operates at several levels including that of the State, where medical doctors are the institutionalised experts in all matters relating to health care and all forms of State patronage are enjoyed.

The State apparatuses such as Parliament and the health bureaucracies have been the site of this struggle. Here the growing dis-junctions between scientific and clinical legitimacy outlined earlier have become increasingly important as the basis for policy decisions over the extent of politico-legal legitimacy. The medical profession has traditionally argued that scientific legitimacy should be the basis for State patronage, and that this patronage should only be accorded to those modalities of which it approved (physiotherapy, for exam-ple). Traditionally, State patronage could only be secured by first securing the approval of the medical profession. The complementary modalities, by contrast, have argued that clinical legitimacy should be the rationale for such patronage and have pressured politicians for the fruits of State patronage. In such a complex situation, governments of the day have found it difficult to resist the conven-tional bureaucratic response to such controversial and complex situations of, 'let's have an inquiry'. Since 1961, there have been a dozen such inquiries in Australia and New Zealand, the last two (VSDC and MBRC) of which have been reviewed here (for details see VSDC, 1986, 1: 14–22). These various inquiries have probed various aspects of the complementary modalities under consider-ation here, though the advisability of either statutory registration for these modalities or entry into State-funded health schemes have been the most common.

While there has been an element of reinventing the wheel about these inquiries, they have been very important to the historical process of political legitimation in several ways. Firstly, the com-missioning of independent research into both basic and applied aspects of these modalities has clarified the picture greatly in a situation where very little was known. Secondly, the recommen-dations while not always consistent, have provided guidelines for the occupational development of these modalities. Though a consid-erable amount remains to be done, between inquiries as it were, they have been able to concentrate on putting their 'house in order' and a gradual process of this nature has been apparent.

Most importantly however, these inquiries have largely accepted the argument that clinical legitimacy should be the basis for politi-cal-legal legitimacy. As such, the State has moved to a position of greater independence in relation to the medical profession. Chiro-practic leads the way in this process, statutorily registered first in Victoria in 1975 and then subsequently in every state and territory, even in the teeth of medical opposition. It has been less successful in those areas of State patronage where medical dominance is most apparent, such as dissemination of research funding, and had its ambitions to receive Medicare schedule items thwarted in consider-able part by the fiscal crisis of the State which restricted the expansion of public funding. Significantly though, in terms of growing politico-legal legitimacy, it did win a recommendation that chiropractors be allowed entry into those bastions of medical dominance, namely hospitals.

State patronage, of course, is directed at attempting to guarantee standards of practice by adequate training on one hand and legally demarcating occupational territory and the occupational title on the other (who may call themselves a chiropractor). Answering the social policy questions of how best to organise these services and guarantee standards of practice, involves considering the extent of State patronage that is appropriate for particular modalities (should they be registered, etc.?). The argument in this chapter has been that in answering both these questions a distinction is necessary between the complementary modalities discussed here and others usually included under the rubric of alternative medicine.

CONCLUSION

This paper has developed a sociological analysis of that area of 'health care' usually called 'alternative' medicine, but which it has been argued here should be called *complementary* health care. In the current context, where the modalities discussed here are a significant and legitimate part of the health care system, the continued use of the term 'alternative' is counterproductive in view of the urgent social policy question of how to organise these modalities so as to serve the maximum number of people to the greatest extent. The basis for this argument has been a trend towards convergence of the different paradigms of health knowledge, not so much in theory but in the day-to-day routine attempts to solve or alleviate health care problems presented. This trend towards convergence has been slow but has been crystallised by the numerous inquiries that have been held.

Much remains to be done. On the part of the medical profession, a continued blanket opposition is no longer appropriate. On the part of the complementary modalities themselves, there are varying amounts of 'putting houses in order' still to be achieved—in particular, restraining their more esoteric fringe elements. For both there is a need to promote an active program of research into both the basic and applied aspects of those modalities' treatments and also a need to seek better working relationships at a day-to-day level so that each may learn from the other. Only in this situation can the overall aim of the health workforce be realised: that of improving people's health.

POSTSCRIPT

My interest in what has broadly been known as complementary or alternative medicine stemmed from the work on chiropractic that formed part of *Medical Dominance* (1989a). In sociological terms, I found it fascinating that, in the face of trenchant opposition from the medical profession, some of these alternative modalities had withered and practically perished while others had flourished. While there are hazards in generalising, in a general sense it can be clearly stated that the modalities discussed in this chapter have something to offer the health of the populace, so that the question becomes: 'How can their integration into the mainstream health system be pursued in such a way as to maximise the benefits to the health of Australians?'.

The call for more research is one commonly made in this field. It is frequently argued, especially by the medical profession, that the assertions of efficacy made by the proponents of these complementary modalities should be subjected to scientific scrutiny. Yet the politics of research are complicated. For one thing, a number of the inquiries that have been held into complementary medicine have recommended that funds be made available for research to be conducted, but this call has invariably fallen on the deaf ears of those medically controlled bodies responsible for the allocation of research monies.

Secondly, there is the question, related to the call for independent research to be conducted in this field of, 'Who is independent?'. If members of neither the medical profession, nor practitioners of complementary medicine can be considered independent, then who remains? Medical scientists, another possible group, are most often employed in medically controlled research laboratories.

In spite of these difficulties, some research *is* conducted. A recent landmark study in the field of chiropractic is the study of the efficacy of spinal manipulation for treatment of low back pain, conducted by Shekelle et al. (1992) at the Rand Corporation in the United States. Using a methodology of health services research known as meta-analysis, they reviewed all known studies of the efficacy of spinal manipulation for this condition and conclude that it is effective.

So, there is growing recognition of the legitimacy of complementary modalities; that they are here to stay and, as evidenced by large numbers of the population who continue to fork over their hard-earned cash to be treated by these practitioners, (even though not corroborated by a great deal of actual scientific research), must be doing some people some good, at least some of the time.

Such recognition even extends to organised medicine. In their

latest diatribe against chiropractic, the Australian Medical Association (1992) in effect gives recognition to the ability of chiropractors
for instance to alleviate musculoskeletal conditions, by calling for
their registration to be limited to the treatment of these conditions,
albeit in a backhand way by arguing that other practitioners such
as physiotherapists are even better at treatment of these conditions.
Although individual medical practitioners may be located along a
continuum of acceptance of complementary healers—from a few
who enthusiastically embrace what these modalities have to offer at
one end, to those few at the other end who still regard complementary practitioners as evil quacks—nonetheless, this AMA document
is strong testament to the ongoing trenchant hostility from the most
public voice of conventional medicine to the very existence of
chiropractic and other complementary healers.

Part 2

TECHNOLOGY AND HEALTH CARE

6 Technological innovation and the labour process in health care
Jeanne Daly and Evan Willis

The publication of Braverman's seminal work (1974) and the consequent reorientation of sociological studies on work towards concerns of political economy, sparked a considerable amount of research activity in the post-Braverman era as the agenda which Braverman set has been explored. Most research in this labour process tradition has involved examining the organisation and control of that labour process in work contexts such as factories and offices where the *direct* capitalist relations of domination and subordination involved in wage labour exist. In this paper, by contrast, the questions that Braverman and subsequent analysts posed about the organisation and control of the labour process are examined in the context of *indirect* wage labour relations of that area of the workforce known as the professions. Taking health care as our case study, and the labour process surrounding diagnostic imaging technology in particular, we examine the professional labour process.

At first glance the medical system seems to contradict Braverman's thesis. Major new health care technologies have tended to be labour complementing and not labour displacing. Commonly, a new technique allows the creation of a new medical speciality skilled in its use as well as a new category of lesser-skilled worker to assist the specialist. So, for example, the introduction of X-ray diagnosis in 1895 had led to the emergence of both radiologists and radiographers working under the direct control of the radiologists (see also chapter 2 for a discussion of this development). Importantly, X-ray diagnosis did not displace earlier diagnostic devices like the stethoscope which remain in use to this day. It is auxiliary workers who have the *potential* to be technologically deskilled with continuing technological innovation. However as Cockburn (1985: 124–5) has shown, while the latest version of X-ray machines, the automated CT scanners are largely 'idiot proof' and thus potentially threaten the skills of radiographers, the greater diagnostic scope of the machines has in fact meant an augmentation of their skills as a greater range of tasks are undertaken.

Radiologists are arguably the most highly technologised of medical specialists but they have been able to resist deskilling with each major technological innovation—first X-rays themselves, then ultrasound, CT scanners and most recently nuclear magnetic resonance imaging. Their dominance has been and is such that they exert a powerful influence over all decisions made about imaging technology. Indeed radiologists have so successfully controlled the market for their services that the Australian state government of Victoria has recently held an inquiry (analysed in this paper) into the effects of the radiologists' control, in particular the 'uncompetitively high' incomes of radiologists in private practice.

The aim of this chapter is to argue that professional labour process involving the medical profession does not stand in contradiction to labour process theory but can be used to analyse the professions. Not the least of the advantages of studying the medical profession in particular is to delineate the social contexts in which technological innovation provides a means of empowering workers.

As has been argued elsewhere (Willis, 1988), one of the major lines of critique of Braverman's work has been that some concepts which are essential to an adequate analysis of the labour process in advanced capitalist societies such as Australia are either missing from or insufficiently developed in his analysis. In this paper we argue, following Burawoy (1985), that two essential conceptual ingredients largely undeveloped in Braverman's work but important to an adequate understanding of the professional labour process in general, and technological innovation in particular, are those of ideology and the capitalist State. Ideology we use here as a complex and contradictory set of ideas, representations, actions and practices grounded in social relations. That is, it consists not only of ideas, rationalisations, justifications, but also has a material force in actual concrete practices (what people do). This argument is developed in the first part of the paper. In the second part of the paper we turn to a more detailed analysis of the *effects* of technological innovation on the labour process in health care. Drawing on earlier work (Daly, 1985; Daly & Willis, 1987; Willis, 1989a) we consider the process of technological innovation in general, and X-ray diagnosis in particular.

THE MEDICAL PROFESSION, IDEOLOGY AND THE STATE

Our starting point is with class analysis in the world of work, an issue which Braverman brought back to the centre stage of sociological analysis from the wings where it had tended to be relegated. Although class relations between the dominant or ruling class and the working class in advanced capitalist society constitutes the major structural relation of domination and subordination which shapes these societies through the social division of labour, any comprehensive analysis also requires an account of intermediary class grouping. The middle class, far from withering under the impact of proletarianisation as Marx predicted has remained and indeed developed as an important structural feature of capitalist societies such as Australia. Our concern is with those occupations recognised as being professions, which constitute an important part of the new middle class. Professionals indeed are defined as 'new middle class' irrespective of their employment status as wage labourers (that is, salaried) or self-employed. Following Gramsci (1971: 12) it is on the basis of their contribution to the maintenance of ideological hegemony, the basis of capitalist social order, that they are so defined. Professionals such as members of the medical profession act as organic intellectuals to the dominant class, mediating the relationship of domination and subordination between classes and reproducing labour power by, for instance, writing medical certificates to legitimate work absences or conducting pre-employment screenings to assess fitness to enter a wage labour contract. Their importance at the level of ideology is that they are 'experts in legitimation' (Merrington 1968: 154) who 'act as the mediators of the realities of capitalism into values' (Davidson 1968: 45).

The conceptual confusion with the terms 'profession', 'professionalisation' and 'professionalism' has been considerable. Whatever utility the term may have in commonsense language it has severe limitations as an analytical category. One response however is to examine the phenomenon historically. The professions as we know them today, originated with the advent of capitalism in the nineteenth century (Laslett, 1971) and their expansion provided a link between the educational system and the occupational order (Schudson, 1980). Their emergence soon attracted the attention of social scientists especially Durkheim (1957) who saw their emergence positively as a source of stability and integration in a modernising world. The tradition of study of professional work which developed reflected this Durkheimian legacy, until recently when it has been argued that professions, professionalisation and professionalism were matters of power and control (Freidson, 1970a; Johnson, 1972). The claim to being a profession was seen as a claim

to a particular form of self-governance of the occupation, to maintenance of internal self-control over the occupation (autonomy).
Professionalism could thus be analysed as an occupational ideology
which legitimates autonomy (see also Larsen, 1977). As Freidson
argues, professionalism is 'a deliberate rhetoric in the political
process of lobbying, public relations and other forms of persuasion
to attain full control over its work' (1970a: 80).

In labour process terms then, professionalism can be seen as a
form of resistance to the imposition of control external to the
occupation itself, a strategy for maintaining the unity of conception
and execution in the performance of work. Importantly, it must also
be analysed as a strategy involving quite explicit gender and class
aspects. Regarding gender, as Versluysen argues: 'theorists of professions ignore the fact that groups which have successfully
professionalised have usually been male in composition' (1981: 22).
While ideology in this or any other context does not operate in a
straightforward, even way, but in a complex, contradictory uneven
fashion, in class terms the ideology of professionalism reproduces
aspects of the dominant class ideology and promotes hegemony. In
particular, professionalism reproduces what Habermas (1970) calls
the 'ideology of expertise', that only those who have specialised
knowledge can adequately make decisions about appropriate courses
of action (such as treatment), despite the ease of demonstrating that
for instance, many medical decisions are made as much on moral
and political grounds as they are on purely technical grounds. The
claim to skill or expertise, furthermore, is articulated as beneficent
power based on the notion of technological rationality, the claim to
effectiveness, and on individualism. Yet in class terms, as Larsen
(1977) has shown for a number of capitalist countries, professionalism legitimates inequality and élitism. Professionalism also has
important ideological consequences in blinding the facts of relative
subordination and powerlessness by the professionals themselves,
thus pacifying them. As Larsen argues:

> as the labour force tends to become totally subsumed under the
> relations of capitalist production, the real and ideological privileges
> associated with 'professionalism' legitimise the class structure by
> introducing status, differential status aspirations and status mobility
> at practically all levels of the occupational hierarchy. (1977: 239)

THE LABOUR PROCESS IN HEALTH CARE

Turning now to the professional labour process in the area of health
care more specifically, two features are immediately apparent. One

is its hierarchical nature, the other its domination by one occupation—the medical profession. The labour process is constituted as a very complex division of labour in part negotiated on a day-to-day basis (see Freidson, 1976) but overwhelmingly formally imposed and codified. The process by which this division of labour developed and medical dominance was achieved and defended has been analysed in detail elsewhere (Willis, 1989a). Briefly though, medical dominance (that is, dominance by the medical profession) is sustained at three levels: autonomy, authority, and medical sovereignty. Doctors dominate the relationship between the health sector and the wider society; doctors are institutionalised experts on all matters relating to health. Thus medical dominance of the labour process in health care as Larkin has argued, is only 'a shorthand concept for a complex historical process of the establishment of control' (1978: 853).

Professional expertise and the issues of skill

In this section we turn to a consideration of skill in the context of the professional labour process, using health care as our example. Our starting point is to note that in the professional labour process, skill tends to be constructed as expertise. Although the two terms are in many ways synonymous, an aspect of the ideology of professionalism is to construct skilled workers as 'experts'. Being 'professional' (rather than amateurish) involves bringing expertise to bear on a particular range of issues. The difference between the conceptions of skill and expertise, insofar as it exists is in the greater emphases on knowledge (mental labour) in expertise. A skilled worker is one expressing a unity of manual and mental labour, of hand, eye and brain. A professional expert by contrast is more likely to be concerned with the design or planning than with the execution of a task. The expertise of a doctor may be more concerned with defining illness and devising a strategy for treatment than with the execution of the treatment. This gives rise to the phenomenon of 'pass-the-task' whereby over time, the more mundane, routine manual tasks are delegated to lower-order occupations. Obvious examples are ward-based hospital care by nurses and the dispensing of drugs by pharmacists.

Nor is this process of differentiation restricted only to doctors but occurs as 'subprofessional dominance' as well further down the hierarchy. The creation of the occupation of State-enrolled nurses (formerly nurses' aides) is a good example of this process, as mundane manual tasks of nursing (such as emptying bedpans) have been delegated as part of the occupational territory or task domain of other occupations.

This mental/manual distinction fails to account for the high value attached to the skill of, for example, a cardiac surgeon and here a useful analytical device is the distinction between elements of technicality and indeterminacy in the work performed by an occupation, made by Jamous and Peloille (1970). The technical aspects are those which are susceptible to codification by rules, procedures and techniques and could be made available to others in the form of a manual (how to bandage a sprained ankle). The indeterminacy aspects by contrast are those which are not codifiable into precise prescriptions of tasks. As Atkinson et al. (1977) argue these personal 'rules of thumb' such as interpersonal skills, clinical judgment, 'flair' or 'knack' cannot be easily taught to others. All occupations contain a mixture of technicality and indeterminacy, of explicit and implicit expertise and it is possible to compare occupations in terms of the ratio of indeterminate to technical elements (I/T ratio). In the health labour process the medical profession has a high ratio of indeterminate elements to technical elements sometimes called 'medical mystique' (Atkinson et al., 1977). It is this claim to uncodifiable indeterminacy in medical expertise which has provided a powerful means of resisting technological deskilling. The more codifiable aspects of clinical practice have, by a process of specialisation of the division of labour, been incorporated into the training of subordinate occupations and it is their susceptibility to deskilling which provides a buffer for the medical profession.

What then is skill/expertise in the medical profession? While not denying objective criteria for the concept—notably the existence of job autonomy—for the purpose of this analysis skill/expertise is best seen as socially constructed, as a form of social status, created and maintained through politically limiting the expertise of other competing occupations by a combination of custom and tradition and collective organisation through trade unions or professional associations. Historically, the Australian Medical Association, in classic trade union fashion has provided resistance to alternative modes of organising and controlling the labour process in health care.

Their strategy for establishing and maintaining dominance and control over the labour process has been two pronged. At the level of their own work, of autonomy, they have attempted to create and defend the direct employment relationship between themselves and their clientele, patients. Two phases of this struggle have been apparent: firstly, to rid themselves of salaried employment with Friendly Societies (see Green & Cromwell, 1984); and secondly to resist the entry of government as a third party in the various proposals for salaried service along the lines of the British National Health Service. Uniquely in Australia, they were able to mount a successful constitutional case against salaried service, succeeding in the High Court in 1949, with the highly questionable argument that salaried medical service constituted a form of civil conscription, something the Australian Constitution proscribes. The direct producer–consumer relationship has enormous advantages for the medical profession since the doctors are able in most cases to define not only their clients' health needs but then proceed to meet those needs themselves and charge a fee for the service (what economists call supplier-induced demand). Combined with first a private, then since 1975 a national health insurance scheme which meets the costs of consultation, substantial financial rewards have been reaped.

The second prong of the strategy to establish dominance of the organisation and control of the health care labour process is at the level of the work of other health occupations, represented previously as authority. Medicine has gained the right to legitimately evaluate and direct the work of many other health occupations while at the same time deny the legitimacy of the converse. Another way of saying this is that doctors monopolise the competence not only to practice but also to judge that practice—a powerful market situation.

Control and the State

This organisation of the labour process in health care does not occur in a vacuum however. Medical dominance operates with legal backing to control the labour process. An analysis of the professional labour process therefore requires taking account of the State as providing the medical profession with a legally enforceable monopoly over the services it provides and those of others (represented as *medical sovereignty*). Briefly we are using the concept of the democratic capitalist State as a balance of forces and relations within a material framework and as an organisation constituted by an array of judicial, legislative, military and coercive institutions that serves the interests of the dominant class through maintenance of the economy, political order and legitimacy, without being directly subordinate (having relative autonomy) from it.

Medical dominance and control over other occupations (authority) is maintained through State patronage of the profession in the form of legislative backing for its dominance. Statutory registration legislation legally defines occupational territories or task domains not only of medicine itself but of other health occupations as well. Radiographers, for instance, cannot legally interpret the X-rays they take. The struggle over licensing legislation at the level of the State has been important to the emergence of the labour process. As Bucher and Strauss (1961) argue, licensing laws are the historical deposits of the exercise of power and authority. Such State patronage is also important to understanding the third level at which medicine is dominant—that of medical sovereignty in the wider societal arena.

State patronage for medicine is therefore central to the organisation and control of the labour process. The autonomy, authority and sovereignty of the medical profession depends upon this State patronage. The question then is why has the State endorsed this medical monopoly? The answer, argued in detail elsewhere (Willis, 1989a) is because of the class compatibility of the paradigm of scientific medicine. In the creation of ideological hegemony, the form of medical knowledge which saw disease as individual and biological rather than mediated in a social and political manner had a definite compatibility with dominant class interests, and State patronage for the dominance of medicine has been the result (see also Berliner, 1985). This historical alliance between 'new middle class' doctors and the dominant class has been the major factor giving shape to the labour process in health care.

TECHNOLOGICAL INNOVATION AND THE LABOUR PROCESS

Having considered the organisation and control of the labour process in health in general, we now turn to the process of technological innovation in particular. This second part of our paper analyses the role of imaging technology in some of the changes that have occurred in the health care division of labour in the last century.

The concept of technology we are using here includes not only a material component, the machines used in health care and those techniques aimed at achieving a planned end; but also an ideological component, the social relationships involved in its use. Here the emphasis will largely be on technology used to image the living body, in particular the various versions of the X-ray machine. However, these machines do not exist independently of the techniques used by their operators. So when we speak of the X-ray machine as a technology we include the machine, the skills involved in its operation and the social relationships that exist between the radiologist, the radiographer, other occupational groups such as chiropractors and the patients in whose interests the technology is used.

This section of the paper has three parts. In the first we argue that imaging technologies played an important role in establishing and maintaining medical dominance. In the second section we analyse the role of X-ray technology in the labour process that developed following its introduction. Lastly, we trace these developments to the relationship between the medical profession and the State, arguing that the technology which helped establish medical dominance may now be providing the State with a justification to intervene in the health arena, a move which some have argued will lead to the end of medical dominance. This, however, is not to argue that the technology in any way determined these changes. Indeed it is specifically against this notion of technological determination that we wish to argue. Instead our argument is for a dialectical relationship between technology and society.

Technology and autonomy

Before analysing in detail the role of imaging technology in medicine, it is necessary to look briefly at the more general development of technology in medicine, particularly its role in the nineteenth century when the profession established itself. It is also necessary to draw a distinction between technologies directly involved in the treatment of disease (therapeutic technologies) and what is our concern here, those involved in the identification of disease (diagnostic technologies).

In the nineteenth century, medicine was revolutionised by therapeutic advances which made surgery safer, and brought vaccines and disease-specific drugs. These medical miracles, like the miracles of steam power and mechanisation that revolutionised industrial production processes, were perceived as having been made possible by the application of the scientific method. This scientific method, derived substantially from Newtonian physics, needed objectively derived data to establish its laws. The real revolution in the perceptions of nineteenth century medicine was therefore to view patients not as authoritative about their own disease but as objects about which objective data had to be collected. The scientific worldview was reductionist in focus, which in medicine meant that doctors had to penetrate the body to gather data about internal organs and processes. Autopsies had long been a means of obtaining such data. So were the various technologies which, like the laryngoscope, were inserted into the body to view its interior. The diagnostic technologies of the nineteenth century—the stethoscope, ophthalmoscope and finally the X-ray machine—allowed living patients to be examined internally, without invading the body, to establish the anatomic facts about disease. These diagnostic findings of anatomical disease came to define the disease rather than the symptoms experienced by patients (Reiser, 1978). Diagnostic technologies were needed to do for the living patient what the microscope had done for the laboratory specimen.

Claims of scientific objectivity have a political function in establishing control over an area of expertise and protecting it from invasion by others. The rising status of the nineteenth century medical profession rested heavily on the claim to being scientific and this in turn led to a sometimes indiscriminate pursuit of diagnostic data (Corrigan, 1828: 588). With only a very few technologies capable of providing this data on living patients, the status of the medical profession rested squarely on the extensive use of such technologies as were available.

Ideological arguments used to justify the autonomy of the medical profession mask the importance of the medical profession to the capitalist State. Diagnostic technology plays a key role here as is aptly illustrated by the importance attached to the use of the ophthalmoscope in nineteenth century medicine. This instrument was not used primarily because its diagnostic potential was markedly higher than that of direct patient accounts, but because it produced objective evidence of disease, that is evidence that was independent of the deceit of 'malingerers, conscripts, applicants for pensions, insurance or society benefits, plaintiffs claiming damages for injury . . .' (Jackson, 1894: 337).

But, above all, medical science is an important component of the ideology of scientific progress and technological advance. The benefits of science can only be delivered by the scientific experts who are able to address the complex problems involved. If we want these benefits then we have no option but to 'trust the expert'. The means by which these benefits are made available to consumers is technology and 'progress' is therefore measured by technological advance. When applied to medicine, this means that the status-enhancing technologies must always be the newest and the most powerful 'weapons' against disease whether therapeutic or diagnostic. With new technologies constantly replacing old, technical skill has constantly to be renewed and is therefore resistant to codification. Esoteric technical skill however, is only one aspect of the expertise claimed by professionals. The other aspect of expertise, the claim to indeterminacy, will be analysed in the next section where we turn to a case study of the use of X-ray diagnosis in medical care.

X-rays: technology and authority

X-rays were discovered by Rontgen, a physicist, in November 1895, and were a mysterious radiation (hence the name) which penetrated the soft tissue of the body but were absorbed by the more dense tissue so that an image of the internal structure of the body could be captured on a photographic plate or a fluorescent screen placed on the opposite side of the body. The X-rays were produced by apparatus available in every physics laboratory: an induction coil and a Crookes tube.

By January, 1896, the first X-ray pictures for clinical purposes were taken by a British electrical engineer (Shanks, 1950: 44) and the diagnostic potential of the rays became clear. X-ray machines became readily available, easy to use and sold in large numbers. It became a popular parlour game to produce images of the internal structure of the human body. Such parlour games rapidly lost their fascination when, within two years of the discovery, it became clear that X-rays were lethal. However, as is evident from the death rate of the early radiologists (Court Brown & Doll, 1958), the medical profession was not similarly constrained.

These early pioneers were well aware of the dangers of their practice but, like the 'men of science' that they professed to be, they continued using the machines and took the opportunity to study the course of their own excruciatingly painful and fatal disease (Brecher & Brecher, 1969). The medical profession rallied to the care of these victims and took every means to alleviate their suffering (Brecher & Brecher, 1969: 171) but failed to implement the one certain means of ending the deaths—the discontinuation of X-ray diagnosis.

The medical profession owed its autonomy to claims of a scientifically based capacity to diagnose and cure, but by the end of the century there were few *in vivo* diagnostic devices and none as spectacular as X-rays. Radiographs also possessed the advantage that a group of physicians could discuss an accurate visual representation of a patient's anatomy without the patient even being present. This degree of objectification of the living patient meant that medicine could both be and appear more scientific—an important ideological benefit. Indeed, popular belief in the scientific effectiveness of the machines was so well established by the 1930s that patients took to demanding 'an X-ray all over' (Reiser, 1978: 163). In such circumstances the early radiologists can be seen as having martyred themselves to the cause of scientific medicine.

Medicine, however, did not have a monopoly over the medical uses of X-rays. The machines were developed by physicists and electrical engineers who, in the early years, commonly interpreted their radiographs for the medical profession. Indeed they were foundation members of the British Rontgen Society, later the British Institute of Radiology. Larkin (1983) argues that the participation of laypersons in the diagnostic process central to the practice of scientific medicine gave them a unique position from which to observe those diagnostic errors (and therapeutic failures) which could discredit it. The medical profession rapidly acted to exclude these fellow scientists from the medical applications of X-rays by the establishment in hospitals of their own physician-controlled X-ray facilities. In Victoria, the physicists who had introduced the technique to Australia had been replaced by hospital-controlled departments as early as 1898 (Eddy, 1946).

The dangers remained however. When Thomas Edison who was manufacturing the devices, made public the extensive radiation-induced injuries which he had suffered, the medical profession derisively dismissed his account as publicity seeking (*Journal of the American Medical Association*, 1903). For the most part, the medical profession itself ignored the hazards (Edsall, 1906) but then made the ideological claim that it alone had the technical expertise, the correct morality and 'professional aptitude' [*sic*] to 'settle these delicate questions' (*British Medical Journal*, 1906). In fact, in the early years, dosage was commonly assessed by the exposure of the user's own hand (Court Brown & Doll, 1958). As the high cancer death rates of early radiologists show, the radiologists themselves are likely to have been exposed to large doses of radiation (Smith & Doll, 1981) and patient doses could not have been controlled in any effective way.

The end of the First World War during which X-ray diagnosis was used in field hospitals, brought a flood of informally trained operators and simpler machines. There was the perception that the market could be swamped. In addition, by the 1920s the deaths of the early pioneers from radiation-induced cancer (100 deaths by 1922) was undermining the claim of the medical profession to being able to control radiation hazard. The early 1920s therefore saw a number of important changes. Firstly, relatively effective radiation protection measures were instituted. These had the effect of sub-stantially reducing the death rate among radiologists (Court Brown & Doll, 1958). Secondly, the medical profession instituted postgrad-uate training in radiology—in Britain their professional organisation was recognised in 1921. Later writers have claimed that this move occurred when it became clear that 'something would have to be done to train radiologists to serve the expanding specialty' (Shanks, 1950: 48), but we argue that the establishment of the specialty was a necessary part of the formal procedures used by the medical profession to license itself as technically expert in the use of diagnostic X-rays. This, in turn was a necessary step to appropriat-ing the production process and establishing medical authority over the large number of other workers skilled in X-ray production.

The subordination of non-medical practitioners had two pur-poses: to deskill the lay workers by removing their diagnostic skills and to enhance the radiologists' own lowly status within medicine by shedding the production role (Larkin, 1983). This hierarchicalis-ation was justified by reference to scientific rationalisation: scientific efficiency called for the delegation of production tasks to lesser-skilled workers while the medical profession retained those higher skills involved in the interpretation of the data (Reiser, 1978: 117). Such 'helpers', radiographers, would be invaluable in helping the medical profession satisfy the increased demand for X-rays but they would be 'extremely dangerous when they seek to practise independently' (Hernaman-Johnson, 1919: 81, quoted in Larkin, 1983).

Hence the second aspect of the professional's claim to expertise. The professionals, through training and experience, claimed a wider, less determinate understanding of a process, which enables them not only to supervise the execution of the technical aspects of the procedure by other less trained workers, but also to interpret the results and integrate them into the clinical process.

Of course, the claim to both esoteric technical skills and to indeterminacy is not a strategy adopted only by the medical profession, but where the medical profession succeeded in establishing its claims, others, such as skilled metal workers, have not. Indeed, when early radiologists laid claim to special expertise which they did not in fact possess, what was there to prevent other skilled groups like physicists and engineers from using the same weapon?

Larkin (1983) recounts how non-medical workers fought back by forming their own representative bodies to promote their own claims. However, when the British Society of Radiographers sought recognition by the State, its application was passed to the General Medical Council for comment. This body determined that radiographers should be recognised conditional on subordination to medical control. Radiographers, lacking the social power of the medical profession, were forced to submit or be excluded from practice. In this way the State recognised the expertise of one group at the expense of the others.

What was claimed on ideological grounds was now to be achieved in fact: medical domination over radiographers' education boards determined that henceforth their training would be confined to the production role, thus excluding them from the interpretive process. At this point, men with an autonomous occupational base like the electrical engineers, left what they acrimoniously called 'The Society of Radiologists' Assistants' and radiography became a largely female occupation. The work of radiography was seen as being peculiarly suitable to women as it called for them to have a 'real, deep, loyalty' to the radiologist. Only in 1960 did British radiographers gain professional recognition (Larkin, 1983). Physicists and engineers, excluded from the diagnostic process, extended their own independent study of the applications of X-ray technology.

Against this background, it is difficult to sustain the claim that technological rationality necessitated the deskilling and subordination of what was to become the radiographer. Even if the machine created the need for technical helpers, this does not explain why they were disproportionately women, working under the control of men at much lower rates of pay. Instead, we argue that arguments of technological rationality and claims to professional expertise serve as the ideological justification for a licensing system based on State patronage, which in turn is based on the compatibility of medical practice with the interests of the capitalist State.

The dominance of the medical profession over the practice of radiology received a setback after the Second World War when the aftermath of the atomic bombs used on Japan focused renewed interest on the control of what was now demonstrated to be an appalling hazard. Internationally, radiation control measures are now determined by the International Commission on Radiological Protection, a body heavily dependent on the expertise of physicists, especially that élite group involved in the nuclear industry (Radford, 1981). This body has raised serious questions about the capacity of radiologists to control the dangers to their patients from the use of unnecessary doses of X-rays and recommended in 1983 that certain common radiological procedures were 'dispensable' (International Commission on Radiological Protection (ICRP), 1982). Today in hospitals, medical physicists have re-established themselves in radiology departments in a long overdue recognition of their skills in controlling radiation hazard.

Using arguments based on radiation hazard, radiographers in Victoria in 1979, also pressed their professional claims arguing, like the radiologists of 60 years ago, that 'ionizing radiation is a highly dangerous tool in untrained hands'. The medical profession, they argued, not only took defective plates but had a profit motive which resulted in the taking of unnecessary X-rays. In 1979, 21 per cent of GPs were said to have X-rayed the pregnant abdomen. Public safety arguments, claimed the radiographers, were used by the medical profession as a reason for refusing radiographers registration when the real reason for the lack of success of their claims was simply that the Australian Medical Association could 'counter . . . responsible submissions by reaching the upper levels of government behind closed doors' (Hospital Radiation Technologists' Association of Victoria, 1979).

There is evidence from the United States that radiographers do take safer X-rays than do medical practitioners (Wochos et al., 1979). However, the same study shows that untrained operators (orderlies and receptionists) also take safer X-rays than medical practitioners but not as safe as radiographers. Despite the question this raises over the role of training, it is primarily these informally trained operators who will be excluded from X-ray practice. The pattern it appears persists: the labour process has developed around a pattern of deskilling less powerful users of a technology.

In 1983 in the *Health (Radiation Safety) Act*, Victorian radiographers finally won their battle for registration. It represents a substantial change in the attitude of the State that, in 1983, radiographers' claims could be granted directly by the State in the face of pressure from professional medical organisations against registration. The change, as we argue in the next section, originates in the problems caused by the rising cost of health services.

Thus we argue that the X-ray machine has not itself created a new division of labour in health care, but it has facilitated the process by which those already in authority have reinforced pre-existing divisions based on class and gender. This authority of the medical profession over other occupations in the health field is legitimated by claims to special (indeterminate) expertise but it originates in State patronage.

Medicine, technology and the State: the case in Victoria

By the 1950s in Britain, there was growing concern that large rises in the number of X-ray diagnoses could undermine the hospital system (Brailsford, 1952: 679). Not only were X-rays being used routinely (on one out of two hospital admissions, Shanks, 1950: 44) but there was growing doubt about the benefit to the patient (Reiser, 1978: 160). Nuclear physicists started claiming that unnecessary exposure to diagnostic X-rays in the United States was causing between 3500 and 29 000 cancer deaths each year (McClenahan, 1970: 453). The financial costs too were rising; by the 1980s the use of diagnostic X-rays in the United States consumed $7.6 billion each year of the $85 billion spent on hospitals (Richardson, 1987).

Radiologists in the 1950s and 1960s were faced with two causes for concern. Firstly, there was the perception that if they did not themselves regulate the use of X-rays, then the State would force it on them (Brailsford, 1952: 679). Secondly, patient demand for technological diagnosis was undermining the indeterminacy of their clinical skills.

> Thus one day the vice president of a big company came in and said, 'Send me for an electrocardiogram; I want to check up on my heart.' Did he care to have me ask him any questions, or even to listen to his heart sounds? No; his idea was that the records made by a machine would tell everything he wanted to know, and that they would do this with an accuracy and infallibility far beyond any attainments of mine.' (Alvarez, 1943 quoted in Reiser, 1978: 163)

This latter problem was to be overcome by the development of spectacular new non-invasive imaging technologies which were to exacerbate still further the first problem of cost. The use of diagnostic ultrasound from the 1960s onwards provided an answer to concerns about the toxicity of X-rays, particularly in the imaging of the pregnant uterus and produced, in the early years, images which were difficult to interpret but diagnostically valuable. Then in the 1970s there was the advent of the CT scanner, a computer-amplified X-ray scanning device which could produce vivid representations of cross sections of the human body including the soft tissue and thus of particular importance in the diagnosis of tumours. But ultrasound and CT scanners are now dwarfed—in diagnostic capacity, complexity of the image produced and cost—by the latest in imaging devices, nuclear magnetic resonance (NMR) imaging.

The cost of CT scanners is high (about A$1m) but there are now 30 such scanners in Victoria alone with a further twelve likely to be installed in the next year (*Australian Doctor*, 28/11/86). Only eleven of the machines are in public hospitals. There is one NMR unit in a public hospital at an installation cost of about A$3m. Since the capital costs of these machines can only be justified by maintaining a high 'throughput' of patients, the number of CT scans in the last five years has risen by over 400 per cent. If we bear in mind that these new technologies only add on to rather than displace the old technologies, then together they pose a clear threat to health budgets. In such a context, the radiographers' claims to being able to contain demand may well have won them registration even though it was granted under the ideologically more acceptable claim to promoting radiation safety. The same radiation safety legislation was used to cover the first 'certificate-of-need' legislation which allows the Victorian Department of Health to regulate the introduction of any radiation device over the value of $80 000.

The reason why the Victorian Government uses such indirect means to control the radiologists' 'tools of trade' is that State intervention in the medical field is strongly resisted. When the Federal Government decided in 1985 to regulate the use of private radiological services in its public hospitals by limiting the fee payable for such services, New South Wales doctors resisted with the well-known industrial tactic of going on strike. The dispute was resolved by the Commonwealth Government agreeing to buy new radiological equipment for public hospitals and by setting up a commission of inquiry into the question of private practice. The Penington inquiry concluded that the arrangements for private practice in public hospitals did not warrant changing because, in some cases, it was more economical.

Any attempt to place controls on the use of radiological high-tech is met with the Royal College of Radiologists' argument that its concern is to 'maintain the highest standards of health care in the area of radiological sciences . . . The issue at stake is community access to modern, proven diagnostic services'. Or more emotively: '1000 people with curable cancer die each year because of a lack of proper equipment' (*The Sun*, 14/12/84). Under such ideological cover, radiologists can apparently expand their technical services and their incomes at will.

The conclusions reached by the Penington inquiry make evident that government intervention is practicable when it is framed in terms of economic rationality. As argued by Duckett (1984) the State has established itself as a force in the Australian health sector using arguments based on economic rationality, that is, the need to constrain health care costs. Corporate rationalists located in the State institutions which fund health care services have developed technocratic solutions to health costs which are a direct challenge to the hegemony of the medical profession. So, for example, the Victorian Parliament recently initiated a study into the labour market for radiologists.

A major finding of the inquiry (Economic and Budget Review Committee, 1986) is that radiologists in private practice earn an average gross income of $400 000, 65 per cent higher than that of other specialists. Such incomes are seen as coming from a labour market shortage of radiologists, created by the labour-intensive new technologies; from a growth in demand particularly in the private sector; and from a restriction of supply induced by the high failure rates in the radiologists' qualifying examinations. The Government's stated concern is to correct the understaffing created in public hospitals due to the drift of radiologists into lucrative private practice. The recommendations set out by the inquiry follow the well-known strategies, as set out by Braverman, to proletarianise workers. Firstly, the number of radiologists is to be increased by State government monitoring of the radiologists' entrance examination failure rates and by recruiting overseas radiologists. Secondly, there is the recommendation that the appropriate authorities consider allowing radiographers to perform a wider range of services including the interpretation of the more routine diagnoses. Thirdly, that private practice incomes be restricted by reviewing the fees payable for radiological procedures.

The radiologists have responded in classical professional style by describing the report as a 'series of bizarre recommendations . . . some of which if implemented would seriously affect the quality of health care Australia-wide' (Letter to the *National Times on Sunday*, 6/11/86.) The inquiry had already been advised that radiographers do not have the training to provide independent radiological services and would at any rate be reluctant to do so. The Royal Australian College of Radiologists (RACR) has also signalled that any such proposal would be strongly resisted. Its argument is simple but effective: 'You wouldn't want someone without medical training reading the results of your X-ray, would you?' The proposal for cutting fees it sees as unworkable (*Australian Doctor*, 28/11/86). However, the economic arguments also have to be countered. The RACR claims that the government is trying to create a mood of public acceptance of government action against radiologists. It was unjustly blaming radiologists for 'excessively high' fees when in fact they argued, the radiologist spent sometimes over 90 per cent of their gross incomes on the operating costs of their practices.

THE JAPANESE EXPERIENCE

The case made by radiologists for non-intervention by the State and technological innovation being left to market forces, makes Japan an interesting comparative example. It gives an indication of what happens when the introduction of a device is left entirely to the discretion of the medical profession. According to Niki (1985), CT scanners proliferated very rapidly (from 85 to 1693 in five years) to the highest distribution in the world (18.5 per million population), a level which he describes as 'anarchically excessive'. The major incentive for this rise was economic and brought about by the entrepreneurial owners of small private hospitals. These private hospitals, lured by the promise of high profits from CT scans, seldom have radiologists in attendance, a point on which they have been criticised by the Academy of Radiologists. Because the bulk of Japanese scanners are head scanners where the technology is 'almost complete', (that is, highly mechanised), the machines, according to Niki, do not require the presence of a radiologist. The technology of the body scanner, he notes, remains 'incomplete' and special knowledge and experience is therefore still needed for the interpretation of the results. Such modifications, detrimental to the radiologist, will be keenly sought by the medical engineering instrument industry which enjoyed a remarkable growth over a period of four years based on the sale of CT scanners.

The Japanese experience provides some indication that the free proliferation of high-tech medicine on a purely entrepreneurial basis provides a powerful incentive to produce machines which eliminate the need for medical expertise. In such a context it would seem that the radiologists' interests are still compatible with that of a cost-cutting State. And once again we return to the argument that the medical profession has not escaped technological deskilling because of any intrinsic quality of their skills but because of the way in which their interests articulate with those of the State.

CONCLUSION

In this paper we have examined the applicability of concerns of the labour process tradition to indirect wage labour relations associated with 'professional' work. We have argued that accounts of both ideology and the State must be more centrally incorporated in order to adequately do this. In the professional labour process, resistance is aimed at preservation of the indeterminacy of professional practice and of autonomy. The case study of the labour process surrounding imaging technology demonstrates how effectively this form of resistance through ideology can operate, particularly when backed up by more traditional forms of resistance such as strike action.

There is, however, nothing intrinsically labour intensive about technological innovation in the health arena which would prevent the deskilling of workers including the medical profession. The preservation of autonomy, and protection of a medically dominated labour process ultimately rests not on technology but on continued State patronage. In the face of the increasing technicality of medical tasks associated with technological innovation, the emphasis on indeterminacy can be seen as an ideological rearguard offensive. In such cases, the ability of professions to continue resisting deskilling depends upon the continuing articulation of their interests with those of the State. The other consequence is the possibility of empowerment of other medical workers against medical dominance and control, as the ideological nature of the claims to indeterminacy in the face of increasing technicality becomes more apparent.

POSTSCRIPT

This chapter, written with my colleague Jeanne Daly, was originally published in *Social Science and Medicine* (1989). It attempted to draw together the work we had been doing over a couple of years on the social relations of medical technology. In addition, it attempted to show the relevance of theoretical developments in the area of the study of work and the role of technology, associated in particular with the re-emergence of what has become known as labour process theory. Applying such a theory to the evolution of the health workforce is useful and instructive in understanding how such an evolution has occurred.

7 The social relations of medical technology: the case of echocardiography
Jeanne Daly, Ian McDonald and Evan Willis

Echocardiography is a technique for producing images of the human heart with ultrasound. First applied as a scanning device for submarine detection during the First World War, ultrasound evolved rapidly under the impetus supplied by parallel developments in radar. This led to the application of ultrasound to medical 'imaging'. In the 1950s, it was used to generate physiological patterns rather than true pictures of the heart—the *interpretation* of the signals required a thorough knowledge of cardiological anatomy and physiology. Development of ultrasound accelerated again in the 1960s with production of two-dimensional pictures of 'slices' of body organs, but it was several years before the technique could be extended to the beating heart.

The modern echocardiogram allows the doctor to 'see with sound'. A fan-shaped beam of high-frequency sound generated by a microphone applied to the body penetrates the tissues, is reflected back and translated into an image of the organ. The strength of diagnostic ultrasound is the imaging of soft tissues. The echocardiogram provides striking images of sections through the beating heart. These show the inside of the heart in detail including valve size, thickness and contraction of cardiac chambers, and abnormalities such as thrombi (clots) or fluid around the heart. Recent innovations based on the measurement of the Doppler effect (the effect which accounts for the drop in pitch as a sound-source passes) have contributed information on blood-flow including flow of blood through holes in the heart and measurement of the severity of narrowing of the heart valves.

Since toxicity has not been demonstrated in humans, ultrasound is seen as a safe alternative to X-rays. Echocardiography provides much more diagnostic information than the electrocardiogram which simply records the electric potentials from the heart, and the chest X-ray which produces a shadow image. The only other technique providing comparable detail is cardiac catheterisation, a potentially dangerous, invasive technique by which a tube is introduced into the heart and fluid injected to make the heart visible on an X-ray screen. Not surprisingly, then, all major hospitals dealing with cardiac disease throughout the world consider echocardiography to be a standard form of equipment. Since the machines are inexpensive relative to other imaging machines—$A50 000 for a portable machine to $A250 000 for the new colour Doppler machines—their spread cannot be controlled by present Australian state regulation. Although it is known that the use is widespread and increasing (Economic and Budget Review Committee, 1986; 15), it is not known how many of the machines are in use in Australia, or elsewhere. Clearly echocardiography is seen as a versatile technique, with a contribution to make to the diagnosis of virtually all forms of cardiac disease. The echocardiogram is, however, complex and difficult to interpret.

This is partly because of the large amount of data generated. But it is also because of the wide range of normal appearances. Particularly in the case of minor lesions in which the difference between normal and abnormal is small, the discriminatory power of the test is reduced and there is an increased likelihood of misdiagnosis from a false positive result (Newburger et al., 1983: 63–4).

Moreover, since echocardiography is the best non-invasive cardiac imaging device available, there is no 'gold standard' for checking suspected problems. With the screening of a large number of normal subjects, some false positive diagnoses are inevitable.

IMAGING TECHNOLOGY: CONSTITUTING THE PATIENT AS 'OBJECT'

Ultrasound is non-ionising and therefore free of the radiation hazard associated with X-rays, the discovery of which in 1895 revolutionised technological diagnosis. As was outlined in the previous chapter, without invading the body, X-ray diagnosis produced the first visual images of living anatomy, images which physicians could discuss without the patient even being present. Unfortunately, the X-rays were toxic, a fact known soon after their discovery. It is a measure of the critical importance of this first imaging device to the medical profession that early radiologists continued using it while hundreds of their colleagues died of cancers caused by the rays. By 1970, influential voices among radiologists themselves were saying that, notwithstanding renewed concern about the risks, X-rays were being wasted because of 'traditional rites of doubtful rationality' such as using the test to 'rule out' disease when the diagnosis could be made by physical examination alone (McClenahan, 1970).

These changes in the diagnostic field occurred at the same time as medicine was learning to locate disease in 'the dark spaces of the mind and social relationships' (Armstrong, 1984: 739). It was becoming possible to think of illness without physical cause and treatment was accordingly coming to include ways of altering the patient's outlook; medical practitioners were turning their attention to the patient as 'subject'. This change was felt in the imaging field with the possibility being envisaged of the test being used to relieve anxiety in both patients and doctors. Together with the professional criticism of some uses of X-rays, this could have been expected to lead to a decline in the use of imaging techniques. In public hospitals in the state of Victoria, Australia, for example, the use of plain film X-rays has declined over the last decade. However, the use of computerised tomography and ultrasound has increased.

The technological context of clinical medicine, particularly the role of technology in the perception of the patient, is an important aspect of the widespread and increasing use of the echocardiogram. During the nineteenth century, medicine came to be associated more and more closely with scientific research and was rewarded with safer surgery and disease-specific drugs and vaccines. These successes raised public confidence in the promise of medical science and lent legitimacy to State patronage of the new medical profession.

In medicine, the scientific method employed was reductionist: disease came to be seen as an anatomical lesion, a localised pathology often in a specific organ. The 'core task of medicine became not the elucidation of what the patient said but what the doctor saw in the depths of the body' (Armstrong, 1984: 738). 'Seeing' inside the body was difficult, requiring a combination of physical examination and the taking of the patient's medical history. The early diagnostic technologies, first the stethoscope and then the ophthalmoscope, disclosed internal signs of disease which were independent of the patients' subjective interpretation and so highly valued that some diseases became defined entirely on the basis of findings produced by technology. Diagnosis ceased to be merely a means of facilitating therapy and became, at the same time, a means of contributing to science (Corrigan, 1828: 588). This was understood as cumulative knowledge of potential benefit to all patients. For clinical practice, however, the sometimes contradictory aims of treating individual patients while maintaining 'progress' by studying them as objects of science was engendered. The dilemma remained clearly evident in the debate over the ethics of randomly allocating patients to control groups in trials of medical procedures. The purpose of the study being reported upon here is to examine the clinical contribution of echocardiography less narrowly than do studies that have attempted to assess the tests in terms of their technical attributes only. In this paper the concern will be the more appropriate one of considering the technology as inseparable from the social context in which it is used.

Since the work of Talcott Parsons, it has been an axiom of medical sociology that illness must be understood not as an event but as a process, and that this process is primarily a social rather than a biological one. It begins with the recognition of signs or symptoms, some of which lead to entry into the medical system in the form of interaction with a number of types of 'health professional'. The process ends with a number of possible outcomes. Between the entry and outcome points of the process, the patient is defined as 'well' or 'ill' as a result of their interaction with medical technology constituted as an event: the recording of the patient's echocardiogram. Although the two sets of relationships are clearly related, there is an important difference. The relationships through which the technology is applied constitute the patients as 'objects' whereas those in which the patients are more actively involved help to form them as 'subjects'. Furthermore, when patients act as subjects, the doctors also become engaged as subjects. Viewing medical technology as a process, means that the experiences of both patient and physician must be considered when an attempt is made to assess the technology of modern medicine. The 'subject' status of doctors and patients is a neglected dimension of technology assessment.

'Technology assessment' has grown considerably in the last two decades. Faced with the wish of manufacturers and medical and paramedical groups to see the most up-to-date equipment employed, the high cost of which has threatened attempts to limit spending in the interest of economic management, governments have been concerned to assess the effectiveness of technological innovation in diagnosis and therapy (Daly, Green & Willis, 1987). Technology is the 'cause', it has been generally assumed, and financial restraint the cure for, the expanding demands of technological medicine.

The methods used to assess the demand have, however, been mainly devised within a quantitative tradition exemplified by the epidemiologically based randomised control trial (Daly, Green & Willis, 1987). Such methods tend to involve treating technology as central, excluding as far as possible questions of subjective assessment. Primarily, this is because the problem is conceptualised in a way that requires their exclusion. As a result, the methods 'do not contain provision for evaluating the complex crucial data that distinguish [people from inanimate objects]' (Feinstein, 1977, quoted in Brorsson & Wall, 1985: 17).

Although technology assessment is important, and randomised control trials are a valuable method for assessing the more material aspects of medical technology, understanding the experience of the patient and clinician is central to understanding the manner in which a technology operates in the clinical context. 'Subjective' factors affect the method and rationale of the doctor's use of a technology and its 'effect' on patients. Understanding the 'experience' of doctors and patients is a necessary precursor to designing more quantitative studies using larger 'populations'. Technology assessment must be directed not only at technical assessments in the strict sense but must cover broader 'social' aspects as well. Although this is widely recognised in principle, the positivistic traditions of the disciplines concerned—medicine, epidemiology, biostatistics and economics—mean that too little recognition attaches to sociological methods of research.

Indeed, the Swedish Research Council survey of technology assessment methods concludes: 'there are today no established criteria to rely on for identifying or assessing, the social consequences related to developing and utilising medical technology' (Brorsson & Wall, 1985: 115). The research project reported here has been informed by these social policy and conceptual concerns.

ECHOCARDIOGRAPHY: TECHNOLOGICAL IMAGING OF THE HEART

For analytical purposes, the technical attributes of echocardiography have been considered separately but they assume significance only within a set of social relations. The extensive use of, and control over, medical technology by specialist medical practitioners, plays an important part in maintaining their dominance over the other groups—general practitioners, ancillary technicians and others—in the health-care division of labour.

Historically, imaging technology has been incorporated into an existing system of health care in a manner that has enabled radiologists to assume a dominant position in the organisation of the work of imaging. When other specialised skills have been needed, however, radiologists—the original imaging specialists—have not always been so successful. This is so in the case of echocardiography in Australia. Radiologists have been almost completely excluded on the grounds that the test 'requires' specialised knowledge of cardiac function. However, the pioneers of the technique—cardiologists and physicists—have been made honorary members of the Royal Australasian College of Radiology. Moreover, although at present any cardiologist prepared to purchase a machine can perform and charge for the test, a new specialty is emerging: the cardiologist formally accredited in the use of cardiac ultrasound. The cost of the machine, though relatively modest, is such that specialists usually practise from imaging laboratories rather than being in individual private practice. In the state of Victoria, echocardiography is increasingly the province of these highly specialised practitioners and their ancillary technicians.

The social relations surrounding the organisation of health care in the narrow sense include the 'social control' aspects of medicine (for example, certifying health for purposes of insurance or employment), patient–practitioner interaction and the social construction of cardiac disability and other implications of the test for the patient's life.

The enhanced capacity of echocardiography to diagnose pathology is beneficial if the pathology is disabling, or potentially so, and treatable. However, with powerful new imaging devices there is a tendency to diagnose illness for which the prognosis is uncertain and the treatment of questionable efficacy. In cases for which treatment is not especially recommended—for example, mitral valve prolapse in the absence of mitral regurgitation—the effect on the patient is likely to be negative.

In addition, there is the risk of false positive diagnosis. It is recognised that, with children, even temporary mislabelling may lead to morbidity from 'cardiac non-disease'. However, while the testing of the heart under these conditions is unlikely to benefit the patient, the test often serves to satisfy an insurance or superannuation board. It is in the interest of such companies to identify asymptomatic applicants with suspected or mild disease—for example, minor valve lesions—having a small or uncertain effect on life expectancy but, in aggregate, affecting insurers' profit margins.

When, therefore, a cardiologist orders an echocardiogram, the action is not determined exclusively by the 'physical' condition of the patient and the possibilities for diagnosis created by the echocardiogram as a 'scientific' technique. The test is valued for the role these technical attributes play in medicine as a social process between patient and cardiologist and between both these actors and other agencies. Of the two types of role, the former—the role of the test in the interaction between cardiologists and patients undergoing the test—is the present focus. Despite the widespread use of echocardiography the present study has few predecessors.

An exception in the medical literature critically examining the test's clinical contribution is a recent Australian study (McDonald et al., 1988). As a first step in the evaluation of the technique, McDonald and co-workers considered clinical utilisation: how the doctors use the test result and the patients' response. Clinical training reinforces the mechanistic notion that better diagnosis will result in improved treatment, and hence, improvements in health. The McDonald et al. study showed, however, that only in approximately nine per cent of patients did the test lead to the technical management plan for the patient being changed, from surgery to intervention, for example, or to drugs. In approximately one-third of cases the test was seen to be useful in reassuring anxious patients but in less than half these cases did the cardiologist consider the test result essential for the reassurance. A simple measure of patient anxiety showed that a 'clean bill of health' did not necessarily provide the expected reassurance and, in a small number of cases, left patients more anxious about their hearts. The results of the study by McDonald et al. show the importance of looking beyond the manifest technical uses of a diagnostic test to perceived social uses: bolstering the confidence of doctors and reassuring patients.

The character of the process of reassurance is imperfectly understood and the benefit to the patient uncertain. The present study therefore aims to analyse the role of echocardiography in the process of being tested for heart disease. To isolate the effects as far as possible, only those patients whom the admitting cardiologist believed on clinical grounds to have normal hearts and who were found to have a normal echocardiogram were studied.

The echocardiogram test is often performed for a variety of reasons: to 'rule out' heart disease, to reinforce doctors' reassurances or to comply with implied or explicit requests of referring physicians. Participating patients—twenty in number in a major Melbourne hospital to be termed 'City Hospital'—were referred consecutively to three cardiologists. The consultation in which the cardiologists gave the result of the test was tape-recorded and use was made, where appropriate, of the patients' medical records. Patients were interviewed at home immediately following the test. The interviews were designed to establish the patients' perceptions of the test results and their understanding of the significance of the results for their health. Cardiologists were also interviewed, on a similar basis, to discover the perceived benefits of the test.

The study by McDonald et al. showed that 'reassurance', used as a justification of the test, was uncertain of achievement: patients were in some cases more anxious after having been reassured.

Considering the quantitative nature of the study, such findings were inexplicable. Cardiologists tended to see the unexpected results as caused by a random factor: the patient's personality. One doctor considered a patient who requested repeated testing for reassurance 'mad as a snake'. The opinion was expressed that this could be demonstrated by the use of psychological tests.

Together with gaining access to the echocardiography laboratory, the most difficult aspect of preparing the research was persuading the participating cardiologists that reassurance could be understood as a social process. They needed to be persuaded that it is not an isolated clinical event in which the patient's personality confronts the evidence of the test, and that qualitative methods of analysis are justified.

In most cases the patient's 'career' started with the detection of a 'sign', usually asymptomatic, when a heart murmur was identified in the course of a routine examination. In about 20 per cent of cases, the medical examination was performed at the request of an employer or prospective insurer.

A murmur is a turbulent flow of blood that is heard with a stethoscope. At the primary care level, particularly with children, such murmurs are usually 'innocent' in the sense that the turbulence originates in the normal function of a healthy heart. Children, for example, commonly have murmurs which persist into early adult life. Concern arises, however, over rare cases of heart disease, in particular valve abnormalities, which also cause murmurs. These have a small statistical impact on life expectancy owing to a low risk of infection which is treated with antibiotic prophylaxis.

General practitioners are usually unable to distinguish the cause of the murmurs. The patient is almost invariably told: 'You have a heart murmur. It's nothing to worry about, but we'll just examine it to make sure.' This involves going to a cardiologist to have the murmur assessed. In the case of insurance assessments the patient is usually sent with a specific request for an echocardiogram. The test is performed in a testing laboratory. City Hospital is unusual in having clinical cardiologists and testing laboratories in one unit.

After the initial diagnosis and referral, patients had had to face up to a two-month wait for the test. During this time they have had to cope with the disjunction between the identification of a sign—the murmur—and the lack of symptoms to match.

Some patients understandably became very anxious. Others focused on the absence of symptoms to remain relatively unconcerned.

> I used to do a lot of aerobics as well, um, so I feel fit and if I was sick I would feel sick. So I [wasn't] worried. (Patient 7)

Sometimes the diagnosis did not correspond with the patient's experience.

> I thought that they were talking rubbish, quite honestly . . . I've
> been under general anaesthetic about half a dozen times, no one
> ever mentioned it before. (Patient 5)

This patient was also reluctant to take on a further problem.

> Yeah, [the problems I've got] are ghastly enough. You can't try on
> things like that . . . You've got to cool it. (Patient 5).

However, in some patients the initial diagnosis allowed other worries to be interpreted as heart problems.

> I can remember a month ago . . . I did aerobics and I just couldn't
> get my breath and I mean, I'm fit so that shouldn't have been a
> problem and I can remember doubling over to get my breath . . .
> But when this heart thing came up I thought, mmm, maybe that's
> why. (Patient 2).

Her murmur was discovered in the course of a pre-employment medical examination. In part because of the doubts raised and in part because it made her feel 'special', she was eager to have the test.

> It was sort of like I was setting out on something new, if you know
> what I mean, a new experience? And, um, even though it might
> have been something serious, I don't think I was worried about it
> . . . (Patient 2)

In another case the mother of a 17-year-old weightlifter stopped him carrying firewood because his grandmother had said:

> It's the finish if there's something wrong with the heart. It's not
> like a leg. (Patient 1)

Clearly, already patients' responses—the meaning they gave to the initial diagnosis in light of their life-situations and personal orders of priority, in which health and the risk of it had different levels of significance—showed marked differences. These differences affected their dealings with cardiologists.

Using the test result

The cardiologists themselves performed the test for a variety of reasons. The most common given were excluding the possibility of disease and reassuring the patient. In eight cases, the cardiologist carried out the test primarily to satisfy the referring doctor and in four of these the test was required for a murmur detected during pre-employment screening.

Cardiologists justify the test by the need to ensure that rare but serious disease has not been missed but admit to some doubt about the real benefits of antibiotic prophylaxis. In the superannuation cases, in the opinion of one of the cardiologists, the patients would derive some benefit from having an abnormality diagnosed, but this has to be set against possible iatrogenic effects and the loss of superannuation or insurance benefits. In such cases the cardiologist concluded, the test is conducted in the interest of the employer or insurer and is a form of 'anti-patient' medicine.

Some patients observed in the waiting-room before the test gave the impression of being extremely anxious. They all accepted the necessity of the test. Yet several had reservations. One, however, calmly read the latest Mills & Boon novel, yawned audibly during the test and later commented:

> You sort of think, I'll let them go ahead, you know, they're going to tell you anyway that there's nothing wrong but, um, they need the practice. (Patient 4)

This patient was gratified by a test result which reinforced her own judgment. In a case like this, 'reassurance' is almost self-induced, on the patient's part.

> [sniggers] No, it just seems like they keep trying to keep their friends employed. (Patient 19)

In fact, cardiologists used the test result in several ways in the consultation with patients whose hearts they regarded as normal, despite having undertaken to administer the test. The authority of the cardiologist is strongly reinforced by the diagnostic capacity of the test, and the 'expert' knowledge required to interpret it. At the same time, patients can 'see for themselves'. Both aspects are regularly emphasised in consultations.

> We're actually looking at the heart chambers pumping. We can see everything going, we can see all the valves working, we can see the blood flowing in the heart so that there is nothing that could escape our view. (Doctor 1)

The emphasis on the machine provides an acceptable reason for supplementing the diagnosis of the referring doctor. A technical rationale is provided, which is indisputable, does not impugn the first doctor's competence and serves to maintain a united professional front in the face of possible scepticism. So effective is the combination that only once was it felt necessary to refer to the discrepancy explicitly in a consultation.

> I don't know why they wanted to check it again, to be honest but

the fact of the matter is that this test overrides everything.
(Doctor 1)

In all cases, the diagnosis was actually made on clinical grounds, with the data from the test—suitably interpreted—as but one element in the overall assessment. However, the emphasis on the machine leads patients to underestimate the cardiologist's clinical skill:

> I thought he must know what he's talking about if he's working with this machine . . . humans can make mistakes but you don't expect machines to make mistakes. (Patient 3)

Unaware of the significant problem of false diagnosis because of machine artefact, this patient would probably have been satisfied with a result by machine printout. Indeed, there is a striking contrast in the way different doctors manage the process of reassurance; one, in particular, regularly gives scarcely more information than a machine printout. The following is the full content of one of his consultations:

> *Doctor*: It's normal, one hundred per cent normal, no doubt about it.
> *Patient*: Good.
> *Doctor*: Any questions?
> *Patient*: Can I have a certificate for work? [To justify a day off work.]
> *Doctor*: Come outside and I'll give you one. (Doctor 2, Patient 11)

This cardiologist describes himself as 'frankly paternalistic' and believes that reassurance is best achieved by stating the essential facts confidently. Interviewed at home, the patient said that her heart was normal but nevertheless feared that the murmur, which she had had since childhood, could cause her to have a 'cardiac' and 'drop dead' as her mother-in-law had recently.

In this brief consultation the cardiologist restricted his comments to technical matters only. The patient was effectively removed from her wider social attachments to be placed in a narrow, technical context, becoming merely a source of technical data to resolve the purely physiological question of whether her heart is normal. This would seem to be a continuation of the search begun in the last century for 'objectivity'. However, the process of objectification is greatly intensified by the specialised setting. The focus of medical attention narrows to one organ: the heart. In addition, the definition of echocardiography as a 'test' means that the patient's condition is decided by a single test 'result'. Despite the perceptible trend in modern medicine to seeing patients more as 'subjects', some doctors utilising powerful new imaging devices in specialist fields may represent a counter-trend.

In these circumstances a patient's symptoms become irrelevant in the light of the test and are disregarded. In the following case the patient, who had been concerned about breathlessness during exercise, was asked about her fitness.

Patient: . . . regularly I jog about three to six kilometres.
Doctor: OK.
Patient: I think it's about three. I find that the hardest, to jog in the morning.
Doctor: So do I. Actually I find it hard at any time but particularly hard in the morning/
Patient: /You see, it's much harder to get my breath in, in the morning/
Doctor: /Yes, OK/
Patient: /which probably is a lot/
Doctor: /All right, so you are a very fit person, swimming, jogging and so on. Any murmurs in the family? (Doctor 1, Patient 2)

The test being definitive in nature, the cardiologist can dismiss as unimportant the very symptoms which led the patient to seek medical help in the first place. The following patient, a 19-year-old, went to the doctor after experiencing repeated bouts of chest pain, one so acute that he felt he was going to faint and his parents took him to Casualty. He was found to have a murmur, referred to a cardiologist and tested. The cardiologist is talking to him on the telephone:

Doctor: Now, the er, you recall that when you came to see me you, you had chest pain/
Patient: /Yes/
Doctor: /which I said was as a result of muscular aches and pains and there was nothing to be really concerned about. Is, has that gone or . . .?
Patient: Um, oh, sort of, kind of . . . I've been noticing that, over the last week or so I seem to be getting slight twinges every now and then/
Doctor: /Yes, yes/
Patient: /and/
Doctor: /So it didn't really worry you?
Patient: Not really, no.
Doctor: All right. Well, that's really of no, er, great significance. Now, you also had a heart murmur . . . (Doctor 4, Patient 13)

The cardiologist would seem to have allayed the patient's anxiety about the murmur. Yet despite the patient's apparent acceptance of the cardiologist's interpretation of the chest pain, he said later that he intended approaching a chiropractor for the treatment of his chest pain.

Providing 'reassurance' clearly takes a variety of forms, and signifies different things to patients, many of whom have believed for the several weeks since referral that their condition is a cause for concern. A further salient feature of the consultation is the manner in which the cardiologist attends to what he sees as features of the patient's situation beyond the immediate circumstances of the test itself.

'Treating' the patient's situation

Consultations sometimes move from the 'technical context' to the patient's 'social context', with reference to which further attempts are made at reassurance. Here, symptoms become important again as the doctor confronts the patient-as-subject. The shift can be abrupt, as in this case of a pregnant woman who said she was breathless:

> *Doctor*: OK, that's good news: the test is normal. OK. Now I want to go over a few things with you, I want to discuss that breathing business. (Doctor 1, Patient 4)

The consultation then becomes what David Silverman (in a personal communication) has described as a 'search-and-destroy mission':

> *Doctor*: Now that is an anxiety breathlessness . . . What that means is that there are tensions around about something, right? Everyone's got some problem that you feel tense about. But that is a tension/
> *Patient*: /mmmm hmm/
> *Doctor*: /a tension problem. Maybe you were worried about the pregnancy, maybe you were worried about your weight, maybe you were worried about things at home/
> *Patient*: /[interruption inaudible as doctor carries straight on]/
> *Doctor*: that's the big thing on your mind . . . I can assure you that that's what it is. It's not a heart breathlessness, not a real one or anything else. (Doctor 1, Patient 4)

The patient later said she had been trying in vain to establish the cause of her anxiety. She recalled—incorrectly—that the cardiologist had suggested she talk to a psychologist.

In cases such as this, echocardiography is not serving a technical purpose; the patients are normal. The cardiologist is, conscientiously, 'reorganis[ing] the patient's problems, symptoms and worries so as to make sense of them' (Armstrong, 1984: 741). In order to do so, any symptoms mentioned by the patient during the taking of his or her history must be linked not to physical pathology but to the patient's feelings or situation. Cardiologists may, however, feel they lack the necessary skill in communicating, leading them to avoid the role of counsellor.

> I just find it, you know, it's, er, it's sad and there has been terrible damage done somewhere and God only knows, I don't even know if it's reversible . . . where you encounter seriously refractory problems frequently unless you are a saint, what you start to do is to cut off. (Doctor 1)

By describing a patient's problems as 'refractory', the cardiologist effectively withholds further medical help.

In the following case the patient is a 23-year-old electrician who came to Casualty with a sinus infection. He suffers severe and intractable pain as the result of a back injury through work and is unemployed in consequence. To obtain relief from the pain he has used heroin but his hospital record shows that he has been assessed as free of addiction. His use of the drug, he believes, leads doctors to classify him as a 'no-hoper':

> It's just like big barriers just put up straightaway, kind of thing, but you've really got to climb up to the top of it and shout down to the guy, 'You know, you've got to listen to me!' (Patient 5)

When the cardiologist finds no murmur and a normal test result, he explains that the patient's heart complaint could have been caused by a high temperature which could be associated with what he suspects may be drug addiction:

> *Doctor*: Well, you know I, I'm not going to lecture to you/
> *Patient*: /Yeah, that is, it's just/
> *Doctor*: /that is a serious risk of the business/
> *Patient*: /Yeah!/
> *Doctor*: /that you can get the, particularly the Staph. infection, on the skin, goes in with the needle and if it does you can get a bad infection of, you know, the tubes of the heart, the valves on the right side of the heart. I'm telling you that, they've probably told you that
> *Patient*: /Yeah [tries to carry on but inaudible]/
> *Doctor*: /I've got to tell you/
> *Patient*: /They told us, I was aware of it before!/
> *Doctor*: /You knew about it?
> *Patient*: Yeah.
> *Doctor*: Yeah, I guess it's around the traps. (Doctor 1, Patient 5)

The cardiologist explained later that 'with that sort of patient I have not the faintest grip on the situation'. He was 'having a quick swing' at the patient's 'pathological' behaviour in the hope that the warning might come back to the patient later.

In this case a gratuitous test performed at the request of the referring doctor has led to the 'treatment' of the patient's suspected drug addiction. Significantly, the real medical problems suffered by the patient were ignored because they lay in other specialist fields. The case underlines some of the pitfalls accompanying the increasing specialisation of medicine.

The patient was seen by a surgeon for his sinus infection, by a cardiologist for the suspected murmur, by the community medicine department in connection with his drug abuse and by the pain clinic for his back complaint. His back injury was not investigated. Each specialty performed tests, and in one, a computed tomography (CT) scan of the sinuses, an arachnoid cyst was discovered on the brain. This, the patient maintains, he was told was 'nothing important', although it now requires monitoring every three months. The patient left hospital without any consultation which could draw together all these separate medical manoeuvres.

After the test

There remains the conclusion of the test process. All the patients interviewed were either relieved by the test result or gratified when it reinforced their own beliefs. For one patient, relief was tinged with regret:

> I thought this was going to be something, not that I wanted to be sick, but that made you different, I suppose. And then when I left [City Hospital], well, I was just like everybody else . . . (Patient 8)

A common problem is that patients had a highly mechanistic conception of the cause of the murmur. One saw it as 'a bit of skin flapping' and another described it as follows:

> It's just like a tube which has got some, what would you say, a bit of rubbish around, rust, so that the blood doesn't flow properly . . . (Patient 1)

There is difficulty in reconciling the idea of a murmur as physical impairment, with the test result showing a normal heart. As a consequence, most patients were left in some doubt as to the murmur's real significance. They could, accordingly, be prone to retesting and recurring anxiety about their 'heart problems'.

After the test, all but one of the twenty patients interviewed regarded their hearts as 'normal'—although with reservations. The mother of the remaining patient—a seven-year-old child—saw the heart as 'more normal', the child being less likely to 'drop dead'. The family was adjusting to living with 'Jenny's heart problem'.

This mother later returned to the referring doctor with a request for retesting, but he refused, clearly regarding her as neurotic.

In one case, while the patient and his family accepted that the heart was normal, the general practitioner who had referred him did not, and proceeded to treat a non-existent valve abnormality with antibiotic prophylaxis, as if the test had never been conducted, 'just to be sure'. In another case, in which the patient mentioned to the cardiologist that she had had scarlet fever as a child, he asked to review the patient again in a year, thereby calling into question the definitive nature of the test.

In the light of these cases, the familiar medical justifications of testing require some re-evaluation. The data presented cast doubt on the bland term 'reassurance', which certainly has the ring of a worthy medical aim expressive of concern for, and conferring benefit on, the patient. In all cases, the test did indeed make the patients feel that their hearts were at least more normal than they were before. The patients commonly fail, however, to make sense of the diagnosis by understanding the sign, which is the murmur.

TOWARDS AN ASSESSMENT OF ECHOCARDIOGRAPHY

The test also serves, with its high capacity to provide images of the inside of the human body, to legitimate medical scrutiny of the patient's life situation. The test provides 'cover' for the exercise of social control in a context in which the patient is particularly vulnerable as a result of the authority which the 'technological context' confers on the cardiologist.

Social control may be present in a particularly intense form when the doctor believes the patient to be neurotic. The benefits the patients gain must, moreover, be balanced against the risk of misdiagnosis or the detection of an insignificant abnormality. If it is borne in mind that in 20 per cent of cases at City Hospital, the heart question is raised in the course of a medical examination conducted at the request of an employer or insurer, the use of echocardiography to exclude the possibility of heart disease begins to look morally doubtful. The tests, furthermore, must be seen against the background of the changing forms of medical practice in which they are located, and which they, in some part, help to engender through the manner of their conception.

The tests are increasingly conducted in a context of highly specialised professional practice in which the physician has only limited authority to treat the whole patient: an opinion about the heart only is sought. Considering the trend in Australian medicine away from general practice, it is likely to become less and less possible for patients to participate in consultations in anything approaching a subject role.

These considerations should not obscure the positive uses of the test. As it is usually definitive, it can be used to correct false positive diagnoses from electrocardiograms that would result in a patient being misdiagnosed as having serious heart disease. The patients selected for study were at the margin of potentially effective medical practice; those cases in which the diagnosis led to life-preserving therapeutic intervention were deliberately excluded. On the other hand, cases of the kind selected represent about one-third of patients undergoing the test in City Hospital, a public hospital.

Echocardiography is one of a new generation of diagnostic tests some of which have installation costs of several million dollars. To run these machines cost-effectively it is necessary to maintain a high rate of testing of patients. Early results from studies being conducted in Australia show that approximately the same proportion of patients as in echocardiography are undergoing other, similarly technically sophisticated tests, to 'exclude' disease. In the case of imaging technologies capable of diagnosing symptom-free pathology even at the molecular level, screening tests may disclose the widespread occurrence of asymptomatic pathology. These screening exercises carry not only a financial cost, but the iatrogenic effect may also be considerable. These broader issues are important in assessing imaging and other medical technologies. The increasing refinement and ability of diagnostic techniques to detect pathology in apparently healthy individuals raises the question of the advisability of such public health programs as mass screening for disease. Increased diagnostic power is two-edged. If it detects treatable pathology at an early stage, treatment may prolong life. The other side of the coin, however, is its ability to detect more of the hidden pathology which every individual manifests with increasing age, a type of 'iceberg phenomenon'. When the test is then used for social control purposes—to deny or limit employment or insurance, to create significant changes in the longer-term social identity of the patients undergoing the test—or to generate iatrogenic effects, the benefits are less clear. The former aspect—detecting disease—may be considered the liberating side of diagnostic technology, the latter—introducing uncertainty—its repressive side. The medical profession's emphasis, almost exclusively, on the beneficial uses serves only to obscure those uses of the echocardiography test from which the patient stands to gain least.

POSTSCRIPT

This chapter was originally a paper, written from a multidisciplinary project, on the social impact of medical technology based at a Melbourne hospital. It was conducted with Jeanne Daly, who was employed as a researcher on the project and Ian McDonald, the head of cardiac investigation at that hospital. A grant from the Research and Development Grants Advisory Committee of the Commonwealth Department of Community Services, Housing and Health (RADGAC) made the research possible and it was the project out of which Jeanne wrote her doctoral dissertation. This chapter was a work-in-progress paper, further extended and developed in Daly (1989) as well as in Daly and McDonald (1993).

The project was an attempt to detail the social relations of the diagnostic medical technology of echocardiography. In this chapter, we have argued that the hallmark of a sociological analysis of technology in general and medical technologies in particular, is to view technological intervention as a process, not as an event. The process is a social one, involving the lead-up and the aftermath as well as the actual event of engagement with the material aspect of the technology—in this case the echocardiogram. The social relations provide the social context in which the specific technological intervention takes place and, we have argued here, are as important in determining the outcome of the process of technological intervention in terms of its impact on the health of the patient as the specific test itself. This is as true for 'high-tech' interventions as it is for 'low-tech' ones such as the subject of the next chapter.

8 The changing social relations of condom technology in the AIDS era

The process of technological innovation is not a neutral question of efficiency of technical imperative but is intimately related to the distribution of power and the exercise of social control. It is necessary to consider the centrality of the social relations of the technology. As used here, technology has dual components, fused in practice, but separable for analytical purposes. It is not only the tools and machines used by society (that is objects used as a means of altering the physical environment), but also the social relationships implied by their use. These social relations result not from the technical imperatives of the machines or tools, but from the wider society: the broader social structure stratified and divided along class, gender, ethnic and other lines. Technology and society influence each other mutually, the social relations are an integral part of the technology and do not follow in a determinist way from the material component.

This chapter focuses upon the technology of condoms; primarily as a prophylactic (that is, disease prevention) rather than a contraceptive technology, though the two uses obviously cannot be separated other than for analytical purposes. The particular interest is in how the threat of ill health mediates social relations, and the role of condoms in that process of mediation of the threat of sexually transmitted diseases, particularly AIDS. The chapter considers how the social relations of condom technology are changing in the AIDS era. The basic argument to be made is that of a continuity in the material component of the technology in the AIDS era, but a substantial discontinuity in the social relations of the technology.

The chapter has four parts: the origins of condom technology are traced, both the material and social component in the pre-AIDS era. Then changes in the social relations of the technology in the last decade are analysed, as well as some of the social policy implications of these changes.

CONDOMS IN THE PRE-AIDS ERA

The history of the technology needs to be considered in two parts. The first is the *material component*. The origins of the condom are unknown. According to a history of the technology by French doctor Jeanette Parisot (1987: 1–5), there is some evidence of ancient use, none of it definitely established. The Chinese used oiled silk paper as a type of condom about 2000 years ago. According to Greek legend, King Minos of Crete (of labryinth and minotaur fame), used a goat bladder. Aristotle was reported as a user, as was Pliny, the Roman author and scientific writer.

In the mid-sixteenth century, Gabriello Falloppio, an Italian doctor (known for naming the tubes) described sheaths made from linen which had been soaked in herbal brews and inorganic salts as a means of disease prevention. Until the use of rubber in the mid-nineteenth century, condoms were made from animal tissue. The appendixes of the sheep, lamb, calf and goat were tried. As well, there is evidence of fish bladders being used and from Japan, tortoiseshell!

Controversy surrounds the re-invention in modern times, though legend attributes it to a Dr Condom, physician to Charles II. Parisot disputes this and suggests instead the inventor was an army physician, Dr Quondam around 1645, who later changed his name to Cundum (1987: 9). In 1666, a witness to the first English birthrate commission testified that they were in widespread use in London at the time of the Great Fire.

Throughout the eighteenth century, most were made from sheep gut. The method of production was laborious and contributed to their high cost and re-use. The 1828 edition of Gray's *Supplement to the Pharmacopoeia*, describes the process of making them from sheep's caeca:

> They were soaked in water for several hours, turned inside out, macerated again in weak alkaline ley (changed every twelve hours), scraped carefully to abstract the mucous membrane, leaving the peritoneal and muscular coats exposed to the vapour of burning

brimstone, and washed in soap and water. Then they were blown
up, dried, cut to seven or eight inches, and finally 'bordered at the
open end with a riband'. (quoted in Fryer, 1965: 28)

Deluxe versions were also available:

'Baudruches Fine' were similarly prepared, but were drawn smooth
upon oiled moulds of a suitable size after being brimstoned. 'B.
superfines' had to be scented with essences, stretched on a glass
mould, and rubbed with a glass mould to polish them. And for 'B.
superfines doubles', a second caecum was drawn over the first on
the mould; being moist, the two insides adhere together'. (quoted in
Fryer, 1965: 28)

Little wonder that the range of affordability was limited to upper-
class men and that the client required a fitting for size before
buying!

The major technological advance came in 1833–34 with the
vulcanisation of rubber. Rubber condoms could now be produced
that were both much cheaper and could be stretched. The earliest
rubber ones however were rather thick by modern standards and
also had a seam, both of which diminished their sensitivity, probably
not unlike wearing a piece of bicycle tube. Nonetheless their invention was hailed by George Bernard Shaw as 'the greatest invention
of the nineteenth century' (quoted in Parisot, 1987: 26). In the 1930s
the latex method of manufacture was developed, where the condoms
could be manufactured directly from the latex sap of the rubber tree
without having to be turned into rubber first. By dipping glass
moulds into latex, the condoms could be manufactured thinner and
more elastic, without the seam and mass production by automation
became the norm. Prices dropped as a result, and latex condoms
became available on a mass scale (Parisot, 1987: 29–30). Product
diversification has seen developments in the construction of the
condom with variations in both taste and shape (the 'ribbers and
ticklers') supposed to increase sexual pleasure. At the same time,
sheep's gut condoms are still made and widely available with New
Zealand being the main international supplier.

The issue of condom safety has always been an important one,
not the least in the AIDS era. Safety relates not only to the technique
of use, but to defects with the product itself. As late as 1930, there
were complaints being made that 50–60 per cent of condoms were
faulty, though according to Parisot, no successful liability case has
ever been brought against a manufacturer. Laboratory testing by the
Australian Consumers' Association in 1982 found substandard
batches in two of the brands tested (*Choice*, 1982: 329). In pursuing
safety, manufacturers have had to strike a balance with sensitivity.
In general, it appears that safety increases with thickness of the

condom, but sensitivity, an important feature of male resistance to their use, declines. The Australian Standard for condom manufacture is a thickness not to exceed 0.16 mm and most models in the *Choice* tests fell within the 0.13–0.16 mm range. This is considerably thicker than a surviving eighteenth-century condom measured at only 0.07 mm, half the thickness of the standard, or one Japanese brand available at 0.03 mm (*Choice*, 1982: 331; Parisot, 1987: 32).

The second aspect of the history of condom technology is the *social relations*. In considering the traditional social relations of condom technology (especially but not exclusively prophylactic use), there are two aspects to analyse.

Firstly, there is the gender relations of the technology. Condoms have been considered to be a male technology, being worn by men and associated with patriarchal social relations. In ancient times, condoms had a variety of social purposes. Fryer (1965: 23) has argued, 'Sheaths were used in primitive times, hardly ever for contraceptive purposes, but to protect the wearer during combat, or against insect bites, tropical diseases, or evil spirits: or, in assorted colours, as badges of rank: or as charms to promote fertility; or as decorations: or simply for modesty's sake'. Then followed a long period until the sixteenth century when there appears to be no mention of the device in the historical records. Parisot argues that the reason for this disappearance was the emergence of a powerful ideology associated with the Church against contraception. Associated with this ideology was the suppression of any healers who may have advocated the use of condoms.

The re-emergence of the barrier device in modern historical times appear to be as a male upper-class response to the threat of sexually transmitted diseases. Parisot argues the reason was that, 'men, who until very shortly before had considered contraception to be worse than murder, suddenly began to feel the effects of this philosophy on themselves—in a very intimate way. Syphilis was reaching epidemic proportions, especially amongst the upper classes, so the doctors began to look for a solution' (1987: 5). Certainly, little early mention is made of its contraceptive usage. Before vulcanisation was employed in the manufacture of condoms, the cost restricted their use to a small section of the population. The contraceptive benefits of the technology were thus not promoted as an early advantage, however Parisot argues that this effect of the use of the technology was soon recognised by upper-class French women who began to encourage its use.

Also part of the traditional social relations of the technology has been the belief that condoms decreased male pleasure. Casanova, an early user, considered it akin to 'shutting himself in a piece of dead skin', though he did use them for contraceptive as well as prophylactic purposes (Parisot, 1987: 14). Within a set of dominant patriarchal social relations, that which decreased male pleasure, easily became defined as decreasing sexual pleasure in general. From the early days of usage, whether used for prophylactic or contraceptive purposes, increasing sexual pleasure was never part of the motivation for use except as a means of reducing premature ejaculation. Condoms have been almost universally assumed to interfere with sensation, as well as with spontaneity and therefore romance because of either the premeditated decision to wear one or the need to interrupt proceedings to fit it.

Partly as a result of these social relations, when the contraceptive pill became available in the early 1960s, it quickly assumed a hegemonic position as contraceptive technology in most countries. This, and the development of drugs to effectively and simply treat sexually transmitted diseases—the avoidance of which had traditionally been a motivation for wearing condoms—lead to a decline in the use of condoms for either contraceptive or prophylactic purposes. The less problematic social relations of the birth control pill meant that the traditional male opposition to the use of condoms largely prevailed. Expressed in the view that 'condom sex is not real sex', or likening use of a condom to 'showering in a raincoat', this attitude has proved a formidable obstacle to encouragement of their use in the AIDS era. The main users were amongst particular groups such as teenagers. A survey conducted by the Australian teenage magazine *Dolly* in 1983 where 6500 teenagers responded to a mail-in questionnaire, 55 per cent of whom were sexually experienced, showed that usage of condoms declined with age as the young women began using the birth control pill (*Dolly*, 1985).

The second major element of the traditional social relations of condom technology and related to the location of this technology in patriarchal social relations regarding sexuality, has been the moral and political objections to their very use in the modern historical context. An important feature of the traditional social relations of condom technology has been the 'anti-condom' lobby who have opposed, if not their very existence, at least widespread availability of condoms. This has been based on concern reflected in both the Church and State that easy availability and any form of public sanctioning of condoms implied by that availability, would have the effect of encouraging sexual expression especially insofar as it entailed the implicit acceptance of sex outside marriage (especially for the young) as well as homosexuality. Such sanctioning represented a threat to erode religious, moral and ethical values of the sanctity of monogamy and the family which have been important values within Judeo-Christian as well as other types of religious thought. Part of this moral and political objection involved young people who were considered a special case—expressed in concerns about vulnerability and innocence. Sex education in general, and availability of condoms in particular, was opposed because it was likely to encourage sexual experimentation.

This traditional objection had a number of effects on the social relations of condom technology. For one thing, it reinforced the male discourse surrounding the technology; condoms became a sort of symbol of teenage male sexuality. For women, and young women in particular, the social relations were problematic; to carry condoms invited allegations of promiscuity. For these reasons the 'blush and giggle' factor has traditionally been a component of the social relations.

These social relations also affected availability. At various times in Australian history the sale of condoms as contraceptives has been banned (Hicks, 1978). Only in the last decade and associated with the general social process of secularisation, have condoms been sold openly. Traditionally, availability had been restricted to pharmaceutical chemists, at first out of sight below the counter, then on display but not in the self-serve area, then on the open shelves. Vending machines, promoted by manufacturers as 'removing the blush factor' gradually appeared in male toilets, often the subject of political controversy and struggle to secure their introduction. Progress in the availability of condoms has been uneven both within Australia and throughout the world. In the Republic of Ireland they were banned from sale until 1980 and then available only on prescription from a medical practitioner, until 1985 when this restriction was removed.

What's in a name has always been important to the social relations of a technology. For condoms, because the origins are uncertain and because of the problematic social relations, the technology has always lent itself to euphemism. Dr Condom himself changed his name to avoid the connotations of the name. In England they became known as 'french letters' while in France they were known as 'english overcoats' (redingotes d'Angleterre). The 1828 edition of Gray's *Supplement to the Pharmacopoeia*, described their manufacture under the heading 'Condoms, Armour, Baudruches, Redingote Anglaises'. Other names by which they have been known include 'machines', 'johnnies', 'frangers', 'rubbers', 'frenchies'.

In similar vein, the brand names under which they have been marketed often tended to express male connotations, reflective of the male discourse on sexuality. These include 'Sheik', 'Trojan', 'Rough Rider' (the last hardly designed to appeal to women). In other cultures, the brand names reflect the place of the condom in the discourse of sexuality. For example, in Japan where condoms have remained the principal form of contraceptive (Coleman, 1981), most condoms are purchased by women. The brand names reflect this, such as 'The Lady Wet', though it's not clear why one major brand name should translate as 'Wrinkle'! The problematic social relations are also reflected in the international marketing strategies: 'Fourex' is a major brand of condom in the United States but a brand of beer in Australia, heavily promoted with a jingle which says, 'I can feel a Fourex coming on'!

Finally, in considering the traditional social relations of the technology it is appropriate to consider briefly the other uses to which the condom has been put. A major one has been their use to facilitate the smuggling of drugs across international borders by their concealment inside the body. Likewise, they have been used by the Australian Army to protect the ends of their rifles in the tropical north of the country!

THE AIDS ERA

Since the identification of the disease in the early 1980s, AIDS has come to represent a major new challenge with profound sociological and social policy implications. It has come into a developed world in which the major focus of health expenditure has become maintaining quality of life in the face of long-term chronic degenerative illnesses. Of infectious diseases there was little experience; it had become widely believed that the problem of infectious epidemic diseases had passed or only occurred in the third world.

The dominant paradigm of knowledge about illness and treatment which had come to be known as western scientific medical knowledge, promoted a biomedical model of disease—that disease was an individual and biological phenomenon that could be alleviated by 'technological fixes' in the form of chemotherapeutic technology (see Willis, 1989a). Part of the ideology of the occupational group that lay claim to this paradigm of knowledge, was the claiming of much of the credit for having conquered these infectious diseases in the past, despite evidence that decreased mortality and increased life expectancy was more the result of public health measures such as improved diet, shorter working hours and better living conditions (McKinlay & McKinlay, 1977). Armed with this biomedical model of disease, medical researchers have concentrated on the search for a 'technological fix' of the chemotherapeutic kind in the form of a vaccine or other treatment. Thus far however, the search for a 'magic bullet' in the form of vaccine or other treatment for AIDS has been unsuccessful. Furthermore, the history of the treatment of infectious diseases in general and sexually transmitted diseases in particular (see Brandt, 1988) suggests that it is unlikely that development of such treatments will easily end the epidemic.

Indeed the AIDS epidemic graphically demonstrates the classic problem and flaws with the biomedical model on which medical practice is based, in particular, the view of diseases as individual and biological entities mitigated by technological fixes rather than social and political solutions. In his work on the history of sexually transmitted diseases, Brandt (1988: 371) argues: 'Diseases are complex bio-ecological problems that may be mitigated only by addressing a range of scientific, social and political considerations'.

The recognition of the current unavailability of a cure for AIDS has led to a realisation that the best chance of controlling the spread of infection is to prevent transmission, by a public education campaign into both knowledge about what causes transmission, and also what can be done to prevent that transmission (practices). Again, however, the 'sense of problem' thrown up by the biomedical paradigm focuses on a technological fix, this time with a change of emphasis from chemotherapeutic to prophylactic (barrier) and diagnostic technology—that is, condoms and testing. It is the appropriateness of this strategy, particularly in relation to condoms that constitutes the social policy implications of this chapter.

In considering the technology of condoms in the AIDS era, it is again necessary to consider both the material and social components.

The material component

This is characterised by a *continuity* from the traditional to the AIDS era. The developments in the material component of the technology that have occurred reflect the changes in the social relations. New products have appeared on the market designed to cope with the increased importance of the prophylactic role of the technology, such as a thicker and stronger condom designed to more effectively withstand sexual practices with a high risk of transmission of the virus, such as anal intercourse. Likewise, condoms are now available treated with a chemical 'nonoxynol 9' which has been shown to kill the AIDS virus under laboratory conditions (Hicks et al., 1985).

Increased demand, amounting to as much as a 50 per cent increase over the last five years in Australia (with total annual sales of 36 million—*Age*, 19/11/92), as well as the related greater fashionableness of condom use has resulted in product diversification: condoms that glow in the dark, condoms that are to be worn by women rather than by men (probably better called sheaths), and the release of a youth product are all reported. Similarly, a return to production of condoms in different sizes has occurred, though reflective of the male social relations of the technology, not marketed as 'small, medium and large' but as 'large, extra large and jumbo size'!

The social relations

While the material component of condom technology is characterised by a continuity, the social component is characterised by a growing and substantial *discontinuity*. A distinction should be drawn however between the changing social relations at the level of official public policy in relation to condom use—what might be termed the macro level—and the private, micro level, of what evidence there is about the changing social relations of the technology in bedrooms. At the macro, official level, there are several indications of this change.

Firstly, the maleness of the social relations of the technology have lessened in the AIDS era. Vending machines are now to be found in female as well as male toilets. Women are being encouraged to carry condoms with discrete holders akin to tampon holders available in a number of countries to reduce the potential embarrassment of accidently tipping over one's handbag!

Secondly, new products which have come onto the market with product diversification, more often have brand names less male in their connotations, such as 'Horizon', 'Lifestyle', 'Mentor' and the American contribution called 'My Pet Rubber'.

Thirdly, the use of condoms is being actively and heavily promoted by State agencies for almost the first time. Condom use is a major component of the official HIV/AIDS prevention strategy the world over. In the United States for example, condom use is urged by the Surgeon-General for groups at risk. The same is true for Australia. The use of barrier technology to prevent infection is considered the best chance of containing the epidemic and especially preventing the spread of infection from current risk groups like gay men and IV drug users to the general heterosexual population. To this end, condoms have been heavily promoted as an integral part of the practice of safe sex. This change in State attitudes to the use of condoms has had and is having substantial implications for social relations of the technology. In particular, it has resulted in a lessening of weight attached to moral and religious objections to its promotion. This has resulted in the placing of condom vending machines in some Australian high school washrooms, something that would have been unheard of only a few years ago. In other words, the threat of ill health is actively mediating the social relations of condom technology in relation to public education.

The emphasis of such public education campaigns is to get sexually active people, both homosexual and heterosexual, who may be at risk, to use them for prophylactic purposes. 'At risk' groups are defined in the United States by the Surgeon-General, for example, as those: having sex outside 'established mutually monogamous relationships'; homosexuals and IV drug users. To encourage their use, campaigns have been targeted at 'socialising' the condom to be more acceptable, overcoming the traditionally problematic social relations of the technology. Reflective of the dominant male discourse of sexuality including male opposition to condom use, the campaigns have encouraged women to be more assertive and insist on their partners wearing them. Campaign slogans such as, 'tell him if it's not on, it's not on', or in the American version 'no glove, no love' have been directed to this end.

There have also been attempts to alter the problematic social relations associated with the nomenclature, by renaming the condom. In New Zealand for example, there has been a public health campaign to identify condoms as 'parachutes'. Television advertisements have featured people jumping out of aeroplanes with the message being 'you wouldn't jump out of an aeroplane without a parachute would you, so don't have sex without a condom'. This euphemistic attempt to make condoms more socially acceptable has affected the discourse of seduction also ('you want to come parachuting with me?').

The aim in these public education campaigns—again related to the male discourse on sexuality—is to change the symbolism of condoms, from being a symbol of male teenage sexuality to being symbolic of caring and responsibility ('if you really cared about me, you'd use a condom'). The effect of these campaigns appears to be that condomless sex is becoming a symbol of true love and status passage in the development of a relationship, along the lines of 'Tom and Sue must really be getting serious now, they've stopped using condoms'. Likewise amongst gay men, Dowsett (1990) has found that couples 'in love' discard the condom.

Knowledge and practice at the micro level

Heavy promotion of condom use at the official macro level is one thing, getting people to modify their sexual practices in the direction of safe sex practices, particularly using condoms, is another thing altogether. In other words, thus far I have considered mainly the promotion of condom technology as risk reduction technology in the AIDS era. Of course, this is only half the story in dealing with the threat to health and longevity. The other side is translating that knowledge about how to prevent transmission into practice, particularly amongst relatively high risk (that is, multi-partnered) heterosexual groups. There has emerged a considerable literature that there exists a disjunction between knowledge and practice. Many people understand quite well what causes HIV infection, but demonstrate little evidence of behaviour change to act in terms of that knowledge. This disjunction has become a considerable problem for health planners and educators.

In relation to condoms, knowledge that condoms at least help to reduce risk of infection is widespread, yet there is little evidence that such knowledge is changing sexual practices amongst heterosexuals. In a study of 419 Sydney university students, Turtle et al. (1989) found that while 70 per cent of respondents said that vaginal intercourse with a casual partner was safe if a condom was used, and 87 per cent thought that condoms should be carried by both men and women, only 7 per cent of the sexually active students have actually changed their method of contraception to using condoms. This type of finding is repeated in the American longitudinal study by Kegeles at al. (1988) where 'sexually active adolescents report placing high value and importance on using a contraceptive that protects against STDs and know that condoms prevent STDs, yet the females continue to intend not to have their partners use condoms and the males' intentions to use condoms decreased' over the year between surveys (Kegeles at al., 1988: 461). A public opinion poll conducted in Australia in September 1987 found that only 5 per cent of respondents said they changed their sexual behaviour because of the threat of AIDS (Bell & Cornford, 1987).

Amongst homosexuals, the disjunction appears to be less— condom use has become widespread and routine amongst homosexuals. In a study of users of homosexual 'beats' in Sydney, Bennet et al. (1989) found more than 70 per cent of respondents reported regular or routine use of condoms and 89 per cent reported intended use in the future. At the same time, the disjunction does still exist to some extent, and being in a monogamous relationship was a major reason given by the respondents for non-use of condoms.

Such a disjunction between knowledge about transmission of the disease and resultant changes in practice towards greater use of condoms would appear to be explainable in terms of some continuation of the social relations of condom technology into the AIDS era. Despite attempts to change these social relations by health authorities, such social relations are proving resistant to rapid change, and traditional attitudes to condom usage persist. In studies of condom usage, the attitude that condom usage reduced sexual pleasure, especially for men, was still widespread and resistant to modification. The study of Bennet at al. (1989) of high-risk homosexual 'beat' users found that the reduction of pleasure was an important reason for non-use. In the Turtle et al. (1989) study of heterosexual young people, 49 per cent of respondents thought the use of condoms reduces sexual pleasure. The persistence of such attitudes suggests that attempts to 'sell' the condom as having improved sensitivity are not likely to be successful and that the best chances are to stress the safety aspects.

Other traditional attitudes towards condoms persist. In a study of young women in Canberra, Abbott (1988) found that many of the young women would not ask for condoms to be used—either because they were too embarrassed to ask or to buy, or did not want to be seen as prepared for or wanting sex.

At the micro level of gender relations therefore, it is clear that aspects of the traditional social relations of condom technology persist and form a considerable problem for health authorities in attempting to contain the spread of the AIDS epidemic amongst the heterosexual population at large. Condoms as a prophylactic technology are embedded in a patriarchal discourse about sexuality whereby males are more likely than females to determine the conditions under which intercourse will occur. In Abbott's (1988) study of Canberra teenage girls, 38 per cent had had intercourse when they didn't want to, and half the sample felt they lacked the communication skills to insist on condoms being used. Such communication skills are important; as Turtle et al. (1989: 375) ask: 'How does one proceed gracefully to find out about a new partner's sexual past?' Being assertive enough to insist on condoms being worn is difficult given what Kippax et al. (1990a) call the 'asymmetry of contemporary heterosexual relations'. Different social construction of sexuality by gender (such as male emphasis on quantity versus female emphasis on quality) mediates the social context in which condoms may or may not be used. Negotiation about the condition under which sex may take place is most likely in situations where women have some control over the situation. To this end they advocate a more female-centred discourse surrounding sexuality. Its possibilities for the prevention of the spread of infection are suggested by a study by Chapman et al. (1990), who found in their sample of 408 respondents with one or more sexual partners in the previous year, only one of the males in the study said he would refuse to use a condom if asked by the women. In the emerging feminist literature on AIDS (e.g. Kaplan, 1987; Richardson, D., 1987), the need for women to take more active steps to protect themselves and their children from the threat of infection is the major theme. Kaplan (1987: 144–9) advocates the Lysistrata strategy to prevent the spread of the epidemic into the heterosexual population. Drawing on the strategy portrayed in Aristophanes' play, of the women refusing all sexual contact with their menfolk until they stop fighting, Kaplan advocates women refuse all sexual contact unless safe sex practices such as exclusivity and condoms are used!

Negotiation over relative risk factors and the need to reduce risk of infection by following safe sex techniques such as using condoms, however, remains problematic. Many of the taken-for-granted assumptions surrounding sexuality need to be carefully examined; what monogamy means to different people, conditions under which trust in one's partner may be justified and when it may not, are all elements of the social context in which condom use occurs. As Chapman et al. argue

> While it is men who wear condoms, the initiation of their use can involve either sex and thus potentially constitutes a minefield of anticipated embarrassment, implied admission or accusation about self or other having an STD or AIDS, diminution of erotic pleasure, and at the base of all these, possible sexual or personal rejection. (1990: 13)

These negotiations constitute an (often tortuous) 'internal' dialogue between sexually active people concerning potential condom use with new partners, to be differentiated from an 'external' dialogue of what is actually said (Chapman et al., 1990: 13). Nor is this aspect of the social relations of condom technology restricted to casual encounters. In established relationships, condom use may be even more problematic; as Kippax et al. (1990a: 540) argue: 'contrary to official wisdom regarding HIV, how can a condom suddenly be introduced into the marital bed?'.

Do they work?

Finally, in considering condom technology in the AIDS era, it is necessary to consider the issue of how appropriate is the official promotion of condoms as a prophylactic technology. This question needs to be considered at several levels: the device itself, the technique associated with its use and in practice in the population at large.

Firstly, at the level of the device itself. Here the basic premise is that condoms provide an effective mechanical barrier to the spread of the HIV virus via semen or vaginal secretions. This proposition is supported by several laboratory studies. In one, condoms were filled with fluid containing a very high concentration of the virus— 5000 times that found in bodily fluids and subjected to pressure. There was no evidence of leakage (Conant, 1986). However, condoms themselves may be subject to manufacturing or packaging defects which may cause leakage. A study for the Federal Drug Administration in the United States found that one in five sample lots leaked (*American Medical News*, 1987). As indicated previously, some batches tested by the Australian Consumers' Association in 1982 were faulty (*Choice*, 1982) and in the issue of the monthly magazine produced by that organisation while this paper was being written (*Choice*, 1990) in the section on 'Recalls and bans', two batches of a particular brand of condoms were recalled for failing the freedom-from-holes test.

The second level at which the effectiveness of condom prophylaxis must be considered is at the level of technique of use; that is, how they are actually used as distinct from the question of manufacture. Two generations of exposure to the hegemony of the birth control pill has resulted in two generations of potential users relatively inexperienced in their proper use. Even with impeccable technique they may not prevent body fluids coming in contact, they may not be put on in time, may break or tear from rough use. All these eventualities may result in infection occurring. In the study by Bennet et al. (1989: 313) of homosexual 'beat' users, 45 per cent of respondents had experienced problems with condoms breaking, leaking or slipping.

Another method of assessing this question is to consider the effectiveness of the condom as a contraceptive technology. Here the conservative estimate is of a failure rate of about 10 per cent amongst couples who use condoms exclusively for one year as their means of birth control (see for example Grady, 1986). When the effectiveness of condoms as a prophylactic against the transmission of HIV virus rather than birth control technology is considered, the situation is more problematic; for one thing women are only fertile and therefore at risk from conception for 4–5 days per month whereas they are at risk from HIV infection every day of the month.

The third level at which the effectiveness of condoms must be considered is in actual use. Studies have examined the continuation of a sexual relationship, using condoms, in couples where the man was HIV positive and the woman not. In one such study (Goedert, 1987) the meticulous use of condoms failed to prevent the infection of three of the eighteen women. He concludes, 'it is clear that the use of the condom will not eliminate the risk of transmission and must be viewed as a secondary strategy' (1987: 1340). In another study of 97 female partners of infected men, Padian et al. found that 23 per cent of the women were infected, though some of this infection may have occurred before the couples began using condoms. They conclude, 'condom use is not significantly associated with protection from infection' (Padian et al., 1987: 789). Based on their review of the literature on the effectiveness of condoms, Feldblum and Fortney (1988: 52–3), conclude:

there exists a widespread assumption that condoms and possibly spermicides can effectively prevent infection with HIV. The evidence for this assumption, however, is not strong . . . While the use of condoms and spermicide is unlikely to be harmful, there is the potential for harm if their use is substituted for abstinence, monogamy or good judgement . . . Necessity has forced recommendations for the use of condoms or spermicides in advance of satisfactory measurement of their potential to interrupt the transmission of HIV, and advice is being given on the grounds of common sense, substantiated by a small amount of less than conclusive evidence.

These findings have led some writers (e.g., Kaplan, 1987; Richardson, 1987) to believe that the safety of condoms has been exaggerated, the effect of which is to give a false sense of security. At the very least it appears clear that condoms are not a panacea for the AIDS crisis. It is not possible to carry on as before with just the addition of condoms. Rather, the social relations of condom technology have changed in the AIDS era. While there is continuity in the material component of the technology of condoms, there is a disjunction in the social relations. Condoms do not represent a 'technological fix' in AIDS avoidance. They do not represent the only strategy necessary but should be seen as part of a comprehensive program that includes not only condom promotion but also education in safe sex techniques.

In other words, while condom use is still important and still to be encouraged, it should be considered as necessary but not sufficient prophylactic strategy. It is appropriate to promote as the symbol of safe and responsible sex, but as a part of such education campaigns it should also be stressed that condom usage alone is not enough. At best, condom use must be considered as a means of reducing the risk of transmission, not eliminating it.

While there is some awareness by health education authorities of the limitations of a condom-only strategy, nonetheless attempts to increase utilisation of condoms can lead to the erroneous perception that condom use is enough, especially when media campaigns demand a short and punchy message ('tell him if it's not on, it's not on') which may not be able to adequately convey the complexity of the preventive strategy. In some quarters the emphasis on condoms as a panacea unfortunately goes further. An example is a publication entitled *The Modern Girl's Guide to Safe Sex* (Cooke, 1988). While the book contains much information that is useful and helpful in preventing or reducing risk of transmission of STDs, it expresses a view of continuity in the social relations of condom technology, basically to carry on as before but use condoms: 'those people who take the trouble to find out how to use condoms properly can relax about the fear of STDs and concentrate on having a good time. The next best thing to winning the lottery is finding a boy who takes wearing condoms for granted' (Cooke, 1988: 8). In the book, the condom is referred to as '. . . the thinking Modern Girl's hero' (1988: 42). The advice is given that '. . . you can have as many partners as you can fit in between sleeping, eating and writing to your maiden aunt if that's what you fancy—just use condoms' (1988: 42). The technological determinist argument being made here does not adequately recognise that the technology is embedded in a set of social and cultural practices. However symbolic the condom is—and its use is no doubt vastly better than carrying on exactly as before—its use is only one of a set of practices to be promoting to control the epidemic.

CONCLUSION

In this chapter the changing social relations of the prophylactic technology of condoms have been analysed. The argument has been that while there is continuity in the material component of the technology, the social relations of condom technology are changing in the AIDS era. Most of this change thus far has been the result of promotion of condom use as a safe sex technique important to reducing the risk of the transmission of the HIV virus. At the private micro level, the continuation of some elements of the traditional social relations of the technology, particularly in embodiment within a male discourse of sexuality in society, is proving resistant to change and represents a considerable challenge to health authorities attempting to prevent transmission of the virus from those engaging in high risk activities such as sharing needles and unprotected anal intercourse, to the population at large.

If the debate over the appropriate place of condoms in the affairs of society has a positive benefit besides containing the spread of infection, it is likely to be the possibilities for the decline in the male-centred discourse on sexuality, and the emergence and acceptance of more female-centred discourse.

POSTSCRIPT

This chapter has been hitherto unpublished. It represents an attempt to apply the sociological perspective on medical technology assessment, not only to the complex, expensive high-tech items like echocardiography, but also to the simple everyday garden-variety instances like the humble condom. The hallmark of that perspective is attention not only to the material component of the technology, but also to the social component. Most often indeed it will be the social relations of the technology which will ultimately determine its 'career'.

Take the example of the recently released female condom/sheath. Whether it will be a successful innovation (from any point of view) will be decided by the social relations of the technology and in particular its acceptability to both men and women. Leaving aside the material component of whether it will effectively protect the wearer (which will only be decided in the longer term), from a woman's point of view the advantage is in giving her control over her own sexual health and reproduction rather than relying on her male partner to provide a condom that has not passed the 'use by' date or whatever. On the other hand, the social relations are similar to those of the birth control pill, that the responsibility for contraception, and in this case prophylaxis as well, falls on the woman. Men are able to avoid responsibility for protecting their partners from unwanted consequences by the use of this technology whereas condoms, worn by males, reflect the opposite attitude.

Finally, taking condoms as an example to analyse from a sociological perspective also illustrates one other aspect of the sociological imagination, that unlike some subjects of study, sociology is not the sort of subject that one can leave in the laboratory at the end of a day of study and not think about until arriving at the bench to begin work the next day. Using a condom may never seem the same again!

Part 3

ILL HEALTH AS SOCIAL PROCESS

9 RSI as a social process

A spectre is haunting Australian business life—the 'epidemic' of repetition strain injuries (RSI) which is undermining the viability of many business enterprises. Consider the following actual case study, no doubt being repeated every day.

> A company involved in the manufacturing industry and located within the suburban area employs approximately 150 people of which 30 per cent comprises of female labour. The company doesn't have an accident prevention programme and a safety officer or facsimile is not employed. The manager of this company finds his workers' compensation premium has dramatically escalated from $80,000 to $200,000, an increase of 150 per cent in one year. During that period, the workers' compensation claims experience included three RSI claims . . . without much foresight (the manager) realises his company will cease to operate if he cannot control his workers' compensation losses. (Dressing, 1981: 1)

The 'epidemic' of concern and claims have been of quite recent origin, in particular since 1982. RSI has become the most common cause of time off work for women since that time and the third most common cause for men (*Age*, 21/11/84). Using New South Wales workers' compensation figures, Fergusson (1984) calculated that the incidence of 'synovitis, bursitis and tenosynovitis' (three of the conditions that are recognised collectively as RSI) had trebled in women in the period 1978–82. Overall, the number of cases in New South Wales has doubled since 1980 (Liddicoat, 1984). Workers' compensation claims represent only a part of the total incidence

133

however; in many workplaces there have been reports of a far higher incidence. At the Australian National University for example, to the end of 1984, one in four of the university's clerical and typing staff had attended the university health service with RSI symptoms (Task Force Report, 1982). Among typists specifically, the number who have had experience of RSI was as high as 60 per cent (Brennan, 1985: 29). Among Telecom operators in Western Australia, one in five has suffered some RSI disability since new equipment was installed in 1980 (*Financial Review*, 25/10/84). In a survey of 108 data process operators in the Melbourne Taxation Office only 20 per cent did not have work-related symptoms of RSI (Taylor & Pitcher, 1984).

Although the existence of repetition injuries has been documented under various names at least since the times of Ramazzini, the father of occupational medicine (1700), the recency of the 'epidemic' is quite startling. As recently as 1979, a large ergonomics conference on the theme of 'Ergonomics and Visual Display Units' did not identify RSI as a particular health hazard associated with their use, and certainly RSI hardly ranked a mention alongside radiation and cyestrain as potential occupational health and safety hazards (McPhee & Howie, 1979).

The recency, the widespread massive reporting and the threat posed to industry together make RSI an important medico-social phenomenon—an instance of what Cohen (1972) calls a 'moral panic' of the 1980s of similar proportions to that other medico-social phenomenon, AIDS. RSI is a phenomenon, furthermore, for which the sociological aspects are quite tantalising and on which the widespread debate thus far has only scratched the surface. The only attempt of any substance that I have found was that of Meekosha and Jacubowicz (1985)

This chapter addresses the sociological aspects of RSI, particularly those associated with the organisation of work and the sociology of (medical) knowledge surrounding RSI. It should be noted that the paper is not based upon formal empirical research, and it must not be read as denying the reality of the symptoms and suffering which victims undergo as a result of RSI. On the contrary, in the tradition of C. Wright Mills (1959) it contends that the personal troubles of RSI sufferers must be linked with the public issues surrounding the injury. The focus in this paper is upon those public issues. It should be noted in addition that many of the propositions advanced in making this argument are empirical ones and open to investigation.

This chapter argues that while the physiological and ergonomic aspects of the phenomenon are important, there is a substantial social aspect *in addition* which needs to be explained. The social environment, in other words, mediates the effects of the physiological and ergonomic factors. A social process is involved, the dimensions of which are not unique or specific. Its explication involves consideration of how illness mediates social relations in general and the social relations of production (that is at work) in particular. In analysing RSI as a social process, this paper draws upon a framework developed by Karl Figlio (1982) in his analysis of occupational illness of miners' nystagmus in Britain in the early twentieth century.

THE SOCIAL ASPECTS

As the process has unfolded, a number of curious and tantalising social aspects of RSI have emerged, all of which are grist to the social scientist's mill. Why, for instance, after workers have used the same equipment for a number of years, have a number of them developed RSI? Then, even after a considerable outlay on state-of-the-art ergonomic furniture, pause strategies and exercises, why do workers continue to develop symptoms? A number of such curious anomalies about RSI have emerged, no doubt many others exist. Why have a quarter of typing and clerical staff at the Australian National University reported RSI symptoms, while a far lower incidence has been reported at other universities such as Macquarie University (Brennan, 1985)? Why did eleven members (20 per cent) of the Basser Department of Computer Science at Sydney University develop RSI in 1984, while the computer centre at the same university, presumably utilising similar technology, have none? (Herbison-Evans, 1984). In some keyboard areas of the public service in Canberra, such as the Defence Department, as many as half the workers have been absent from work with RSI at one time, (*Canberra Times*, 19/8/1984), while in sections of the Health Department the rate is much lower. Amongst Sydney hospital cleaners, RSI is a common complaint at the new Westmead Hospital but uncommon at the older Royal Prince Alfred Hospital (Brennan, 1985). Clearly there is much about the phenomenon that is not yet understood. This paper attempts, in a schematic fashion to go some way towards a better understanding.

THE FIGLIO FRAMEWORK

Figlio (1982) develops a framework for analysing the parallel historical example of miners' nystagmus. Symptomatised by oscillation of the eyes, giddiness, headaches, being dazzled by light, and depression, miners' nystagmus was the basis for a large increase in compensation claims around that period. Its emergence coincided with changes in the social relations of production: liberalisation of workers' compensation Acts in 1897 and 1906, on one hand, basically widening the liability of employers for their workers; and technological changes in the organisation of work on the other. The introduction of safety lamps in 1890 made previously unworkable seams of coal workable, though these lamps made the work more difficult and, paradoxically, more dangerous. The major technological change however was mechanisation of coalmining; disrupting a long-established work pattern, increasing supervision, the pace of work and the noise and danger of working conditions. Figlio's interest is in the way illness mediates social relations; in this case how the changing social relations of production led to discontent amongst workers on the one hand and increased sickness absence by workers on the other. Furthermore in this mediation process, the disease or injury itself becomes an object of negotiation.

Figlio's argument (codified with some effort!) is that the mediation of the social relations of production by illness, occurs as a three-stage process:

1 the appearance of the disease or injury, represented as a set of symptoms;
2 the appearance of observers of the disease or injury who set in operation various medical, legal and administrative apparatuses to 'cope' with the disease or injury;
3 negotiation of the socioeconomic and political meaning of the disease or injury—at its most basic this is workers' compensation, paid in place of wages, but the negotiation goes much further than this.

This chapter applies Figlio's framework to RSI. It enquires how a set of symptoms set in motion a medical, legal and administrative apparatus the result of which, so far, has been compensation on one hand, attempts at prevention on the other, and continuing negotiation over the socioeconomic and political meaning of the injury.

SYMPTOM APPEARANCE AND THE ERA OF SCEPTICISM

Since 1982, the social process has developed to a considerable extent. Some of the earlier wilder claims about RSI which were made have been laid to rest, but those knee-jerk attempts to account for the curious nature of the injury should be examined for the partial insights they may have provided, which can be reinterpreted within a wider approach.

An early response was the technological innovation thesis—the 'blame-the-equipment' explanation, epitomised by the press article (*National Times*, 12/10/84) on the issue entitled, 'Hi-Tech Epidemic: victims of a bright new technology that maims'. RSI was viewed as an occupational health consequence of technological innovation—particularly in computer technology—which had not been adjusted to Australian conditions and had been rapidly introduced without appropriate time for adjustment.

The 'blame-the-worker' explanation, or 'malingering' thesis, developed at much the same time. This has been put forward by some employers and some sections of the medical profession, in considerable part in response to frustration over the complex epistemology of RSI. The crucial link was with the workers' compensation system, for which doctors were required to certify symptoms. This led to a lively debate about the possibilities of malingering in order to secure income without working for it. In classic victim-blaming style, RSI has been termed 'golden wrist' (*Business Review Weekly*, 17–23/11/84), the latest excuse for bludging, and its sufferers labelled 'work shy' (*Sydney Morning Herald*, 21/2/85). It has been likened to an infectious disease where 'the main mode of transmission has been by example' (Pillemer, 1979: 4). In the tradition of racist medico-legal stereotypes such as 'Greek back' and 'Mediterranean guts ache', RSI has also been called 'migrant arm' (Pillemer, 1979: 4). As one occupational health medical practitioner commented on the basis of thirteen years' experience, 'it is more related to our ethnic population . . . we must not forget that it is an excellent source of income for struggling families . . . to purchase their dream home at a rapid rate' (Furey, 1982: 29).

For the most part, however, this era of scepticism about whether RSI existed or not, has passed. On many issues surrounding the affliction, speculation has been superseded by evidence gathered particularly in the course of two inquiries published in July 1985: the RSI committee of the National Occupational Health and Safety Commission (the NOHSC *Interim Report*, 1985), and the Task Force Report on RSI in the Australian public service (Task Force Report, 1982).

Repetition injuries, we know now, are not just a result of recent technological change but have been recorded both in Australia and overseas for many years. Previously the incidence had mainly been amongst blue-collar workers and had been called by a variety of names such as 'telegrapher's cramp', 'packer's wrist', 'writer's cramp', 'Ericsson's arm' and 'process worker's arm'. RSI is not just an Australian affliction (dubbed 'kangaroo paw') but is known by other names in other countries where its existence is well documented over a considerable period of time. While RSI suffered by white-collar keyboard operators has received most publicity, it has existed—though was often misdiagnosed—for a much longer time amongst blue-collar workers performing highly repetitive process work. In post-war Australia, migrant women, in particular, performed these tasks. RSI is not related in any simple way to technological innovation; the relationship is a complex one.

In Figlio's terms, the appearance of RSI symptoms is not a new phenomenon, indeed the 'epidemic' appears to be as much a function of differential reporting as it does of differential incidence over time. Observers of the injury have emerged including doctors, lawyers, ergonomists, psychologists, biomechanical engineers and—sociologists! The legal and, particularly, medical response has been confused initially but now appears to be developing in a more coherent manner. The administrative response to the threat to the social order engendered by RSI has been the two inquiries indicated. RSI has been defined as a priority area for the new NOHSC and a program of research is being instituted.

NEGOTIATION OF THE SOCIOECONOMIC AND POLITICAL MEANING OF RSI

This third stage of Figlio's framework is currently underway. While the symptoms have existed for a long time, it is the redefinition of their socioeconomic and political meaning that has led to the 'epidemic' in a complex process. The key question, from this perspective, is: 'Why has the epidemic occurred at this historical conjuncture?' The answers are social, economic and technological. In the wider context an important area of social change in post-war Australian society has been the workers' health movement, a social movement that arguably ranks in importance with the women's movement and the peace movement. From a situation where the hazards of work were accepted fatalistically, considered inevitable and compensated directly either by 'dirty money', or 'danger money' or compensation after the event of injury or accident, concern has arisen with the provision of safe and hazard-free working conditions and the prevention of injury and occupational disease.

Occupational health and safety has increasingly become an industrial relations issue between capital and labour; in other words, it has increasingly come to mediate the social relations of production. Governmental responses (in also attempting to mediate these social relations) have been to create the NOHSC to operate on a tripartite basis with employer, union and governmental representatives. RSI has become one of the 'glamour' areas of occupational health and safety (along with asbestos) in an area of social relations increasingly important in shaping the structure of work relations.

It appears that the economic times have contributed to RSI becoming more visible. High unemployment has meant less mobility between jobs. Whereas in times of low unemployment, a traditional blue-collar response to the aches and pains associated with highly repetitive work has been to move on to another job requiring similarly repetitive movements but perhaps different muscles, lack of alternative employment has lessened this possibility. In addition, with the rate and length of female participation in the paid workforce increasing, protection of one's occupational health becomes more important, leading to greater opposition to obstacles to a continued career outside the domestic sphere.

The consequence of rapid technological innovation involving microchip technology in particular, has diluted to a certain extent the sexual and ethnic stereotyping of jobs. Keyboard technology was introduced into white-collar clerical workplaces where Anglo-Saxon women worked. Repetition injuries amongst these workers could not be dismissed with the racist stereotypes that could be made about migrant women. In addition, keyboard technology transformed the work of some traditionally male and strongly unionised occupations such as the printing trade and men have begun to suffer from RSI as well. This last point is not to argue, in a technological determinist fashion, that the new technology itself was the source of RSI; rather the social relations associated with its introduction must be considered.

In summary though, these three factors constitute the changing socioeconomic meaning of RSI and are necessary aspects of the explanation for the epidemic nature of the condition at this particular time. They are not a sufficient explanation however, but must be augmented by a discussion of political aspects.

THE POLITICAL MEANING

The political meaning of RSI has become increasingly the object of negotiation as the seriousness of the threat both to the individual sufferers and to employers has gradually become apparent. RSI represents a qualitatively different type of occupational health and safety hazard from others in the past. Combined with legislative changes concerning workers' compensation and rehabilitation, this means that the rules for coping with employment health hazards are effectively being rewritten.

The traditional employer responses to such hazards are patently inadequate. The response, summed up by the phrase 'fix the worker not the workplace' (for example, issue earmuffs rather than install quieter machines) has been ineffective in coping with the problem. For a start there is no easy way, no 'magic bullet' to alleviate RSI without reducing production, at least. Attempts at devising biomechanical tests to evaluate predisposition to RSI as pre-employment screening were scotched by the National Health and Medical Research Council (1982) which argued that, 'at the present time there is no known technical equipment which could detect individuals likely to suffer adverse effects from stressful movements and postures. Information generated from such equipment has no diagnostic value and these devices should not be used.'

The ability of employers to externalise the cost of damage to their workers' health has been lessened by the huge increases in workers' compensation premiums discussed earlier. Claims from more highly paid white-collar workers make payouts and future premiums much greater. In addition, an employer knowingly continuing to injure their employees' health, faces the possibility of common law claims for failing to provide a safe workplace. Furthermore when legislative changes make rehabilitation of the injured worker legally mandatory, through the provision of light duties, but the amount of light duties work that can be found is finite, the probability is increased of a claim of total incapacity, with much higher payouts as a result. The potential payout for each young data-entry worker totally disabled in this way could exceed one million dollars, although no successful claims have approached this figure so far.

Because the stakes are so high, it is little wonder that the doctors, lawyers or ergonomists who are called upon to mediate the social relations of production have become entangled in controversy and are frequently put in the position of providing contradictory evidence. Workers' compensation claims for RSI have been reported to be disproportionately represented in the 'disputed' category of claims (Mulvaney, 1984). Indeed, even the definition of RSI has become the object of negotiation and mediation. Prior to an 'official' definition being provided by the NOHSC RSI committee, the debate showed there was indeed a lot in a name. Some medical practitioners have objected to the term RSI as being too general (Wilson, 1984). Some employers objected to the term 'occupational overuse injuries', which had been suggested by Stone (1984), because it laid the blame for the condition on the jobs and on the employer when it was sometimes contributed to by repetitive leisure activities such as knitting. 'Muscular fatigue' has been suggested as an alternative which 'does not attempt to lay the blame . . . it is simpler and less emotional' (MacGeorge, 1984). The official definition adopted by the NOHSC RSI committee in their interim report (1985) plotted a relatively neutral middle course, defining RSI as 'a soft tissue disorder caused by overloading particular muscle groups from repeated use of the maintenance of constrained postures'.

RSI AND THE LABOUR PROCESS

Negotiation over the definition of the condition has constituted a relatively early stage of the social process involved in establishing the political meaning of the condition. Much more important to that negotiation process has been the relationship between RSI and the labour process.

From the early stages of the RSI process, it has been patently obvious that the way work was organised was a major contributory factor in causation. Calls for job rotation, rest breaks, and work-adjustment periods, have featured virtually from the start. The NOHSC RSI committee addressed this issue carefully in their Model Code of (Work) Practice proposed as a strategy for the prevention and management of RSI. As well as involving considerations of elements such as work pauses/task variation, technology selection and equipment design, work adjustment periods, and training and support, the strategy also proposes attention to job and task design. This includes limiting repetitive movements, mixing repetitive and non-repetitive movements, monitoring work demands and providing variety. The Model Code of Practice also targets another area for consideration, an area crucial to the political meaning of RSI. Prevention of RSI involves paying attention to factors such as deadlines, peak demands, machine pacing, bonus systems, incentive payments, electronic monitoring and work rates. The NOHSC RSI committee concluded that, 'work rates must not place excessive demands on workers and the work groups'. These factors go to the heart of the capitalist labour process.

It is possible to argue that RSI is an inevitable consequence of the development of this labour process and demonstration, if any was needed, that the human body is not a machine. First, however, it is necessary to go back a little and examine the labour process approach which provides the basis for this argument. This approach developed in the 1970s, particularly from the work of Braverman, as a means of analysing the nature of work in capitalist societies in general and the process of technological innovation in particular (see, for example, Braverman, 1974). It is especially critical of technological deterministic accounts of the process of technological innovations ('but we have no choice'), arguing instead that the social context and social relations need to be examined to understand the process (see, for example, Willis, 1985).

Broadly speaking, from this perspective, two features have governed the historical development of the capitalist labour process: the search for greater 'efficiency' on one hand, and more effective means of control over workers on the other. The logic of capitalist production relations, crystallised initially by Frederick Winslow Taylor and later by other 'scientific management theorists', has seen work develop in the following way: the use of time and motion studies to eliminate 'inefficiencies', specialisation of work into discrete tasks, with a more extreme division of labour and, frequently, deskilling as a result; the gradual mechanisation of work tasks, so that the individual worker increasingly became defined as an extension of the machine and work required a greater consistency of physical movements but less physical labour as a result; and increased work rates, with the development of piece rates and bonus systems. On the control side, technical developments permitted measuring the productivity of individual workers and timing absences of operators. The labour process has not evolved in a vacuum, however, but in the context of relations between capital and labour. Attempts by capital to develop control over the labour process have met with resistance from labour. Sometimes this has taken an individual form, such as sabotage, but more often it has been represented by trade union action.

The application of this perspective to understanding RSI is obvious. Indeed it has been suggested in discussion that one of the reasons why RSI has been a much greater issue in Australia than elsewhere is because of a stronger trade union tradition of resistance, particularly in the public service. Certainly there has been some action by trade unions over RSI. In 1981 the Public Service Association, by no means a militant union, took industrial action in the Melbourne Taxation Office in an attempt to reduce what they regarded as excessive productivity demands and to protect themselves from occupational injuries such as RSI. The data operators restricted output and upset surveillance over them by moving from machine to machine and refusing to key in their personal identity numbers (Brennan, 1985).

Incentive, bonus or productivity schemes have often been opposed by the trade union movement. The likely implications of such schemes for workers' occupational health and safety in general, and for RSI in particular, has been a feature of this opposition. Indeed on this issue, the NOHSC RSI committee (1985: 45) was divided, revealing incidentally the major limitation of tripartism. They could not agree on the use of incentive payment schemes and their effects on workers' health and safety, concluding only that 'such schemes should not operate where the sole criterion for their operation is speed of production'.

The significance of these developments for industrial relations are profound. Occupational injury or illness mediates the social relations of work in that it provides a means of resisting 'managerial prerogative' by arguments about the consequences of a particular form of work organisation for the health and safety of workers. This point is further evidenced by the long dispute in Victoria over proposed new health and safety legislation, which gave the appointed health and safety official the right to stop a job if workers' health and safety were endangered. Employer and conservative political parties expressed concern that this right would be used as an industrial relations tactic.

Negotiation over the political meaning of RSI has already produced some interesting results. A credit card company in Sydney, for example, is reported to have abandoned its bonus scheme and established industrial health and work enrichment committees in an attempt to cope with RSI. In an antispecialisation move, to break down the extreme division of labour that had developed, a large Sydney law firm is reported to have reintegrated its specialist word processing section with other secretarial functions (*Business Review Weekly*, 17–23/11/84).

In a startling development reported from the 'RSI capital' of Canberra, which would have Frederick Taylor turning in his grave, an electronic warning device called Key-Care has been developed which attaches to electronic keyboards and monitors to restrict the operator's output:

> It measures both the operator's key-stroke rate and how long the operator has been using the keyboard. A warning tone is emitted to alert the operator that a danger level is being approached. Should the operator continue work, the alarm continues at a rate calculated to upset the key-stroke rhythm. (*Weekend Australian*, 25–26/5/85)

In other words it tells you when you're working too hard!

Perhaps not too much should be read into these developments but they do represent countervailing tendencies to the development of the capitalist labour process. An overwhelming feature of this development has been the gradual dehumanisation of work and, while the initiatives above may be limited in scope, they represent at least some slowing of the process by which work is being dehumanised.

The political meaning of RSI is being negotiated in this wider context. The negotiation is intense because the stakes are high. They involve possibilities for such broad developments as worker participation, work enrichment and industrial democracy aimed at counteracting the alienating and dehumanising direction in which work has been developing. By analogy with Susan Sontag's (1978) excellent analysis of 'illness as metaphor', perhaps the key to understanding RSI is as a metaphor for alienation.

This last argument is not as speculative as it might appear. Anecdotal evidence comes from the workers' compensation arena, where there is a developing awareness that RSI may provide a vehicle for recognition of stress at common law by articulating the symptomatology for making stress claims. Since stress can be seen as a symptom of alienation and it is possible to argue that alienated workers are more likely to develop RSI, then the links in the argument should be clear. Certainly a careful empirical analysis of the relationship between stress and RSI is needed.

THE SOCIOLOGY OF MEDICAL KNOWLEDGE ABOUT RSI

Social control agencies such as medicine and the law are called upon to mediate between the competing demands of capital and labour in the social relations of production. Since illness mediates these relations, doctors become the arbiters of the mediation process even though medical knowledge itself is couched in the medico-legal process and must be understood in that context.

The medical knowledge about RSI is complicated. For a start there has been debate in the medical profession about whether RSI existed at all. Secondly, RSI has been the object of a demarcation tussle about which medical specialty (mainly rheumatologists or orthopaedic surgeons) should deal with it. The conditions that collectively make up RSI may be the result of a variety of causes other than work. Tenosynovitis, for instance, may be of infective origin (syphilis), metabolic or immunological origin, the result of a penetrating wound or congenital abnormality (Fergusson, 1984). Since only work-related injuries are compensable, the difficulty is in assessing what caused the condition.

Some of the frustration about RSI that has been apparent in medical circles is because few of the treatments attempted have met with much success. There has been no 'magic bullet' which could be applied as a remedy. A large number of treatments have been reported including analgesics, steroid injections, occupational therapy, chiropractic, counselling, acupuncture, immobilisation by splints, plaster, physiotherapy, hot wax and surgical operations. These treatments have had poor results. A survey in 1979 at the Workers' Health Centre in Sydney (1979) of patients with what would now be called RSI showed that when asked which treatment helped the most, the most common response was 'none at all'. In the phone-in by RSI sufferers conducted by the Task Force (1985), 37 per cent of the 801 sufferers who responded indicated that none of the treatments worked, while another 30 per cent indicated only rest helped the condition. The only treatment that helped more than a tiny fraction of these sufferers was physiotherapy, which helped in 10 per cent of cases. Rehabilitation of sufferers has proved difficult and time consuming, being complicated by 'external' factors such as patriarchal sexual division of labour in which women sufferers have been expected to maintain their 'domestic responsibilities' while recuperating.

In many respects, the key complexity in terms of the medico-legal process is the lack of measures of RSI independent of the patient's subjective reporting. Some measures are available when conducted on a fully blind basis, leading to what the NOHSC RSI committee has termed 'semi-objective' measures but this complexity has led to the frequent observation that the symptoms and disability claimed by the patient seem out of proportion to the objective signs the doctor can detect. It is this observation that, when located in the medico-legal process, has resulted in the suspicion of malingering and compensation neurosis. All these complexities make the state of knowledge about RSI controversial. As a result, the medico-legal process surrounding RSI has been hotly contested and polarised and the medical disagreements laid bare. Summing up in the landmark workers' compensation case for RSI (*Lashford v. Plessey*, No. 13603 of 1983, Supreme Court of NSW), Mr Justice Roden commented, 'the truth of the matter has to be that one, at least, of the doctors is completely and utterly wrong'.

What kind of argument will account for these complexities? The possible dissonance between subjective and objective evidence of ill health, or between symptoms and signs, has a long history. Foucault (1973), in his analysis of the development of clinical medicine, argues that the key feature in the development of what he calls the 'clinical gaze' was a shift in emphasis from subjective to objective determination of symptoms. The key question being asked of patients changed from, 'How do you feel?', to 'Where does it hurt?' The new biomedical paradigm could avoid the subjective reporting with its psychological components, a diagnosis could be made objectively, preferably by instruments. Such a paradigm made important assumptions about the mind–body duality; in particular stressing the priority of the body (object) over the mind (subject). One consequence of this assumption in modern medicine is that the term psychosomatic, which originally indicated the unity of psyche and soma, mind and body, in ill health has been lost. Instead psychosomatic has come to mean 'all in the mind'.

A useful semantic distinction has recently been drawn by Stagoll

(1981) between *illness* which patients suffer (the subjective state of distress or affliction) and *disease* which doctors treat (an abnormality in the structure or functions of the body organ systems). A large part of the practice of medicine is unproblematic; the 'illness' and 'disease' match and the patient is 'transparent' to use Foucault's term. Diagnosis and treatment become problematic however when there is a dissonance between illness and disease. This may be of two types according to Stagoll:

1 disease without illness, such as hypertension, where a person may have objective signs of high blood pressure without feeling 'ill';
2 illness without disease, where the patient reports suffering but no underlying pathology is objectively determinable.

Illness without disease is an important category for understanding RSI. The absence of detectable disease to match the reported illness of RSI, when couched in the medico-legal process, is what has given rise to suspicions of malingering. Historical examples of analogues to RSI are common. 'Hysteria' is perhaps the best known (see Smith-Rosenberg, 1972), 'shell shock' is another and miners' nystagmus is a third. Such conditions have often been described medically as 'baffling', probably because they constitute anomalies (in the Kuhnian sense) and cannot be easily explained in terms of the logic of the biomedical paradigm of medical knowledge. The anomaly is the result of an overly mechanistic notion of the relationship between mind and body or the person and environment. Likewise, the notion of malingering is too mechanistic. As Figlio (1982: 214) argues of miners' nystagmus, that condition shows the inseparability of psyche and soma, 'mind and body jointly participated in illness and jointly suffered the pathogenicity of the person's living situation'. Miners who developed nystagmus became ill in 'active engagement with their natural and social environment'. Of course this anomaly does not exist only in the field of occupational medicine. A wider example is the 'placebo effect' which, under the dominance of the biomedical paradigm, tends to be relegated to the 'too hard basket' despite tantalising indications of its importance in many areas of medical practice.

This paradigm of medical knowledge does not occur in an idealist vacuum and it is important to understand its materialist context—as Figlio does and as an earlier section of this paper did—and the effect of its materialist context on the labour process. It is necessary to understand the social process by which this paradigm of medical knowledge became dominant and the manner in which certain types of medical knowledge served dominant class interests and were sponsored by capital as a result. The biomedical paradigm became articulated in capitalist societies in corporatist terms. Disease came to be understood in individual and biological terms rather than social and political terms and the industrial analogy developed, viewing the body as a machine with replaceable parts and requiring engineering and ergonomic solutions.

To return from these lofty heights to RSI, the significance of the issue of the medical knowledge surrounding RSI is a classic demonstration of the anomalies and inadequacies of the existing paradigm of medical knowledge. The negotiation over the political meaning of the condition is crucial to its understanding. To see RSI as an individual and a biological phenomenon for which engineering solutions alone—or, indeed, any of the individual and biological treatments alone—are sufficient, is patently inadequate. Rather it is necessary to examine the social structural context associated with the development of the capitalist labour process for social and political causation. If RSI is a metaphor for alienation it is because the unity of psyche and soma together mediate the social relations of capitalist production.

CONCLUSION

This analysis raises many more questions than it answers. It does, however, attempt to redefine the 'sense of problem' about RSI in the context of which empirical investigations can proceed. If this analysis is useful, then the rewriting of the rules about occupational health and safety and their industrial relations over RSI is a taste of things to come—RSI at least arguably, has an organic base. Other 'moral panics' are not difficult to contemplate, especially if the organic base is uncertain. Take, for example, the suspicions about the relationship between visual display units and adverse health consequences, particularly visual ones—despite continual reassurances that no evidence of any health hazards exist or at least have been detected—the uncertainty, suspicion and subjective feelings about adversely affecting the health of operators persists. All it would take would be a trigger article of the sort that Walker's (1979) seems to have provided in the case of RSI and the social process would develop.

VDU nystagmus, anyone . . .?

POSTSCRIPT

Of the essays that appear in this book, this has undoubtedly been the most controversial. In particular, given that there were a number of people around arguing that RSI did not exist, but was a conscious or unconscious device to gain some sort of financial reward. When this article appeared in the midst of the controversial epidemic, attempting to demonstrate the relevance of a Figlio-style social constructionist analysis, the potential for misunderstanding was great. Indeed following its publication, I received letters from a couple of the most explicit protagonists of the position that it was not a 'real' injury, assuming I was a fellow-traveller. Probably the most judicious sentence I have written was the one in this paper indicating that 'it must not be read as denying the reality of the symptoms and suffering which victims undergo as a result of RSI'. The paper was also criticised for perpetuating the use of the term RSI despite its argued inappropriateness. My response remains the same; to paraphrase a famous quote, 'a sore wrist called by any other name hurts just as much!'. Besides, RSI is the name by which this set of occupational health and safety hazards are overwhelmingly known by the majority of people.

Now that the dust has apparently settled on the epidemic, what can we say about it with the benefit of hindsight? I am inclined to agree with the argument made by Andrew Hopkins (1990) that RSI was an epidemic of reporting visibility rather than of incidence. The extent of occupational injury and disease that gets reported and acted upon may be likened to only the tip of an iceberg. Changes in the context of this ill health, may lead to that iceberg rising out of the water more, or sinking further. In the period to about 1987 the acceptability of reporting sore wrists and shoulders improved. After that time, and the Susan Cooper case was the turning point, more of the iceberg sank back under the surface of the water. Some of the reasons for the sinking of the iceberg are to do with decisions not to collect incidence data any longer as has happened in the Canberra public service. But where data has continued to be collected, a continuing high incidence continues. Figures provided by the Victorian Workers' Compensation Authority, at least until data collection was abandoned there as well, showed incidence of half the peak rates of the mid 1980s.

Susan Cooper was a young data entry operator in the Melbourne Taxation Office. Through her union, she took action on a claim of total and permanent disability. This claim was quickly recognised by all parties as a landmark case. The full story of the case is yet to be told, and unfortunately the account of the case remains unpublished (Campbell, 1987). The State was in a contradictory position. On one hand, through its occupational health and safety body, Worksafe, it had defined RSI as a priority area for research. On the other hand, the basis of the case was that RSI did not exist.

Part of the extraordinary lengths gone to by the Commonwealth included calling witnesses such as the official from the United States tax office who indicated that the particular ill health conditions which came to be known collectively as RSI did not exist in the Internal Revenue Service (IRS).

The judgment was in favour of the Commonwealth, and, on the precedent set by this landmark case, signalled a change in direction of the epidemic. In Figlio's terms, the court case represented a resolution of at least some of the negotiation over the social and political meaning of the disease. RSI was defined as an individual and biological phenomenon, rather than a social and political one. The threat eased to the profitability of many enterprises, had the Susan Cooper case opened the floodgates to many other substantial claims. Workers who had been prepared to report sore wrists and arms, again went back to suffering them in relative silence. Other factors were at work also. No doubt the huge investment in ergonomically designed furniture and equipment had some benefits in reducing the incidence of repetition injuries, as did the attention paid to work processes in many industries. In addition, a worsening economic climate in the late 1980s, as the western world slipped towards recession and the Australian economy underwent structural readjustment towards deindustrialisation, took a heavy toll on jobs. For many workers, keeping out of the ranks of the unemployed became a higher priority than maximising one's occupational health and safety. The well-documented reluctance by employers to re-employ any worker who had a history of workers' compensation claims added to this change. Incidence has seemingly again been concentrated in less visible blue-collar women of non-English speaking background where it has continued scarcely abated by events of the 1980s (see Bammer, 1990).

For many, however, the sore wrists and arms continued. The irony is that what we would recognise as RSI began to appear in record proportion in overseas countries including the American IRS (see Hopkins, 1990). We all know fellow workers who struggle on with the help of thermoskin bandages and such aids. I remain convinced that there is an underlying biophysiological basis to the condition; that it cannot be dismissed as some of the requiems for the epidemic have done, where the apparent decline in incidence is given as proof that it was all along 'all in the mind'. The work of the Melbourne surgeon Hunter Fry is important in this respect, demonstrating as he did differences in the muscle tissue under microscopic investigation between sufferers and non-sufferers.

My original article ended with a prediction that other epidemics of the RSI sort were possible and indeed likely. My suggestion at the time was that VDU nystagmus was the most likely. The question then is, 'Why have these not occurred?'. The economic climate is clearly of major importance, though the potential always exists. The latest candidate it seems to me is the so-called 'sick building syndrome'; the consequence of controlled atmosphere modern buildings where infections such as Legionnaire's disease, resulting from poorly maintained heating and cooling systems, may affect workers working there.

The potential of Figlio-style social constructionist analyses of other occupational health and safety hazards remains. Only one subsequent attempt to utilise this framework has been made that I am aware of; that undertaken by Kippen (1992) to historically analyse miners' phthisis in the Bendigo mining region of Victoria.

Finally, the conclusion of the article began by observing that as many questions were raised by the application of a Figlio framework of analysis, as were answered. This remains the case. In particular, the field of the sociology of medical knowledge remains an undeveloped one, as the example of RSI demonstrates (see Bammer & Martin, 1992). Ripe for analysis are the so-called 'syndromes'; in particular the way in which they have become a sort of grab-bag for expressing uncertainty over the aetiology and treatment of these baffling conditions. As RSI has gradually become known as 'occupational overuse syndrome', so too with others like chronic fatigue syndrome (CFS), sudden infant death syndrome, autoimmune deficiency syndrome (AIDS) and sick building syndrome. Labelling them as a 'syndrome' appears to be a label that is reached for, taxonomically speaking, when negotiation over the social and political meaning of the disease occurs. Another way of saying this is while all ill health mediates social relationships, some ill health conditions do so more than others. There is much useful work to be done in this field.

10 The industrial relations of occupational health and safety: a labour process approach

The aim of this chapter is to analyse and trace the emergence of occupational health and safety as an increasingly important terrain of industrial relations, with special reference to technological innovation. In order to do this, I will draw upon two conceptual traditions of sociology: medical sociology on one hand, and on the other what has come to be known as labour process theory. More specifically, what is being investigated is the relationship between the capitalist labour process (especially work organisation), technological innovation and occupational health and safety. Such an attempt to marry these diverse conceptual traditions is quite rare. As Quinlan (1988: 200) has recently commented, '. . . it is significant that there has been little discourse between those sociologists seeking to understand occupational illness and those engaged in one of the most productive re-evaluations of industrial sociology, namely the labour process debate'.

The paper draws upon a sociohistorical study of the emergence of the occupational health and safety 'movement' in Australia, focusing upon different industries and hazards.[1] It is necessary to begin with several caveats. I am aware that the industrial relations of industrial injuries operate differently in some respects from the industrial relations of occupationally induced disease; my focus here is broader and includes both injuries and disease under the more general focus of what might be called occupational ill health. Secondly, this paper does not address the industrial relations of occupational ill health with reference to the institutional mechanisms

151

of industrial relations—a major project in its own right. Thirdly, none of the following should be read as denying the reality of the pain and suffering experienced by workers in the workplace.

In order to make the analysis, it is necessary first of all to outline the conceptual framework drawn from the two areas of sociology outlined above, medical sociology and labour process theory.

ILL HEALTH AS SOCIAL PROCESS

The question to be focused on here, is how ill health mediates social relations—in general but particularly in the workplace. This question has been thrown clearly into focus by the recent work of Karl Figlio (e.g., 1982). The importance of ill health to social relations has been part of the contribution of medical sociology since the original work of Talcott Parsons. Indeed the spelling out of how illness acts as a social process to mediate social relations has been an important part of whatever unity the diverse subdiscipline of medical sociology has had. Ill health, appropriately legitimated, provides absolution from normal role expectations, be they domestic ('not tonight dear, I have a headache'), educational ('yes, you can have an extension') or in other spheres of social life. Ill health mediates social relations in all societies through such diverse means as 'pointing the bone', to incarcerating political opponents in mental institutions.

In the work sphere, more specifically, ill health mediates the social relations of production in a number of ways. 'Sickies' for instance are a source of conflict or point of contestation in many organisations. On one hand they may be an important means by which workers are able to deal with psychosocial pressure at work. Industrial conflict among air traffic controllers at Sydney airport in the mid-1980s is a good example, where rates of absenteeism have become a source of conflict over whether the number of air traffic controllers needs to be increased. On the other hand, there are also instances where injured workers do not take duly certified sick leave in the case of actual injury, let alone the occasional 'sickie', because of fear of losing their jobs. Ill health mediates the social relations of production in other ways as well: pre-employment medical screenings for instance (see Johnstone, 1988); likewise what seems to be a growing de facto acceptance by employers that workers are able to use their own sick leave to look after their sick children.

My main concern here, however, relates directly to injury and disease in the workplace, in particular how the changing social relations of production associated in particular with technological innovation, have been mediated by ill health. In this *social* process of mediation, as Figlio (1982) has shown, the ill health itself has become the object of negotiation and has become a terrain of industrial relations. Mediation in other words occurs socially: medical and scientific 'experts' play a role in setting health and safety standards but the process of, for instance, evaluating risk, always occurs within a social context (see Mathews, 1985a: 198). In order to understand these changes however, it is necessary to consider the organisation of work, and in particular its reorganisation in the context of technological innovation.

LABOUR PROCESS THEORY

The other conceptual tradition drawn upon to analyse the emergence of the industrial relations of health and safety is what has come to be known as labour process theory. This has provided a useful means of theorising issues related to the contemporary organisation of work including technological change. At the outset it should be said that it is difficult to talk about labour process theory in general. Since the original seminal work of Harry Braverman (1974), a great deal of research has identified legitimate problems with his formulation of many of the issues involved, and there have been a number of developments in somewhat different directions which together make up a tradition of labour process studies. As I have argued elsewhere (Willis, 1988), Braverman's importance lies more in the questions asked than in the answers given, and that what gives this tradition a considerable degree of unity is that writers within it are working out the agenda largely set by the original Braverman formulation.

Labour process theory has been an important development in serving to reorientate the sociological study of work away from traditional industrial sociology and psychology towards greater concern with the political economy of work in capitalist societies. It also served to reintegrate what had become largely separate academic approaches—via economics, politics, sociology and psychology—to the study of work. As Littler (1987: 2) has argued:

> Braverman's major contribution . . . was to smash through the academic barriers and offer the potential for the birth of a new and integrated approach to the study and history of work. An integrated approach which provided an (apparent) coherent theoretical framework and which also directed attention to a range of issues and problematics both within and beyond the workplace, which had previously been seen as unrelated.

Labour process theory has also provided a useful framework for understanding the interaction between technology and work, in particular for opposing 'technological determinist' explanations (summed up by the phrase 'but we have no choice'). Braverman argued that the issue of control was inseparable from the issue of efficiency, in understanding the process of technological innovation at work. Technological change must thus be understood as a social process and the outcome of struggle—including but not only—class struggle. Likewise the occupational health and safety consequences of technological innovation must be seen not in some predetermined way but as the outcome of choices made, the effect of which is to require analysis of the *social shaping* of the introduced technology which may have implications for the health of workers (see Mac-Kenzie & Wajcman, 1985).

Along with a materialist assumption, labour process theory also operates with the assumption not of *consensus* in the organisation of work (as much of traditional industrial sociology has done), but of *coercion*. Applied to the field of industrial relations or occupational health and safety, likewise there is no assumption of consensus but a focus on conflict of interests between capital and labour.

From this point of view, coercion is the answer to the key question of how control of the labour process is achieved, as potential labour power is transformed into actual labour power. Although Braverman himself did not greatly analyse it, as subsequent writers have since pointed out (for example Stark, 1980) an adequate account of the capitalist labour process also requires consideration of worker resistance or contestation to the imposition of managerial control over the labour process. In this paper, the aim is to analyse occupational health and safety as part of the ongoing negotiation over the organisation and definition of work, in that it has increasingly become a terrain for resistance or contestation. In arguing for the utility of labour process theory in analysing the industrial relations of occupational health and safety, the rest of the paper attempts to spell out how this has occurred.

MANAGERIAL PREROGATIVE

The nature of the wage labour contract under capitalism has enshrined 'managerial prerogative' as a key component of the structure of work relations in capitalist societies, recognised in law through the State apparatus of the Australian Industrial Relations Commission. The conversion of *potential* labour power into *actual* labour power in order to generate surplus value requires the entrepreneur to organise labour. A worker may thus be asked, within certain limits, to do anything the employer requires. What those limits are has always been the subject of resistance and struggle.

Occupational health and safety has always been part of the contestation around the issue of what are the limits to which an employer can go in damaging the health of their employees as part of the employment contract in pursuit of surplus value. Such contestation over the limits has not simply been based on attempts by employers to control the labour process, but also on creating the conditions under which workers may consent to the limits negotiated.

Traditionally, that is until the last decade or so, the centrality of the emphasis on 'managerial prerogative' determined the dominant class and State response to occupational health and safety. Part of the structure of control was to deny the existence of the terrain of occupational health and safety for industrial relations. As Carson (1985) has cogently argued, underpinned by the dominant State response to hazards of work, codified and enshrined in the Robens Report (1972), the nature of the relationship between work and health in capitalist societies was obscured and mystified, and the field of occupational health and safety defined very narrowly.

By making disputes over health and safety the subject of apparently classless State regulation, it avoided a difficult area of industrial relations. Instead, disputes could be resolved by 'experts' who could be relied on to provide impartial advice even when employed by employers or institutions of the capitalist State.

Legitimated by 'managerial prerogative', concerns about occupational health and safety could and have traditionally been subsumed under production goals. The whole discourse of occupational health and safety reflects this; for example, the enshrining of the 'so far as is reasonably possible' approach, usually meaning 'so long as it does not conflict with production goals'. As a long-time union official reported in an interview: 'In the 1960s when we went in to talk to management about hazards we always ended up talking about production'. Costs to capital could be externalised as *compensation* payments, either directly to injured workers or indirectly by monetarily compensating for hazards faced in the form of 'dirt', or 'danger' money.

Compensation rather than prevention has constituted the main response to work hazards. With some notable exceptions, this situation was largely accepted by unions through what they perceived to be a lack of alternatives. Again with the notable exception of a few individuals, it was also largely treated with fatalistic resignation by workers because of a combination of lack of alternative employment opportunities and lack of knowledge of the damage being caused to their health by various agents and substances in the workplace. One retired boilermaker interviewed became a boilermaker after five years of unemployment in the depression of the 1930s. He was aware of the problem of noise but there was no feasible alternative except to try to find a less noisy boilershop. These attitudes often occurred in combination with an unwillingness of many employers to share with workers what knowledge was available.

For all of these reasons, occupational health and safety has not traditionally constituted a terrain of industrial relations. Concomitant with this approach has been a concerted campaign by the dominant class, and largely accepted within the capitalist State, to individualise occupational ill health thus mystifying its structural causes. As Carson (1985: 74–5) has shown, collusion between the ruling class and the apparatuses of the State has led to an artificial separation of the categories of health and safety and industrial relations and an enforcement system which 'institutionalised the toleration of contravention'.

This hegemonic approach to occupational health and safety problems in the workplace can be summed up by the phrase: 'fix the worker not the workplace'. Hazards in the workplace were defined as being the problem of the worker not of the process of production itself, and if remedial action was required it should be directed at the worker him or herself rather than the organisation of production. Earmuffs were issued rather than quieter machinery installed, fertile women excluded from dangerous areas of the production process, workers who complained or made workers' compensation claims were dismissed to intimidate others from action (see Creighton & Micallef, 1983; Kreigler, 1980). Where injury or ill health did eventuate, a victim-blaming ideology operated to individualise the problem, through blatant stereotypes such as 'accident proneness', 'Mediterranean guts ache', 'Greek back' and 'migrant arm' (see Quinlan, 1986).

An appalling lack of information existed; few statistics were collected on the extent of industrial ill health and as a medical specialty, occupational medicine remained very undeveloped (see Biggins, 1986). As a result of all this, the nature of the relationship between work and health remained obscured by the hegemony of capital in the workplace.

RECENT EXPERIENCE

In the last couple of decades however, and particularly since 1980, there are a number of signs which might be taken as evidence that the situation is changing. There has been a growing emphasis on prevention rather than compensation, what Carson (1985) calls a 'reconflation of categories' as occupational health and safety has emerged as an important terrain of industrial relations.

There are undoubtedly a number of reasons for this apparent change which have interacted in a cumulative fashion. Also important in this process, and not analysed to any great extent here, are informal factors including grassroots political movements such as the women's and peace movements, as well as the sustained pressure of worker resistance such as expanded compensation claims and strikes over occupational health and safety issues. The most important reasons for change, however, seem to be as follows. First of all, some of the notable disputes over the extent of hazards have been resolved either through a longer latency period or further research. Taking asbestos as an example, time *has* told its terrible story as the long latency period necessary for asbestos-related ill health such as mesothelioma has gradually been revealed, though the hazards have been known since at least the 1930s if not earlier (see McCulloch, 1986). Likewise, the long debate about what was an 'acceptable risk' in the form of a safe level of exposure to asbestos in the atmosphere (measured by fibres per cubic centimetre of air) has been resolved as it has become clear that *any* level of exposure is harmful to health. The debate about what was a safe level of exposure to set as the standard occupied many years, and the health of many workers has suffered while the debate between 'experts' raged.

Secondly, there does seem to have developed a widespread perception that the traditional approach outlined above has had relatively little success in achieving what it was supposed to, namely reducing the extent of ill health in the workplace. As Carson (1985: 75) argues, 'By all accounts the arbitrary separation of occupational health and safety from the sphere of organised industrial relations has not been conspicuously successful in terms of controlling the rate of occupational disease and injury in our society'.

The improvement in data collection about ill health in the workplace as a result of State initiatives has revealed the extent of the continuing problem and has done a considerable amount to demystify the relationship between work and health in capitalist societies. Opening an ergonomics conference, the then federal minister with responsibility for occupational health and safety, Mr Ralph Willis, indicated that the annual occupational death toll exceeded 500 deaths and 300 000 work-related injuries at an estimated cost to the country of more than $6 billion annually (*The Australian*, 2/8/88).

Thirdly, there has been a gradual widening of definitions of occupational health and safety internationally. The International Labour Organization has gradually widened its definition to legitimate workers being more actively involved in it themselves, promoting the humanisation of work and defining within the ambit

of occupational health and safety, all health problems of workers
(World Health Organization, 1980, 1982).

Fourthly, the attitude of trade unions has gradually changed.
There are a number of reasons for this change in attitude: some of
the more important ones would seem to be the activism of notable
individuals such as Stan Willis and George Seelaf in the Victorian
context, who insisted on occupational health and safety issues
having a higher priority in union affairs. Occupationally induced
deafness is a good example. Active individuals within industries
where hearing loss has been a chronic problem such as boilermaking
pursued workers' compensation claims which succeeded for the first
time in 1962. After a case lasting nearly two years, Ballarat boilermaker and union activist Bert Black succeeded with his own claim
which set a legal precedent for others to follow and also raised
consciousness among other workers in noisy industries about the
hazards of industrial deafness.

Another reason for the change in the approach that unions took
to occupational health and safety issues was the election both at
federal and state levels in the early 1980s of Labor governments to
the legislative arm of the State. The implementation of a prices and
incomes accord soon after their election resulted in pay increases
being tied to movements in the Consumer Price Index. With a
substantial part of the traditional trade union work of maintaining
and improving living standards of their members thus taken care of
at the level of the State, many trade unions turned their attention
to attempting to improve the non-monetary or social wage of their
members. Campaigns around issues like occupational health and
safety along with occupational superannuation and redundancy pack-
ages have been common in the late 1980s.

In addition, the general historical process has continued by which
trade unions have gradually externalised their functions to State
apparatuses under Labor governments. For instance, unemployment
benefits were traditionally provided by trade unions themselves from
members' contributions and then subsequently externalised to the
level of the State and funded from general taxation revenue as part
of a social welfare program. Likewise the Hawke Labor Government
was elected in 1983 with a mandate to establish a State apparatus
to oversee, research, collect data on and deal with occupational
health and safety problems. An initial budget of $12 million was
provided in 1985 for this purpose. In a number of Australian states,
legislation has been passed which has instituted a system of worker
participation on health and safety issues in the workplace.

The fifth reason is the emergence of a public/environmental
health movement which is related to and has had a substantial
impact on the occupational health movement. Indeed the occupa-

tional health and safety movement might be seen as part of a general public/environmental health movement which has seen a greater emphasis in general on prevention rather than cure; an emphasis on healthy lifestyles, nutritional campaigns and so on. Public health campaigns focusing on pollution, dangerous chemicals, herbicides, smoking, nuclear power and many other contentious issues have had the dual effect of both raising worker and trade union consciousness and rendering ineffective the traditional managerial means of coping with health and safety hazards in the workplace outlined earlier in this paper.

As a result, there has been a blurring of the distinction between public health and occupational health issues. Tobacco is an example of current relevance with the landmark legal case recently in Victoria resulting in a bus driver with lung cancer, allegedly caused by passive smoking at work, receiving $65 000 in an out-of-court compensation settlement. Flowing from this case is the decision—reached by tripartite representatives from employers, unions and government—of Western Australia, the first state government to ban smoking in all workplaces, including the hospitality industry such as hotels and restaurants (*Age*, 28/7/88). General community concern about, for instance, toxic substances such as herbicides and their alleged relationship to birth defects, led to workers' questioning of the substances and demands for such things as proper labelling and handling procedures. Similarly, AIDS poses a major health hazard not only in the general community but also specifically an occupational health and safety hazard to those working in the sex and health industries.

The sixth and final reason to be explored here is the process of technological innovation and I propose to deal with that in some detail.

TECHNOLOGICAL INNOVATION

As argued earlier, the process of technological innovation must not be viewed as an autonomous phenomenon as part of some technological imperative, but in the context of a profound reorganisation of the capitalist labour process. The relationship between technology and work is a dialectical one; each affects the other. Technological innovation thus represents a series of choices to be made about what technology to be introduced and with what effect. Furthermore, technology should be seen as entailing not only a material component (tools and machines) but also a social/ideological component involving the social relationships that go with those tools and machines (see Dickson, 1974).

Technological innovation it should be said has done a considerable amount to eradicate hazards in the workplace. The availability of lifting equipment for instance, no doubt has done much to decrease the incidence of strains and sprains especially from lifting and bending. The introduction of the chain system of disassembly in meat processing did a great deal to remove bad backs as a traditional occupational health hazard faced by meat workers (see Willis, 1985).

Yet it should also be said that technological development is often a fortunate but at times unintended by-product of the process of innovation. Lead poisoning, for instance, had been a traditional occupational health hazard for printers utilising hot metal linotype technology. Apprentice printers traditionally were socialised into the need to drink a pint of milk a day to minimise the effects of lead on their bodies. The removal of lead from their work environments has been a consequence of the introduction of 'cold type' keyboarding technology.

Technological innovation, however, has also exposed them to new hazards, in particular repetition injuries of which Australia has suffered an epidemic in recent years (see chapter 9). Another example of hazards being unleashed by technological innovation are organic solvents used in new machinery. Furthermore, when technological means are available to reduce hazards they may not be available within specific workplaces. In a recent study of the traditional health hazard of back injuries faced by nurses, Griffin (1987: 73–4) concluded:

> Nursing is a labour intensive occupation, and the particular
> financial constraints of the health industry led to attempts to
> minimise labour costs by simple understaffing and/or use of lesser
> and unqualified nursing staff. A combination of factors led to the
> conclusion that back injuries were an integral part of nursing work.
> These included changes in nursing practice requiring more patient
> lifting and handling, lack of sufficient staff so that each individual
> was required to lift more frequently, lack of lifting devices to
> minimise lifting tasks and lack of lifting instruction.

In other words, the use and availability of technological means for reducing this hazard must be understood in its social context, the major factor of which as Griffin argues was the relative powerlessness of nurses, especially in relation to other (male) workers who had managed to win safe lifting agreements with employers.

Reorganisations of the labour process associated with technological change have done much to change the manner in which occupational ill health is dealt with in the workplace and it is in this context that much of the resistance that has been a feature of the industrial relations of occupational ill health has appeared. The introduction of computer technology into workplaces has been particularly important here. The Australian 'epidemic' of repetition injuries known by various names, earlier as repetition strain injury and more recently as occupational overuse injury is an instructive case study, analysed in detail in chapter 9. The cost has been enormous; in Telecom Australia alone, the *direct* costs only have been calculated at $15 million (Fergusson, 1987: 213–4).

From the early stages of that 'epidemic', it has been clear that the way work was organised was a major contributory factor in its causation, in particular the general direction in which work was evolving. The logic of capitalist production relations—identified by Braverman and others, crystallised by Frederick Winslow Taylor and subsequent management theorists in the search both for greater efficiency and greater control over workers—had seen work in capitalist societies evolve in a particular direction: specialisation of work tasks into an often extreme division of labour, the gradual mechanisation of work tasks, the requirement of greater consistency of a narrower range of physical movements, and increased work rates paid by piece rates and bonus payments. On the control side, technological advances permitted the detailed measurement of the productivity of individual workers and the timing of absences from their machines.

The social shaping of technology to serve the twin aims inherent in the capitalist labour process of greater efficiency and control have had their consequences in the damage to the health of workers of which Australia's epidemic of RSI is just a particularly obvious example. For workers, the consequences of such developments have been reduced reliance on skill in many workplaces, reduced job satisfaction with a decline in *intrinsic* job satisfaction and a concomitantly increased emphasis on *extrinsic* sources of satisfaction (see, for instance, Reed, 1988).

For employers, hazards such as RSI have represented a qualitatively different type of occupational health problem and have threatened the viability of some businesses. Workers' compensation premiums (the cost of companies insuring themselves against occupationally induced ill health of their employees), jumped by as much as 150 per cent in a year at the height of the 'epidemic' in the mid-1980s. The traditional management approach of externalising the cost of injury and disease in the workplace by 'fixing the worker not the workplace' clearly has not worked in this instance. There is no quick fix cure, screening for predisposition was not available, and the white-collar predominantly Anglo-Celtic ethnic origin workforce could not be victim-blamed in the same way as other ethnic groups. Instead, it has been necessary for employers to actually confront the conditions and organisation of work. Installing more comfortable ergonomically designed furniture was one early response, a necessary but by no means sufficient means of preventing injury occurring. Instead, work organisation itself had to be confronted.

The costs of no longer being able to externalise the effects of injury and disease to workers have been substantial. A Melbourne clothing company plagued by occupational injuries is reported to have developed its own in-house rehabilitation program where injured employees are provided with light duties as well as given individual counselling. The cost of such a program which is made up largely of 'unproductive' labour costs is $300 000 per year (*Age*, 28/7/88).

RESISTANCE

Technological innovation has opened up new avenues of resistance or contestation to reorganisations of the labour process. Such an awareness of the possibilities of contestation has been a crucial part of the emergence of occupational health and safety as an industrial relations issue in the 1980s. Previously, resistance to unsafe working conditions in the face of managerial prerogative was a fairly limited individual phenomenon, a situation which suited employers' interests. Workers had the option of leaving a job they found too unsafe, such as the boilermaker looking for a quieter workplace. 'Sickies' discussed previously were also a means of *individual* resistance. The change in recent years in the manner in which occupational health and safety hazards are dealt with in the workplace has come about through the development of *collective* strategies for resistance. These occur at a number of levels of formality: from informal 'understandings' to more formal agreements at workplace level, to insertion of health and safety clauses in industrial awards, as well as legislation; both at the level of the State.

Resistance has not been limited only to issues associated with the provision of safe and hazard-free workplaces however. Rather there is discernible the beginnings of a trend to use occupational health and safety issues as a lever to promote other industrial ends such as co-determination of issues associated with the organisation of work, worker participation and industrial democracy. The importance of the industrial relations of occupational health and safety lies in the grounds it provides for challenging managerial prerogative over the labour process in general, in which reorganisation associated with technological innovation is particularly significant. As Mathews (1985b: 108–26) has argued, technological innovation represents an opportunity for workers and unions to struggle to achieve alternative equipment and work designs. Negotiations about the likely health and safety consequences of such technological innovation presents itself as a lever around which other goals such as some reintegration of the labour process directed at humanisation of work, may be pursued.

Resistance is possible because arguments about health and safety constitute a terrain on which managerial prerogative may be contested. The historical process surrounding occupational health and safety has developed to the point where the boundaries of managerial prerogative can be challenged; it is now much more accepted than previously that managerial prerogative does not extend to damaging a worker's health to anything like the degree that existed previously. Occupational health and safety has become a terrain for industrial relations as a result of this process of struggle by workers. The limits on employers as to what workers might be asked to do under the capitalist contract have been redrawn to some extent. Arguments about occupational health and safety consequences are often claimed to be 'natural' ones; those about managerial prerogative, by contrast, are more often seen as 'cultural' ones.

Resistance to reorganisations of the labour process and increased occupational health and safety consequences as a result, have taken a number of forms. Not all of them are the *direct* result of action taken by workers themselves; others are *indirectly* the result of initiatives taken by management to prevent occupational ill health occurring or to forestall industrial disputation. The examples outlined earlier are relevant here: reintegrating work processes, modifying supervisory styles, giving workers greater autonomy, abandoning bonus schemes, and keeping injured workers on the payroll while rehabilitation occurs. Williams (1985: 1074) identifies a trend towards discontinuing output incentives and machine monitoring of performance. The provision of rest breaks, eye tests and consultation on lighting and seating arrangements have all been negotiated within, for instance, the printing industry in Melbourne, as has agreement not to monitor keystroke rates (Reed, 1988: 45–6).

Willingness to modify work processes, however, has on occasions been achieved by direct industrial action. Such industrial action (detailed in chapter 9) was taken by the Public Service Association in the Melbourne Taxation Office in 1981 in an attempt to reduce what members regarded as excessive productivity demands and to protect themselves from occupational overuse injuries. Data operators restricted output and upset surveillance over them by moving from machine to machine and refusing to key in their personal identity numbers (Taylor & Pitcher, 1984).

Negotiation on the issue of managerial prerogative on working conditions has centred in particular around the issue of the 'right to stop a job'. Under traditionally defined managerial prerogative over the labour process, the worker has no such right, indeed any attempt to impose it would have led in many cases to instant and legitimate dismissal. Gradually, however, some workers in different industries have won this right. The first appear to have been Sydney watersiders in about 1974. It was subsequently formalised in their industrial award in 1977 (Creighton, 1986: 123). It should be noted that this right cannot really be said to constitute worker control; stoppage represents a holding off (without loss of pay) while dispute settlement procedures are instituted. Such a right has existed in Scandinavian and a number of other countries for some years (see Parmeggiani, 1982). It was passed as an ILO convention as long ago as 1974.

In recognition of the need for specialised training to deal with hazards in the workplace, the strategy has also developed of appointing health and safety representatives from among workers who are empowered under agreements to do the actual stopping of the job. Health and safety representatives are empowered to participate in decisions about working conditions, promoting a model of co-determination. As outlined earlier, understandings have gradually given way to more formal agreements. At present these mainly cover workers in particular industries such as state enterprises in Victoria, (electricity generation, shipbuilding etc.). Pursuit of them, however, has become official trade union policy and the extent of the workforce covered appears likely to increase.

EMPLOYER RESPONSE

As a strategy of resistance however, attempts to modify the reorganisation has met with sustained opposition from capital, and attempts to maintain the more traditional interpretation of managerial prerogative. The election of Labor governments federally and in most Australian states in the early 1980s saw a flurry of legislation formalising into legislation those gains made by the labour movement in the preceding decade (see Creighton, 1986: 115–21). Only in the state of Victoria did legislation go beyond the hegemony of the Robens model. The Victorian legislation went further in proposing the right to stop a job. A campaign of opposition to the legislation was organised by conservative political parties and employer groups. The fear was that the right would be used to pursue industrial objectives other than purely health and safety ones. After much controversy in which the bill was brought back more towards the Robens model, it was passed in October during the brief period in which the Victorian Labor Party had control of the Upper House of the Victorian Parliament.

Overseas experience has shown, in general, that the right to stop a job has in fact been used carefully. Based on a review of the evidence, Biggins (1988: 29) concludes that:

> Experience shows that where this right has been granted it has not been abused. There has, in fact, been considerable peer group pressure preventing misuse of such powers. The right to stop unsafe work has been used infrequently: its use has been well justified and it has prevented potentially serious injury.

THE STATE RESPONSE

The capitalist State has always been a terrain upon which conflicting interests of capital and labour were struggled over. Labor parties coming to occupy the legislative arm, as well as the need to preserve the legitimacy of capitalist social order, have made the State's response at times a contradictory one. In the Susan Cooper case which received huge publicity in 1986–7, the Commonwealth government successfully argued—in a case brought against it by a white-collar union on behalf of a young woman clerical worker severely disabled by RSI—that the condition did not exist and therefore the Commonwealth was not liable (see Campbell, 1987 and see also postscript to chapter 9). At the same time, the State apparatus established to mediate the social relations of occupational health and safety, the National Occupational Health and Safety Commission (Worksafe), defined RSI as a priority area for investigation.

Furthermore, it is becoming increasingly apparent that even with Labor governments occupying the legislative arm of the State, that State has only a form of *relative* autonomy from the interests of the dominant class. The Labor governments' commitment to occupational health and safety has been actualised in the creation of three new institutions based upon a tripartite model directed respectively at policy making, education and information operations and research. As Biggins (1988: 30) argues, criticisms are emerging about the character of these reforms:

> The fundamental criticism is that the new structures do not adequately recognise the political nature of occupational health. Because the Robens assumption of 'identity of interests' fits so happily with the Labor Government's ideology of consensus, it has been accepted uncritically. The opposing interests of employers and workers are not adequately allowed for, mechanisms for bargaining and negotiation are being seriously compromised . . . The rights

and responsibilities accorded workers and employers are unequal
with employers retaining the upper hand.

Although one of the rationales for the establishment of these
State apparatuses was to increase worker participation, Biggins goes
on to argue that their very remoteness is likely to be problematic.
In fact, he argues the overall effect of such initiatives is likely to
be in the opposite direction from that identified here: to depoliticise
occupational health and remove it from the industrial relations arena
by presenting occupational health and safety issues as basically
technical rather than political problems.

CONCLUSION

Whether Biggins' pessimism is proved justified or not, clearly the
struggle for a safe and hazard-free working environment will continue. The struggle to end the artificial and ideological separation
between health and work and to have occupational relations
recognised as a legitimate terrain for worker involvement and therefore within the industrial relations sphere has been a long one. In
its latest phase, the process of technological innovation associated
with reorganisation of the capitalist labour process has provided new
opportunities, not only to resist such reorganisation but also to
promote such forms of empowerment of workers as co-determination of issues, worker participation and industrial democracy.

The likely success or otherwise of such processes remains to be
seen. Already evident however are some countervailing factors
which are slowing the rate at which progress towards these goals
is being made and may indeed undermine some of the gains
achieved. The re-emergence of wage bargaining in negotiations over
efficiency and award restructuring is again diverting and soaking
up union resources which had been employed in occupational health
and safety. Furthermore, in the emergence of debates over work
practices, occupational health and safety issues have had a conspicuously minor role.

Against the background provided by this paper, detailed analysis
of the concrete industrial relations contestations can proceed. Some
writers (e.g., Griffin, 1987; Quinlan, 1986) have touched on this
aspect but it needs to be developed. What is needed are concrete
case studies of resistance over occupational health and safety on the
industrial front via direct negotiations or through arbitrated decisions in the formal institutional mechanisms such as the Industrial
Relations Commission.

POSTSCRIPT

This paper was originally written in an attempt to show how issues concerning occupational health and safety could be understood in theoretical terms. It followed a long-standing interest in occupational health and safety, including a period of involvement with an activist group in Melbourne in the late 1970s and early 1980s known as the Workers Health Action Group which was a forerunner to the ACTU establishing a full-time unit in this field. In the field of occupational health and safety, ill health in the form of occupational injuries and disease mediates social relations especially between employers and employees in a manner that can only be described at times as brutal.

Since this paper was written, occupational health and safety has continued to be an active field of industrial relations. David Biggins was justified in his pessimism, it can now be said. The advent of recession, the rise of economic rationalism as an ideology promoting the withdrawal of the State from areas of economic activity, the decline in the 'social wage'—all have had a considerable impact in reversing at least some of the gains of the previous decade. The National Occupational Health and Safety Commission itself narrowly avoided abolition with the unexpected return of the Keating Labor Government in the federal election of March 1993.

The brutal effects of the moves to reduce government expenditure on protecting the health of workers in the name of fiscal responsibility is seen most clearly in the state of Victoria following the election of the Kennett conservative Government in 1992. The gains made in the previous decade to ensure employers build the costs of a safe and hazard-free work environment into their production costs have been swept away as employers are again able to externalise these costs, in this case onto workers. One example is the reform of the labour market, with the abolition of awards and the imposition of 'sign or resign' labour contracts. Workers' health is again a resource to be exploited by employers; workers are again responsible for their own safety and health. Some employment contracts reported, for instance, make workers responsible for providing their own safety gear such as hard hats and steel-capped footwear. Failure to provide the required gear is grounds for dismissal. Secondly, in the rehabilitation field, the zeal to balance the books of the workers' compensation authority has again led to many workers losing their compensation entitlements as well as many other rights in relation to their occupational health and safety. This is a new phase in the industrial relations of occupational health and safety and clearly an important one for the trade union movement as it struggles to hold its membership and appear relevant.

NOTES

1 Funding was received from the Australian Research Grants Council.

11 Hierarchies, bureaucracies and professions: the Medicare review (part 2)

This paper is both a personal account and an analysis of the Medicare review (part two) that took place in 1985–86, to which I acted as Consultant Adviser. It considers what took place, the history of events leading up to the review, the complexities of the review process, issues of implementation as well as the wider context. The aim in the paper is to systematically move from the descriptive to the analytical level to explain and interpret the review process from both a sociological and social policy point of view. It should also perhaps be said from the outset that the views expressed in this paper are personal ones.

THE REVIEW

The Medicare Benefits Review Committee (MBRC) was established in July 1984 to review the operation of the Universal National Health Insurance Scheme, Medicare. Its work was in two parts: the first to review the existing level and scope of benefits paid to medical practitioners under the scheme; the second, the subject of this paper, to consider extensions to the scheme. It should be noted that the issue of whether the levy on taxable income used to pay for the scheme, should be increased above the current 1.25 per cent was not part of the terms of reference.

The review committee was chaired by Ms Robyn Layton, at that time Deputy President of the Administrative Appeals Tribunal in

Adelaide. Dr Brian Shea, psychiatrist and former Chairman of the South Australian Health Commission was the other member of the committee throughout both parts of the review. In the first part, two nominees of the Australian Medical Association had been members of the committee but had stood aside for the second part, their places taken by Dr John Deeble, then head of the Australian Institute of Health.

The second part of the review had as its terms of reference: 'To consider and make recommendations on whether the current scope of the Medicare arrangements should be extended to provide benefits for certain paramedical groups'. In the early deliberations of the committee in the first part of the review considering the existing Benefits Schedule, it was decided to delay until the second part of the review the benefits already paid under the existing scheme to health practitioners other than the medical profession. These were benefits for optometrical and certain dental services, mainly oral surgery and the treatment of cleft lip and cleft palate conditions.

The committee then had three questions to consider:

1   Should the existing optical and very limited dental benefits scheme be modified?
2   Should benefits be recommended for any other paramedical groups or, as the committee chose to describe them, modalities?
3   If so, which modalities?

When the committee began its deliberations in June 1985, almost 100 submissions had been received from organisations and another 60 from individuals. In all, the case for entry into the scheme made by 20 different modalities was considered by the committee. Of the paramedical modalities of the nation, only the bulk of nursing was missing and indeed conspicuous by its absence. A questionnaire was sent to all these modalities requesting a range of data and the inquiry probably represents the most comprehensive picture ever constructed in Australia on what the paramedical workforce does.

The committee met on more than twenty occasions, and held public hearings between September and December 1985 in Adelaide, Canberra, Melbourne and Sydney. The report (henceforth referred as MBRC, 1986), was submitted to the Minister of Health in June 1986, containing four broad types of recommendations:

1   that minor amendments be made to the existing optical and dental schemes.;
2   that no modalities be funded for entry into the Medicare scheme on a fee-for-service basis;
3   that two modalities (chiropractic and homebirth midwifery), receive some level of public funding on a very limited basis. It

was recommended that some chiropractors should be publicly funded to work on a salaried or sessional basis in public hospitals and community health centres. A Health Program Grant was recommended in the case of independent midwives to evaluate a trial of homebirth midwifery;

4 that a scheme be established to assist the elderly to remain living in their own homes, providing on a salaried basis, certain paramedical services: dietetics, occupational therapy, podiatry, physiotherapy and speech pathology. This was called the PAIL (Paramedical Assistance for Independent Living) scheme.

Of the recommendations only some of the first set have subsequently been implemented.

BACKGROUND

The Universal National Health Insurance Scheme, then called Medibank, was introduced by the Whitlam Labor Government in 1975. In the negotiations surrounding the establishment of the Scheme in 1974, optometrists stole a march on other modalities by gaining entry into the scheme from the beginning. Optometry has remained in the scheme throughout the various changes which have followed, and has benefited substantially from its involvement.

From the inception of Medibank, however, other modalities had lobbied government to be included in the scheme. In the late 1970s the Australian Medical Association (AMA) moved to a position of opposition to any inclusion of other modalities within the scheme. With the return of the Hawke Labor Government in 1983 and the reintroduction of a modified National Health Scheme, Medicare, other modalities again lobbied to be included. The review undertaken was the result, carried out in conjunction with a fine tuning of the existing schedule.

OPPONENTS TO EXTENTION OF MEDICARE

When the review was established in July 1984, the composition of the committee was to include representation from the Australian Medical Association. As indicated above, it was decided early in the life of the review to separate consideration of the terms of reference into two parts. For the second part the AMA withdrew its formal representation from the committee while retaining the right to make submissions to this second part. This decision followed questioning from some of the paramedical modalities, particularly those conventionally known as 'alternative', about the appropriateness of the medical profession sitting in judgment of other modalities. In the light of this concern, the committee also appears to have decided it would be appropriate to engage a consultant adviser who could be seen to be independent of the vested interests involved.

The AMA eventually declined an invitation to make a submission to the review, instead writing to reaffirm its policy against any extension of the existing scheme. This would appear to be a strategic move: by not having been part of the process of the review itself, it enabled the AMA to more effectively make direct representations to the minister should the recommendations suggest a course of action the AMA felt was not in its best interests.

In addition, there were a number of direct submissions opposing the extension of the scheme to include other modalities. A number of organisations such as the Australian Consumers' Association and the Royal College of Medical Administrators warned of the dangers of fraud and overservicing should the scheme be extended. Others like the Australian Hospital Association argued that any expansion should not be on a fee-for-service basis but by increasing funds to provide these services on a salaried basis through the public hospitals, and community health centres.

Other submissions against the extension of the scheme came, not surprisingly, from the organisation with a direct interest in not seeing the scheme expanded—the Voluntary Health Insurance Association (VHIA). Its members, the private health insurance funds, provide some insurance cover for most of the paramedical services under their 'extras' or 'ancillaries' tables consideration. About 38 per cent of the population held some form of cover of this type, payments under which amounted to $324.4 million in 1983–84 (MBRC, 1986: 71).

The VHIA submitted that an extension of the scheme was never part of its original design, it could not be funded under the existing level of levy on taxable income and that an extension would have 'substantial employment effects' with up to a third of its 5000-strong workforce employed in administering insurance for ancillary services (MBRC, 1986: 350).

THE SUBMISSIONS

The information provided to the review by the different modalities was of three sorts: their original written submissions; their oral submissions in the public hearing phase; and their responses to the request for information from the committee, particularly the questionnaire mentioned above.

From this material, it was immediately obvious that some of the modalities are much more experienced in undergoing a review process of this kind than others. A modality such as chiropractic, for instance, has been the subject of numerous reviews over the last couple of decades, knew the sort of data the committee would need and had commissioned a survey of chiropractic services by an independent research organisation.

A number of others, however, particularly the well-established conventional paramedical modalities appear to have never been publicly reviewed by external criteria. In a number of cases, they were unable to supply much detail on such basic issues as utilisation rates which would be needed to begin to calculate the approximate cost, at current levels of utilisation, of their entry into the scheme. Nor in a number of cases were they able to provide much by way of evidence on the effectiveness of the services they provide; stating on more than one occasion that their effectiveness was more or less obvious, that in effect 'everyone knew' their services were effective. The Australian Dental Association, indeed, found the whole idea of being asked to provide the sort of information requested by the questionnaire, 'offensive and irrelevant to the content of the Association's submission . . .' (MBRC, 1986: 400), although it could supply utilisation data.

From the information provided, several themes emerged in the rationale provided by the different modalities to support their submission for public funding of their services through entry into the scheme. Many submissions, both from organisations and individuals pointed to the discriminatory nature of the existing scheme, that services provided by the medical profession were provided under the scheme because each taxpayer was levied a portion of their income, but if patients chose to attend a practitioner other than a medical practitioner then the fees were not covered. This 'injustice' was usually couched in terms of 'freedom of choice', that is to attend the practitioner of one's choice without financial penalty. This view was articulated most vigorously by the homebirth midwives and the groups supporting them.

Some submissions pointed to the fact that some of the services provided by their members were already publicly funded and argued that therefore it was appropriate that private practice should be also. Physiotherapists, for instance, argued that because their services provided in settings such as the Motor Accident Board, Veterans' Affairs and Workers' Compensation were publicly funded, then private practice should also enjoy public funding.

Almost without exception the modalities claimed to be holistic and preventive in their approach, and not a few claimed to be preventative as well! Benefits should most appropriately be provided on a fee-for-service basis but fraud and overservicing was not likely to be a problem because their codes of ethics and other mechanisms such as peer review would ensure against such problems. All espoused a teamwork approach; many felt that utilisation rates would not change greatly if public funding were to be provided to the extent that the service became free at the point of delivery. Indeed, the strong impression left by many of the submissions was that the only thing standing in the way of a massive improvement in the health of Australians was the allocation of provider numbers to practitioners of this or that modality so that services could be provided under the scheme!

Certainly the review process was at times an educative one. It was learnt from podiatrists for instance that whereas in most states a foot begins at the ankle, in South Australia, by contrast, it officially begins below the knee! Likewise, it was learnt that breast augmentation was one of the services provided by hypnotherapists and sought as a service recognised under an expanded scheme!

THE COMPLEXITIES OF THE REVIEW PROCESS

In the process of answering the terms of reference, the committee faced a number of complexities in reviewing the scheme and making recommendations about extensions to it.

Firstly, almost without exception, the submissions requested entry into the scheme on a similar basis of remuneration to the medical profession, that is the payment of universal cash benefits on a fee-for-service arrangement; usually along the lines that, if it was good enough for the medical profession to be funded in this way, then it was good enough for other modalities. However, this is only one type of funding that the scheme provides. Others include Identified Health Grants to the states for the provision of 'free' public hospital care or community health services. Furthermore, a recommendation for the provision of some paramedical services on a cash benefits basis contained the possibility that, if implemented, it could lead to the denuding of paramedical services currently provided within public health settings as practitioners left for the greener pastures of private practice. The committee responded to this complexity by deciding, 'we could not limit our considerations to Medicare cash benefits alone . . . we decided to interpret our Terms of Reference to include all of the funding arrangements available' (MBRC, 1986: 71). The outcome of the review process indeed was that no modalities were recommended to receive cash benefits. What recommendations were made for public funding were on other funding bases.

Secondly, the variety of paramedical modalities making submissions for public funding raised the issue of whether some distinctions should be made between them. This review was probably the first time that the whole range of health occupations other than medicine, both what are conventionally known as 'conventional' and 'alternative', have been considered together. Problems exist with the terminology of either 'paramedical' or 'ancillary' occupations in describing the range of occupations under consideration in this review. For this reason, the committee decided to use the more neutral term 'complementary health services' in the sense of 'those which complement the services of the medical profession without implying any relationship of either superiority or inferiority' (MBRC, 1986: 72).

Thirdly, a range of types of submissions were made and it was necessary for the committee to decide exactly what should be considered for inclusion in any expanded scheme. Submissions were received from national professional organisations, state branches of organisations, different organisations competing to represent occupational groups, segments of organisations, individual practitioners and service organisations. An early decision of the committee was to concentrate on occupational groups rather than services provided and to deal wherever possible only with national professional associations. This was not only because of the need to ensure the competence of providers in any expanded scheme in the interests of standards of practice, but also because of the fact that the same service may be provided by a large number of practitioners. Dietary advice for instance is provided by many of the modalities that made submissions as well as by the medical profession. Likewise spinal manipulation is performed by physiotherapists, chiropractors, osteopaths as well as by some medical practitioners. For this reason the emphasis had to be on which groups of providers should be eligible for public funding rather than which services.

In this vein also and in the interests of uniformity, the committee chose to use the term 'modality' to refer to 'a recognisably distinct health occupation and the services provided by its members' (MBRC, 1986: 72). This decision evoked a strenuous response from the Australian Dental Association, arguing that dentistry 'is not a modality. It is an autonomous, independent, ethical profession' (MBRC, 1986: 400).

Fourthly, there is the administrative difficulty of defining what is a service for which benefits might be paid. In its existing form, Medicare is primarily a medical scheme. Submissions received from some modalities sought benefits for services which are health services in the broadest sense, such as marriage guidance counselling, counselling about job satisfaction and financial guidance. While these would easily qualify as health issues on a very broad definition of health such as that of the World Health Organization ('a complete state of mental, physical and spiritual wellbeing'), the cost implications of including such services within a health insurance scheme would be prohibitive and certainly not possible without a substantial increase in the percentage of taxable income levied to pay for the scheme.

This complexity also relates to the likely implications for utilisation rates of inclusion of these services under the scheme. Taking dentistry as perhaps the example of the modality with the greatest electoral appeal for entry into an expanded scheme, the Australian Dental Association estimated the cost of dental services being included under Medicare *at then current levels of utilisation* at approximately $600 million. Utilisation rates could be expected to soar if dental services were provided free at the point of delivery. Likewise, the cost of entry for the services of clinical psychologists at 1985 levels of utilisation was approximately $30 million.

Of course the question of what health services would best be publicly provided is a philosophical one, even if it can be agreed what the criteria are for assessing what is 'best', such as for instance social justice aims of the redistribution of resources to redress the effects of the marketplace. Would the extra billion dollars necessary to include even a small number of modalities on Medicare, be better spent raising pensions and benefits of various sorts up to the poverty line, for instance?

THE METHODOLOGY

In the early stages of the review process, quite a lot of time was spent developing a methodology for assessing the claims for entry into the scheme made by the various modalities. In what may well prove to be the most substantial legacy of the review to the debate about the provision of health services in this country, a methodology was hammered out to provide the framework for the review process.

A starting point was reviewing the methodologies used by other inquiries into different aspects of paramedical services. There have been a number of these both in Australia and elsewhere in the last few decades. From these the committee identified as a useful starting point what have come to be known as the 'McKinlay Guidelines', presented by Professor John McKinlay to the New Zealand Commission of Inquiry into chiropractic (1979). These are designed to assess how best to utilise available resources by determining priorities for the allocation of funds. Building on and developing these guidelines, the committee developed its framework for evaluating the submissions made to decide its recommendations.

In what came to be known informally as 'the baseball analogy', four sets of criteria were developed in stages, (see appendix 1 at the end of this chapter) each of which had to be satisfied before being considered for the next:

> The first stage criteria were essential requirements to be fulfilled by all modalities. The second stage criteria helped to identify and evaluate the specific areas for which funding was sought, the relative cost benefits of the services as well as the context in which any funded services would be provided. While these criteria individually were not essential prerequisites for funding, they were important reference points which we expected to be satisfied in some measure in order to be considered for the next stage. The third stage criteria considered the mechanisms by which Medicare funding could be considered, not all of which are relevant to all modalities and all types of funding. The final stage was the process by which we arrived at our recommendations as to which of the services merited public funding. (MBRC, 1986: 81)

GETTING TO FIRST BASE

In order to get to first base, the modalities had to satisfy the four criteria of effectiveness, social acceptability, cost efficiency and standards of practice of providers. The task of assessing effectiveness, in particular, was a difficult one. The committee had neither the time nor the resources to commission its own research into questions of effectiveness; and in many areas basic research on the effectiveness of the services provided by various modalities has not been done. As a result, reliance had to be placed upon such research as existed as well as the material supplied by the different modalities in support of their claims to effectiveness. For the most part, the committee accepted this in good faith. The effectiveness of the different modalities, it was decided, could be assessed not only on the basis of scientific evidence, but also upon clinical evidence. The committee followed the convention developed in other inquiries of this nature in doing this.

Social acceptability meant 'standing the test of time', since those modalities that are unable to sustain a clientele over a period of time will cease to exist. The criteria of cost efficiency, while quite simple in theory, was complicated to assess in practice because of the difficulty of making cost comparisons. Its difficulty also reinforced the wisdom of an early decision of the committee to focus on modalities rather than services. It would have been possible to recommend for instance that the treatment of low back pain by manipulation be included in the Medicare schedule, but the administrative difficulty of doing this would be enormous given that this health service is provided by manipulative physiotherapists, chiropractors, osteopaths, and naturopaths as well as medical practitioners who perform manipulation. Currently, the performance of this service attracts a Medicare benefit only when performed by the last of these practitioners.

'Standards of practice of providers' relates to the need to protect the public from poor-quality services by ensuring minimum levels of competence amongst providers. Statutory registration legislation is the usual means of doing this and has been the principal term of reference of a number of previous inquiries into complementary modalities. However, the absence of registration did not automatically disqualify a modality from further consideration since:

> Whether or not a modality has secured registration is the result of a complex historical process in which power and authority have often played a major part and its status as a legitimate form of healing, a minor part. (MBRC, 1986: 86)

Where statutory registration did not exist, the committee looked for 'evidence of appropriate education, training, and self-regulation' (MBRC, 1986: 363).

After applying these first-stage criteria, the modalities which were adjudged not to make it to second base were: acupuncture, biochemistry, and medical science (that is, clinical biochemists and medical scientists), clinical perfusion, childbirth and parenting education, natural therapy and osteopathy.

GETTING TO SECOND BASE

To get to second base, five further criteria had to be met: needs, unmet or inadequately met needs, relationship with other modalities, scope for cost saving, and availability.

Need, while of course a difficult concept to define and measure, was preferred to 'demand'. To satisfy the criterion of unmet or inadequately met need, the modality had to be able to show that existing demand was not being met by already publicly funded services. 'Relationship with other modalities' was aimed at fostering teamwork, since:

> the underlying principle of this criterion is that the goal in any health system should be that each modality should contribute what it does best. No single modality, medicine included has all the

answers to promoting, restoring and maintaining health. Neither do the modalities collectively have all the answers. (MBRC, 1986: 88)

At the same time, the committee rejected the idea that Medicare funding for complementary health services should be conditional on referral by the medical profession. 'Scope for cost-saving' meant the saving of public expenditure in other areas, such as to the elderly, which may enable them to remain in their own homes rather than more expensive publicly funded nursing homes.

'Availability' was taken to mean both geographical availability across the country since Medicare is funded by a levy paid by all taxpayers, and availability of a reserve of practitioners so that public facilities would not be denuded if public funding was recommended.

Applying the second-stage criteria, the modalities that were adjudged not to make it to third base were audiology, nursing, psychology and social work. Those that remained and did make it to third base were: chiropractic, dentistry, dietetics, midwifery, occupational therapy, orthoptics, physiotherapy, podiatry and speech pathology.

THIRD- AND FOURTH-BASE CRITERIA

Third-base criteria relate to the ability to control overservicing and willingness to enter into a participating agreement with respect to fees. The committee decided that none of the modalities had the ability to control the levels of service provided and that therefore recommendation of fee-for-service benefits was not appropriate for any of the modalities that remained. For this reason, other forms of limited public funding were recommended for those that made it, with the exception of dentistry, which had actively opposed the extension of the Medicare scheme to include a comprehensive dental scheme anyway; and orthoptics where it was considered that in the face of an existing shortage in public hospitals, meeting institutional needs should take priority.

In the case of chiropractic, the committee gave only qualified support on the important issue of effectiveness; being satisfied in relation to the treatment of musculoskeletal conditions but unsatisfied about its claims to be able to treat conditions of an 'organic' or 'visceral' nature. It recommended:

> That, upon application, the Commonwealth fund on a salaried or sessional basis, a limited number of appointments of chiropractors in public hospitals and/or community health centres . . . We believe that this would provide the best opportunity to fully evaluate the benefits of chiropractic, and to ensure the kind of professional and

peer review which practitioners of other modalities face in a group setting. (MBRC, 1986: 377)

This finding appears to reflect an assessment of the political reality of the situation; that it is impossible to continue the situation where a modality, now registered in all states, and trained within the State-funded tertiary education system, continues to be excluded from other forms of public funding. Whereas under federal governments of more conservative political persuasion, the influence of medical attitudes to chiropractic had no doubt been a part of the exclusionary basis, under a Labor government which has had quite different relationships with the medical profession, at times even hostile, such an exclusion could not be sustained forever. The recommendation in effect gave chiropractic a 'foot in the door'. While it did not actually explicitly call for applications for funding to allow the recommendation to be implemented, it nonetheless in effect encouraged chiropractors, hospitals, community health centres, or all three to come forward with proposals.

For independent, homebirth midwifery, the committee decided that a recommendation to expand the scheme to add this independent modality was not justified, but it did recommend a Health Program Grant to allow the outcome of independent midwifery to be evaluated. It suggested $2 million be allocated over a five-year period for a pilot program and linked to an agreed research program. The committee endorsed a proposal made by the Monash Medical Centre and included it as an appendix to the report, as the sort of pilot program suggested.

The remaining modalities—what became known as the 'gang of five'—were all considered worthy of public funding, not in general but in the context of a package related to the care of the aged (the PAIL scheme). It was recommended that additional funding be provided under the Community Health Program to employ practitioners from these modalities on a salaried or sessional basis.

To finish with the baseball analogy in summary, if no modalities scored a home run, then a number just made it to home base in terms of recommendations.

THE DIVISION OF LABOUR

What did the review mean for the division of labour in health care in Australia? As argued elsewhere, such a division of labour is characterised by two features: contestation over occupational territory and hierarchy dominated by the medical profession with State endorsement.

As the submissions to the review make abundantly clear, scarcely anywhere in the health system of the nation is there consensus over appropriate occupational territory or task domains, with demarcation disputes remaining a major feature of health politics. On many occasions in the public submissions, background music of the 'anything you can do, I can do better' variety would have been highly appropriate.

Not surprisingly, the modalities saw the review as a opportunity to advance their professional interests, both vis-à-vis medicine as well as other paramedical modalities; indeed the submission process was characterised by a certain coyness about the competitive and financial basis to the process. Securing a recommendation for entry into the scheme for that modality would facilitate a stand-alone independent status, thus greatly enhancing occupational development and professional ambitions by providing a secure financial basis for the modality from the public purse. In this sense of course, the State underwrites medical dominance through the Medicare scheme by creating a secure financial basis for the medical profession.

The committee decided very early on in the review process that its job was not to encourage such professional ambitions nor to tamper with the existing division of labour. Nor did its terms of reference in part two of the overall review require or indeed allow it to consider the existing scheme with relation to level of State support for the medical profession. Rather it was required to look only at the issue of expansion of the scheme.

In addition, the review took place against a backdrop of a changing political climate; one which increasingly stressed restraint, indeed reduction in the amount of public spending in the economy as a whole. As the review process unfolded, the committee was increasingly made aware of this; being encouraged to pay close attention to the likely cost implications of recommendations for expansions of the scheme. As a result 'fourth stage' criteria outlined above gradually came to play an increasing role in deliberations! This of course had the unintended consequence of supporting for the most part the policy of the AMA which represented the modality with a vested interest in maintenance of the status quo.

Nonetheless, the narrowness of the terms of reference did create considerable problems in a number of ways for the committee as it attempted to judge the relative merits of the cases for inclusion in an expanded scheme put by the various modalities.

Firstly, problems arose in attempting to assess the cost-efficiency of services provided by the various modalities; or, more particularly where the same service was provided by several modalities including the medical profession. As the report comments: 'it was difficult to consider the issue of funding for complementary modalities without considering what they were complementary to' (MBRC, 1986: 358).

This relates, secondly, to the assumption of 'universal competence' of the medical profession that the existing scheme assumes, in part at least because of the bureaucratic difficulty of defining exactly what is a 'medical service'. Under existing arrangements, anything performed by a medical practitioner can be claimed on Medicare. It is one of the major anomalies of the existing scheme, and was pointed out to the committee by a number of the modalities, that Medicare funding can be claimed by the medical profession for services that are also performed by other modalities, and often, in their view, better. The training and competence of medical practitioners was challenged in a number of specific areas by modalities who argued they were discriminated against as a result.

This argument was most forcefully made by 'lay' acupuncturists who claimed with considerable justification, that they were better trained (often for up to seven years), whereas most medical practitioners, who could be reimbursed under the scheme for providing acupuncture services, had undergone only very short training courses by comparison. Indeed the traditional acupuncturists labelled the training undertaken by most medical practitioners as 'akin to a first aid course' (MBRC, 1986: 358).

Similar arguments were and could be made for other modalities with considerable justification; that dietitians are better than most medical practitioners at providing dietary advice, that chiropractors and manipulative physiotherapists are better at treating bad backs than most medical practitioners, even that midwives are probably better than general medical practitioners and perhaps also obstetricians at assisting in *uncomplicated* deliveries.

The terms of reference furthermore combined with the political realities of restraint of public spending to restrict the extent of the possible recommendations the committee could make. An example is clinical psychologists; they may be more effective than psychiatrists for some of the services they both provide, but unless benefits for psychiatrists for providing this service were dropped (even assuming the greater effectiveness of psychologists could be definitively established), the cost of the scheme would only increase and therefore a recommendation to publicly fund the services of psychologists would be very difficult to make.

While the committee gave recognition to these difficulties, it could see no alternative:

We must observe there are no clear alternatives to the present broad definition of medical services . . . We were not required to take any position on the matter and we could not see how a public program like Medicare could either. Our recommendations are therefore limited to areas in which we could identify unmet or inadequately met needs, or for which effective and cost efficient services, other than medical services, could be made available. (MBRC, 1986: 359–60)

Nonetheless the submissions for Medicare funding by several of the modalities provoked opposition from whichever section of the medical profession was most likely to be affected. The Royal College of Psychiatry opposed the extension of the scheme to include the services of clinical psychologists, likewise the submission from midwives for independent status to perform homebirth elicited opposition from the Royal College of Obstetrics and Gynaecology. In the case of clinical perfusionists (that is, those performing cardiovascular perfusion in cardiac bypass surgery), their submission was for independent provider status alongside their medically qualified colleagues, to be reimbursed under the schedule item on the Medicare Benefits Schedule rather than on a salaried basis. This proposal generated a number of hostile medical complaints including one from the Australian Society of Anaesthetists who argued in their submission opposing the expansion of the scheme to include perfusionists, that the submission represented 'more the aspirations than the reality of practice' for most clinical perfusionists (MBRC, 1986: 166). The committee was moved to comment in its report:

While the claims made by medical perfusionists are undoubtedly genuine, there would also appear to be a dispute about territoriality between the differently trained professionals; one we have seen in a less overt form between other modalities. The right to charge is seen by many as evidence of independence which may or may not be true and the presence of a pecuniary interest increases the complexity of the dispute enormously. (MBRC, 1986: 167)

The other sociologically interesting issue reflected in the review process is the effects of technological change upon the practice of health care. Modalities working in highly mechanised areas of health care, that is clinical biochemists and medical laboratory scientists, submitted to the review as part of their justification for seeking provider numbers for inclusion in the scheme, the changing nature of pathology services. In effect, they submitted that restriction of direct payment only to medically qualified pathologists, was no longer justified because the increasingly highly mechanised and automated nature of most pathology services reduced the need for the full extent of the pathologists' skills to effectively interpret the results. Technological innovation in this field, as in many other areas, in other words was eroding the justification for existing social relations, in this case, medical dominance of the pathology field of medicine. This opened the way in this field, as in many others, for the more technical aspects of the work to be excised and parcelled out to lower-order participants at a cost saving, leaving to pathologists only those areas of work that have a level of indetermination requiring the skills of a pathologist—an application in the medical field of the Babbage principle.[1] Certainly for a government seeking to restrain the escalating costs of pathology—a part of the Medicare scheme which had little rational basis as it had grown, and was considered a major problem area for the government because of concerns about possible abuse and overservicing—such a proposal would seem to have great advantages.

In this context it was surprising that the submission from the modalities seeking funding in pathology services, did not offer a sweetener to encourage such an arrangement by suggesting lower rates of reimbursement than those paid to pathologists. Biochemists and medical laboratory scientists asked to have entry into the scheme at the same fee levels as pathologists rather than challenging the existing division of labour on the basis of lower fees and thus a cost saving to the government. Without such a saving, giving access to another occupational group to public funding would complicate still further an already complicated situation without improving it. Recommending entry for clinical biochemists and medical laboratory scientists could well have added to an already messy situation when instead the need is more to revise the existing pathology scheme. As a result the medical scientists scored low on the criteria of 'scope for cost savings'.

IMPLEMENTATION

None of the recommendations, modest as they are, have been implemented except for the minor recommendations fine-tuning the existing optometrical and limited dental schemes. The major recommendation anyhow was to preserve the status quo and not extend the scheme to provide cash benefits for any of the modalities.

On the chiropractic front, despite a virtual invitation for chiropractors and hospitals and/or community health centres to put in proposals for funding to allow the employment of chiropractors in such settings, none have been forthcoming. Chiropractic associations have however been actively seeking such an arrangement so that a proposal for funding can be presented. Most activity has been centred in South Australia, but approval of the medical staff remains a problem. In other words, it is not for want of trying on the part of chiropractors that this recommendation has not succeeded. The recommendation of a 'foot in the door' of public funding has been indirectly useful in other ways as well in terms of occupational advancement. In mid-1989, a chiropractic organisation received the first substantial grant of public money for purposes of education or research, ever given by any Commonwealth or state body to a chiropractic organisation, no doubt helped by the legitimacy accorded by the recommendation of the committee. Over $80 000 was received over two years by the modality's research arm, The Australian Spinal Research Foundation, under the Community Health Program to develop a spinal awareness program. This was in effect implementing, albeit in a small way, one of the recommendations of the Webb committee of inquiry (1977) which had taken place more than a decade earlier.

On the homebirth midwifery front, application for funding as recommended in the study detailed in the report of the committee (MBRC, 1986: 247) has not been successful. The reasons for this are not clear, though the study as outlined, being still medically dominated, may have meant that the proposal has not been supported by the homebirth and independent midwifery lobby. The 1989 budget did however contain an allocation of $6.4 million to the states and territories for alternative birthing services including 'outreach' and homebirthing services. The PAIL scheme to employ practitioners from five different modalities in promoting independent living for the elderly has not so far (1990) made any headway.

CONCLUSION

What did the Medicare review achieve then? Was its main achievement only to keep modalities lobbying for extension of the Medicare scheme off the government's back for about five years?

Though direct effects in the form of recommendations implemented are few, the importance of the review is able to be considered more in terms of indirect effects. The review forms part of an historical process which includes many such reviews; since 1961 there have been a dozen such inquiries into complementary modalities in Australia and New Zealand. While there has undoubtedly been an element of 'reinventing the wheel' about these inquiries (almost all have identified the need for more research for instance), they have been important to the historical process of growing legitimacy for the complementary modalities.

For many of the modalities under consideration, the recommendations have represented a set of guidelines for occupational development in order to 'put their collective houses in order' and an incremental process is apparent. For a modality like naturopathy for instance, the inquiries have been very important not only in giving guidelines but also in helping to overcome some of the internal factionalism which has frequently existed. Recommendations made on what the modality has to do in order to be more favourably considered the next time an inquiry takes place, have been important internally to the modality in promoting unity and restraining some of the more esoteric elements amongst practitioners.

Even with the more established modalities there are given guidelines to be followed, should the issue ever arise again of possible extensions to the scheme. Certainly the need is for those modalities to collect much more data about such things as utilisation, as well as to encourage research, both theoretical and applied.

In terms of legitimacy, the historical process of review of the complementary modalities has also been important in establishing that clinical legitimacy should be the basis for politico-legal legitimacy as reflected in State patronage. Such State patronage takes several forms particularly in the spending of public money: subsidised training of the occupation through the State-funded tertiary education system, statutory registration of practitioners to provide a legal basis to occupational territory, reception of research funds and ultimately entry into State health insurance schemes such as Medibank and Medicare.

Medicine has traditionally argued that the only basis for politico-legal legitimacy and State patronage can be scientific legitimacy and that this patronage should only be accorded to those modalities of which it approved, so that traditionally such State patronage could only be achieved by first achieving approval of the medical profession. Those modalities that did not meet with the approval of medicine have traditionally been opposed at all levels.

The site of this struggle for politico-legal legitimacy has been the apparatuses of the State, the Parliament and the health bureaucracies. Here the increasing reliance on clinical rather than scientific legitimacy as a basis for making policy decisions has been symptomatic of the State moving to a position of greater independence vis-à-vis the medical profession.

The outcome of the review has been not to tamper with the existing division of labour in health care and not to challenge medical dominance of the health care system. The preservation of the existing division of labour, however, has been not so much the result of continued State endorsement of medical dominance, but the result of attempts to limit increases in public sector spending by not extending the scheme to include other modalities.

The social policy question remains, of what is the appropriate level of State patronage to best organise these modalities, guarantee standards of practice etc., in the interests of improving the health of Australians. In the longer term, by reason mainly of the methodology developed to assess the advisability of State patronage, the Medicare review will be seen to have made a contribution to that social policy process.

POSTSCRIPT

This chapter was written to reflect upon the experience of having been an adviser to this committee of inquiry. For someone interested in the social structure of health care delivery in Australia, it was an extremely worthwhile experience. The paper attempted to make the sort of 'fly-on-the-wall' type observations of an observer as participant. At the start, I was interested to find out how I came to be invited to participate. My interpretation is that there was a perceived need to have someone involved who was and who was seen to be, independent of the vested interests being paraded in the inquiry. Obviously this was important to the overall legitimacy of the outcome report.

The inquiry was undoubtedly the most comprehensive analysis of the division of labour in health care that has been undertaken in this country. Although relatively little of the recommendations have subsequently been implemented, the report provides an account of the state of occupational development of all the modalities that made submissions; as well as, in many cases, reasonably subtle and gentle indications on where those modalities might develop in future. As a result, it is an important document in the history of health policy.

Subsequent events have raised the possibility, at least, of developments in this area that were not recommended by the Medicare inquiry. In the 1993 election campaign, a promise was made by the Keating government to introduce dental services for Australians with health care cards (welfare beneficiaries primarily). After their unexpected return to government, the implementation of this promise has been delayed at least once. Another development is the reported consideration being given to independent nurse practitioners in rural and remote areas where medical resources are scarce, to have entry to the Medicare scheme. The 1993 budget contained a plan to remove Medicare benefits for sight-testing by optometrists, justified on cost saving grounds though this measure was withdrawn after pressure from Government backbenchers. None of these proposals were part of the recommendations.

As always in these sorts of inquiries, and I have subsequently had other experiences that confirm this observation, the political process operates in a particular way. Think of the issues involved as a continuum; at one end are the technical issues like, 'What is the evidence that this or that treatment works?'. At the other end are the political considerations like: 'Is there room within the funding arrangements for Medicare to increase expenditure further, given that at that time, the funding basis of a levy of 1.25 per cent of taxable income was already not meeting the cost of the Medicare scheme?'. This was represented in the form of several missives from the higher echelons of government, enjoining the committee to pay careful attention to the financial implications of any recommendations.

The outcome of the policy-setting process, the recommendations, can be understood as a meeting of the two considerations (technical and political) at a point on the continuum somewhere in the middle, though probably closer to the political than the technical end. In other words, on balance, my personal assessment is that political considerations were more important than purely technical ones. At times though, political decisions were dressed up as technical considerations; that a basically political decision having been made, a technical rationale was developed to justify that decision. This observation, supported it should be said by a considerable literature in the sociology of science, is just another way of saying that policy determination in general, and health policy in particular, is basically a social process in which technical and scientific arguments have an important role but are, in the end, not determining of the outcome.

NOTES

1   The Babbage principle consists of dividing up a work process into its component elements and paying individual workers according to the skill required for that particular job rather than an overall amount for the job as a whole, thus making a saving on the overall cost. The success of pathologists in resisting this process is another example of the ability of powerful occupations to resist the deskilling potential of technological innovation, in contrast to their blue-collar comrades.

APPENDIX: EVALUATIVE CRITERIA

1. First-stage criteria

1.1 Effectiveness

The modality must demonstrate that its services have a reasonable ability:

   i   to promote and maintain the health of people; or

   ii to beneficially alter the natural course of a defined condition; or

   iii to beneficially alter the symptomatic effects of a defined condition.

1.2. Social acceptability

That there has been acceptance of the services of the modality over a reasonable period of time by a reasonable proportion of the relevant subsections of the society affected.

1.3 Cost efficiency

   i   Costs of the services of the modality should reflect the preventive, curative or palliative benefits provided.

   ii Where services of approximately equal effectiveness for similar people are provided by one or more modalities, the least costly alternative should be preferred.

1.4 Standards of practice of providers

That there should be established standards of practice of the modality as evidenced either by statutory registration or by appropriate and adequate education, training and self-regulation.

2. Second-stage criteria

2.1 Needs

The extent to which there is either:

   i   a general need, i.e. a need of a significant proportion of the population; or

   ii a special need, i.e. a need of a particular group of the population.

2.2 Unmet or inadequately met needs

That those needs are not presently met or are inadequately met by an existing publicly funded facility or existing coverage by Medicare funding.

2.3   Relationship with other modalities

The extent to which the services provided by a modality may be appropriately coordinated with the services provided by other modalities.

2.4   Scope for cost-saving

The extent to which the preventive, curative or palliative benefits derived from the services of the modality may lead to a reduction of expenditure in other areas.

2.5   Availability

That adequate services be reasonably provided by the modality throughout the country to satisfy the unmet or inadequately met needs without adversely affecting existing publicly funded facilities.

3   Third-stage criteria

3.1   Ability to control levels of servicing

3.2   Willingness to enter into a participating agreement in relation to either fees or the condition of funding

4   Final Stage Criteria

Budgetary and political considerations.

(MBRC, 1986: 81–92)

Bibliography

Abbott, S. 1988, 'Talking about AIDS', *AFAO National AIDS Bulletin*, August, pp. 24–7

ACA, 1982 *See under* Australian Consumers' Association

American Medical News, 1987, 'FDA: one in five sample lots of condoms failed standards', September 4, p. 37

Australian Bureau of Statistics, 1983, Australian Health Survey: Health related action taken by Australians, No 4358.0, AGPS, Canberra

Armstrong, D. 1984, 'The patient's view', *Social Science and Medicine*, vol. 8, pp. 737–44

Atkinson, P. , Reid, M. and Sheldrake, P. 1977, 'Medical mystique', *Sociology of Work and Occupations*, vol. 4, no. 3, pp. 243–80

Australian Consumers' Association (ACA), 1982, 'Condom tests', *Choice*, September, pp. 329–31

——1990, 'Recalls and bans', *Choice*, April, p. 15

Australian Medical Association, 1992, *Chiropractic in Australia*, Sydney

Balint, M. 1964, *The Doctor, His Patient and the Illness*, Pitman Medical, London

Bammer, G. 1987, 'How technologic change can increase the risk of repetitive motor injuries', *Seminars in Occupational Medicine*, vol. 2, no. 1, pp. 25–30

——1990, 'The epidemic is over . . . or is it?', *Australian Society*, vol. 9, (April), pp. 22–4

Bammer, G. and Martin, B. 1992, 'Repetition strain injury in Australia: medical knowledge, social movements and defacto partisanship', *Social Problems*, vol. 39, no. 3, pp. 219–37

Bell, G. and Cornford, P. 1987, 'AIDS: the worst is still to come unless. . .', *The Bulletin*, October 6th, pp. 58–67

Bennet, G., Chapman, S. and Bray, F. 1989, 'Sexual practices and "beats": AIDS-related sexual practices in a sample of homosexual men in the western area of Sydney', *The Medical Journal of Australia*, vol. 151, September 18, pp. 309–14

Berliner, H. 1975, 'A larger perspective on the Flexner report', *International Journal of Health Services*, vol. 5, no. 4, pp. 573–92

——1984, 'Scientific medicine since Flexner', *Alternative Medicine: Popular and Policy Perspectives*, ed. W. Salmon, Tavistock, New York

——1985, *A System of Scientific Medicine*, Tavistock, New York

Biggins, D. 1988, 'Focus on occupational health: what can be done', *New Doctor*, no. 47, pp. 6–10

Boven, R., Genn, C., Lupton, G., Payne, S., Sheehan, M. and Western, J. 1977, 'New patients to alternative health care', *Report of the Committee of Inquiry into Chiropractic Osteopathy, Homeopathy and Naturopathy*, (Western Report No. 1), AGPS, Canberra

Brailsford, J. F. 1952, 'Factors which influence the value of a radiological investigation', *The Lancet*, vol. 1, pp. 679–83

Brandt, A. 1987, *No Magic Bullet: A Social History of Venereal Disease in the United States*, rev. edn, Oxford University Press, New York

——1988, 'AIDS in historical perspective: four lessons from the history of sexually transmitted diseases', *American Journal of Public Health*, vol. 78, no. 4, pp. 367–71

Braverman, H. 1974, *Labour and Monopoly Capital: The Degradation of Work?*, Monthly Review Press, New York

Brecher, R. and Brecher, E. 1969, *The Rays: A History of Radiology in the United States and Canada*, Williams Wilkins, Baltimore

Breen, A. 1971, 'Chiropractors and the treatment of back pain', *Rheumatology and Rehabilitation*, vol. 16, pp. 46–53

Brennan, P. 1985, *RSI Explorers Guide Book*, Primavera Press, Sydney

Brewer, A. 1983 'The failure of a new communications technology in a large hospital organisation', *Prometheus*, vol. 1, no. 2, pp. 350–65

British Medical Journal, 1906, Special Correspondence, 27 January, p. 231

Brorsson, B. and Wall, S. 1985, *Assessment of Medical Technology: Problems and Methods*, Swedish Medical Research Council, Stockholm

Bucher, R. and Strauss, A. 1961, 'Professions in process', *American Journal of Sociology*, vol. 66, pp. 325–44

Burawoy, M. 1985, *The Politics of Production*, Verso, London

Campbell, S. 1987, 'The Susan Cooper case', unpublished paper presented to the Conference of the Sociological Association of Australia and New Zealand, Sydney

Carchedi, G. 1977, *On the Economic Identification of Social Class*, Routledge & Kegan Paul, London

Carson, W. G. 1985, 'Hostages to history: some aspects of the occupational health and safety debate in historical perspective', *The Industrial Relations of Occupational Health and Safety*, eds B. Creighton & N. Cunningham, Croom Helm, Sydney

Chalmers, A. 1976, *What is this thing called Science?* University of Queensland Press, St. Lucia

Chapman, S. and Hodgson, J. 1988, 'Showers in raincoats: attitudinal barriers to condom use in high-risk heterosexuals', *Community Health Studies*, vol. 12, no. 1, pp. 97–105

Chapman, S., Stoker, L., Ward, M., Porritt, D. and Fahey, P. 1990, 'Discriminant attitudes and beliefs about condoms in young, multi-partner heterosexuals', unpublished paper, Dept of Community Medicine, University of Sydney

Chow, E. P. Y. 1984, 'Tradititonal Chinese medicine: a holistic system', *Alternative Medicine: Popular and Policy Perspectives*, ed. W. Salmon, Tavistock, New York

Cockburn, C. 1985, *Machinery of Dominance: Men, Women and Technological Change*, Pluto, London

Cohen, S. 1972, *Folk Devils and Moral Panics*, McGibbon & McKee, London

Coleman, S. 1981, 'The cultural context of condom use in Japan', *Studies in Family Planning*, vol. 12, no. 1, pp. 28–39

Colliere, M. 1986, 'Invisible care and invisible women as health care providers', *International Journal of Nursing Studies*, vol. 23, no. 2, pp. 95–112

Committee for the Study of Professional Issues in Nursing (F. Marles, Chairperson) 1988, *Report of the Study of Professional Issues in Nursing*, Ministry of Health, Melbourne

Conant, M. 1986, 'Condoms prevent transmission of AIDS associated retrovirus', *Journal of the American Medical Association*, vol. 255, p. 1706

Cooke, K. 1988, *The Modern Girl's Guide to Safe Sex*, McPhee/Gribble, Fitzroy

Corrigan, D. J. 1828, 'Aneurism of the aorta', *The Lancet*, no. 1, pp. 586–90

Coulter, H. 1984, 'Homeopathy', *Alternative Medicine: Popular and Policy Perspectives*, ed, W. Salmon, Tavistock, New York

Court Brown, W. M. and Doll, R. 1958, 'Expectations of life and mortality from cancer among British radiologists', *British Medical Journal*, 26 July, pp. 181–7

Creighton, W. B. 1986, *Understanding Occupational Health and Safety Law in Australia*, Croom Helm, Sydney

Creighton, W. B. and Micallef, E. J. 1983, 'Occupational health and safety as an industrial relations issue: the Rank-General Electric dispute, 1981', *Journal of Industrial Relations*, vol. 25, pp. 14–26

Daly, J. 1985, 'Assessing the hazards from diagnostic radiology', unpublished M.Env. Sci. thesis, Monash University

——1989, 'Innocent murmurs: echocardiography and the diagnosis of cardiac abnormality', *Sociology of Health and Illness*, vol. 11, no. 2, pp. 99–116

Daly, J. and McDonald, I. 1993, *The social impact of echocardiography: opening Pandora's box—medical motivation and patient responses when a non-invasive test is used for "reassurance"*, Australian Institute of Health and Welfare monograph, Canberra

Daly, J. and Willis, E. 1987, 'The social relations of medical technology:

implications for technology assessment and health policy', *Technologies in Health Care: Policies and Politics*, eds J. Daly, K. Green & E. Willis, AGPS, Canberra

Daly, J., Green, K. and Willis, E. 1987, *Technologies in Health Care: Policies and Politics*, AGPS, Canberra

Davidson, A. 1968, *Antonio Gramsci: The Man, His Ideas*, New Left Publications, Sydney

Dickson, D. 1974, *Alternative Technology and the Politics of Technological Change*, Fontana, Glasgow

Dolly Magazine Promotions Pty Ltd, 1985, 'Teenage girls and sex: the Dolly survey 1983', *Healthright*, vol. 4, no 2, pp. 20–5

Doran, M. and Newell, D. 1975, 'Manipulation in treatment of low back pain', *British Medical Journal*, 2 April, pp. 161–2

Dowsett, G. 1990, 'Reaching men who have sex with men in Australia. An overview of AIDS education, community intervention and community attachment strategies' *Australian Journal of Social Issues* vol. 25, no. 3, pp. 186–98

Dressing, P. 1981, 'A risk management approach in dealing with repetitive movement type claims', *Tenosynovitis, Repetitive Stress Injuries and Other Twentieth Century Work Related Problems*, Occupational Health and Safety Series, Melbourne Chamber of Commerce

Drury, N. 1981, *The Healing Power: A Handbook of Alternative Medicine and Natural Health in Australia and New Zealand*, ANZ Book Company, Sydney

Duckett, S. 1984, 'Structural interests and Australian health policy', *Social Science and Medicine*, vol. 18, no. 11, pp. 959–66

Durkheim, E. 1947, *The Division of Labour in Society*, Free Press, Glencoe, Ill.

——1957, *Professional Ethics and Civil Morals*, Routledge, London

Economic and Budget Review Committee of the Victorian Parliament 1986, *Fourteenth Report to Parliament: A Labour Market Study for Radiologists*, Government Printer, Melbourne

Eddy, C. E. 1946, 'Fifteenth anniversary of the discovery of x-rays', *Medical Journal of Australia*, 2 Feb., pp. 138–41

Edsall, D. L. 1906, 'The attitude of the clinician in regard to exposing patients to the x-ray', *The Journal of the American Medical Association*, vol. 47, no. 18, pp. 1425–9

Feldblum, P. and Fortney, J. 1988, 'Condoms, spermicides and the transmission of the human immunodeficiency virus: a review of the literature', *American Journal of Public Health*, vol. 78, no. 1, pp. 52–3

Fergusson, D. 1984, 'The "new" industrial epidemic', *The Medical Journal of Australia*, vol. 140, pp. 318–9

——1987, 'RSI: putting the epidemic to rest', *The Medical Journal of Australia*, vol. 7, 7 September, pp. 213–4

Fett, I. 1975, 'Australian medical graduates 1920–1972', unpublished Ph.D. thesis, Department Anthropology & Sociology, Monash University

Figlio, K. 1982, 'How does illness mediate social relations: workman's compensation and medico-legal practices 1890–1940', *The Problem of Medical Knowledge: Examining the Social Construction of Medicine*, eds P. Wright & A. Treacher, Edinburgh University Press, Edinburgh, pp. 174–224

Fisk, J. 1980, 'A controlled trial of manipulation on a selected group of patients with low back pain favouring one side', *Journal of Manipulative and Physiological Therapeutics* vol. 3, no. 2, pp. 20–4

Foucault M. 1973, *The Birth of the Clinic: An Archaeology of Medical Perception*, Panthean, New York

Fox, E. and Melzack, R. 1976, 'Transcutaneous electrical stimulation and acupuncture comparison of treatment for low back pain', *Pain*, vol. 2, pp. 141–8

Frankenberg, R. 1974, 'Functionalism and after? Theory and developments in social science applied to the health field', *International Journal of Health Services*, vol. 4, no. 3, pp. 411–27

Freidson, E. 1970a, *Professional Dominance*, Aldine, Chicago
——1970b, *Profession of Medicine*, Dodd Mead, New York
——1976, 'The division of labour as social interaction', *Social Problems*, vol. 23, February, pp. 304–18

Fryer, P. 1965, *The Birth Controllers*, Secker & Warburg, London

Furey P. 1982, (Letter to the editor) 'Understanding needed of tenosynovitis', *Occupational Health*, 24 May, no. 29

Gardner, H. and McCoppin, B. 1988, 'Nursing and politics revisited', *Shaping Nursing Theory and Practice*, ed. L. Pittman, Monograph No. 1, Lincoln Dept of Nursing, La Trobe University, pp. 87–107

Goedert, J. 1987, 'What is safe sex?: suggested standards linked to testing for human immunodeficiency virus', *The New England Journal of Medicine*, vol. 316, no. 21, pp. 1339–42

Goldie, N. 1977, 'The division of labour among mental health professions—a negotiated or imposed order', *Health and the Division of Labour*, ed. M. Stacey, et al., Croom Helm, London

Grady, J. 1986, 'Contraceptive failures in the United States: national survey of family growth', *Family Planning Perspectives*, vol. 18, pp. 93–102

Gramsci, A. 1971, *Prison Notebooks*, International Publishers, New York

Green, D. and Cromwell, L. 1984, *Mutual Aid Or Welfare State: Australia's Friendly Societies*, Allen & Unwin, Sydney

Griffin, V. 1987, 'The social production of occupational injury: a case study of nurses' work-related back injuries', unpublished Master of Science, Technology and Society dissertation, Griffith University, Brisbane

Habermas, J. 1970, 'Technology and science as ideology', *Toward a Rational Society*, Beacon Press, Boston, pp. 81–122
——1976, *Legitimation crisis*, Heinemann, London

Herbison-Evans, D. 1984, *RSI: A Cautionary Tale*, Basser Dept of Computer Science, University of Sydney, Technical Report No. 244

Hernaman-Johnson, F. 1919, 'The place of the radiologist and his kindred in the world of medicine', *Archives of Radiology and Electrotherapy*, vol. 24, pp. 181–7

Hicks, D., Martin, L., Getchell, J., Heath, J., Francis, D., McDougal, J., Curran, J. and Voeller, B. 1985, (Letter to the editor) 'Inactivation of HIV/LAV-infected cultures of normal human lymphocytes by Non-oxynol-9', *The Lancet*, no. 2, pp. 1422–3

Hicks, N. 1978, *This Sin and Scandal*, Australian National University Press, Canberra

Hopkins, A. 1990, 'The social recognition of repetition strain injuries: an Australian/American comparison', *Social Science and Medicine*, vol. 30, no. 3, pp. 365–72

Hospital Radiation Technologists' Association of Victoria, 1979, Submission and Draft Legislation on Radiographer Registration

Illich, I. 1975, *Medical Nemesis*, Calder & Boyars, London

International Commission on Radiological Protection (ICRP), 1982, *Protection of the Patient in Diagnostic Radiology: Annals of the ICRP*, 9, 2/3 (ICRP 34), Pergamon, Oxford

Jackson, E., 1894, 'Report on the values objective tests for the determination of ametropia, ophthalmoscopy, ophthalmometry, skiascopy', *Journal of the American Medical Association*, vol. 88, pp. 337–9

Jamous, J. and Peloille, B. 1970, 'Professions or self perpetuating systems: changes in the French hospital system', *Professions and Professionalisation*, ed. J. Jackson, Cambridge University Press, Cambridge, pp. 102–52

Johnson, T. 1972, *Professions and Power*, Macmillan, London

——1977, 'The professions in the class structure', *Industrial Society: Class Cleavage and Control*, ed. R. Scase, Allen & Unwin, London

Johnstone, R. 1988, 'Pre-employment health screening—the legal framework', *Australian Journal of Labour Law*, vol. 1, pp. 115–46

Journal of the American Medical Association, editorial, 1903, vol. 41, p. 499

Kane, R., Olsen, D., Leymaster, C., Woolley, F. and Fisher, F. 1974, 'Manipulating the patient', *The Lancet*, no. 7869, pp. 1333–6

Kaplan, H. 1987, *The Real Truth about Women and AIDS: How to Eliminate the Risks without giving up Love and Sex*, Fireside, New York

Kavanagh, J. 1984, 'Keyboard cripples: the avalanche looms', *Business Review Weekly*, 17–23 November, pp. 37–52

Kegeles, S., Adler, N. and Irwin, C. 1988, 'Sexually active adolescents and condoms: changes over one year in knowledge, attitudes and use', *American Journal of Public Health*, vol. 78, no. 4, pp. 460–1

Kelman, S. 1975, 'The social nature of the definition problem in health', *International Journal of Health Services*, vol. 5, no. 4, pp. 625–42

Kippax, S. Crawford, J., Waldby, C., and Benton, P. 1990a 'Women negotiating heterosex: implications for AIDS prevention' *Women Studies International Forum*, vol. 13, no. 6, pp. 533–42

Kippax, S., Crawford, J., Dowsett, G., Bond, G., Sinnott, V., Baxter, D., Berg, R., Connell, R., and Watson, L. 1990b, 'Gay men's knowledge of HIV transmission and "safe" sex: a question of accuracy', *Australian Journal of Social Issues*, vol. 25, no. 3, pp. 199–219

Kippen, S. 1992, 'The Silent Disaster: Miners Phthisism, Bendigo' unpublished MA in Health Studies thesis, La Trobe University, Melbourne

Kreigler, R. 1980, *Working for the Company*, Oxford University Press, Melbourne

Larkin, G. 1978, 'Medical Dominance and Control: Radiographers in the Division of Labour' *Sociological Review* vo. 26, no. 4, pp. 843–58

——1983, *Occupational Monopoly and Modern Medicine*, Tavistock, London

Larsen, M. 1977, *The Rise of Professionalism: A Sociological Analysis*, University of California Press, Berkeley

Laslett, P. 1971, *The World We Have Lost*, Scribners, New York

Leatherwood, P. , Chauffaud, F., Hecke, E., Munz-Box, R. 1982, 'Aqueous extract of valerian root improves sleep quality in man', *Pharmacology, Biochemistry and Behaviour*, vol. 17, pp. 65–71

Liddicoat, K. 1984, 'The Health Implications of Screen Based Equipment for Women Workers', unpublished paper presented to ANZAAS Conference

Lindahl, O., Lindwall, L., Spangberg, A., Stenram, A. and Ockerman, P. 1984, 'A vegan regime with reduced medication in the treatment of hypertension', *British Journal of Nutrition*, vol. 52, pp. 11–20

Littler, C. 1987, 'What difference has the Labour Process debate made?' Unpublished paper presented to the Sociological Association of Australia and New Zealand conference, Sydney

Lupton, G. and Najman, J. 1989, *Sociology of Health and Illness: Australian Readings,* Macmillan, Melbourne

MacGeorge, M. 1984, 'RSI and the experts', unpublished address to PANPA seminar, Melbourne, 7 November

MacKenzie, D. and Wajcman, J. 1985, *The Social Shaping of Technology: How the Refrigerator got its Hum*, Open University Press, Milton Keynes

Mackey, K. 1985, 'RSI a Joke', (Letter to the editor) *Sydney Morning Herald*, 21 February

Maddocks, I. 1985, 'Alternative Medicine', *Medical Journal of Australia*, vol. 142, 13 May, pp. 547–61

Marx, K. 1963, *The Poverty of Philosophy*, International Publishers, New York

Mathews, J. 1985a, 'Trade union occupational health and safety initiatives', *The Industrial Relations of Occupational Health and Safety*, eds B. Creighton & N. Gunningham, Croom Helm, Sydney, pp. 190–202

——1985b, *Health and Safety at Work: Australian Trade Union Safety Representatives' Handbook*, Pluto Press Australia, Sydney

MBRC, 1986 *See under* Medicare Benefits Review Committee

McClenahan, J. L. 1970, 'Wasted x-rays', *Radiology*, vol. 96, August, pp. 453–6

McCulloch, J. 1986, *Asbestos: Its Human Cost*, University of Queensland Press, Brisbane

McDonald, I. G., Guyatt, G. H., Gutman, J. M., Jelinek, V. M., Fox, P. and Daly, J. 1988, 'The contribution of a non-invasive test to clinical care: the impact of echocardiography on diagnosis, management and patient anxiety', *Journal of Clinical Epidemiology*, vol. 41, pp. 151–61

McKinlay, J. 1977, 'The business of good doctoring or doctoring as good business: reflections on Freidson's view of the medical game', *International Journal of Health Services*, vol. 7, no. 3, pp. 459–82

——1981, 'From promising report to standard procedure: seven stages in the career of a medical innovation', *Millbank Memorial Fund Quarterly*, vol. 59, pp. 374–411

McKinlay, J. and Arches, J. 1985, 'Towards the proletarianisation of physicians', *International Journal of Health Services*, vol. 15, no. 2, pp. 469–78

McKinlay, J. and McKinlay, S. 1977, 'The questionable effect of medical measures on the decline of mortality in the U.S. in the 20th century', *Millbank Memorial Fund Quarterly*, vol. 55, no. 3, pp. 405–28

McPhee, B. and Howie, A. eds, 1979, *Ergonomics and Visual Display Units*, Proceedings of Conference of Ergonomics Society of Australia and New Zealand, Melbourne and Sydney

Medical Journal of Australia (MJA) 1938, Report of the Queensland Royal Commission on Modern Methods for the Treatment of Infantile Paralysis, 29 January, pp. 187–219

Medicare Benefits Review Committee (MBRC), Chairperson Judge Robyn Layton, 1986, *Second Report*, AGPS, Canberra

Meekosha, H. and Jacubowicz, A. 1985, 'Women suffering RSI: an examination of the hidden relations of gender, the labour process and medicine', paper presented to Behavioural Medicine Conference, Sydney

Mendelson, G., Selwood, T., Kranz, H. 1983, 'Acupuncture treatment of chronic back pain in double blind placebo controlled trial', *American Journal of Medicine*, vol. 74, pp. 49–55

Merrington, J. 1968, 'Theory and practice in Gramsci's Marxism', *Socialist Register*, eds R. Miliband & J. Saville, Monthly Review Press, London

Millen, N. 1989, 'The factors behind the emergent militancy of nurses in the pursuit of work satisfaction and professionalism', *Sociology of Health and Illness: Australian Readings*, eds G. Lupton & J. Najman, Macmillan, Melbourne

Moore, M. and Berk, S. 1976, 'Acupuncture for chronic shoulder pain', *Annals of Internal Medicine*, vol. 84, pp. 381–4

Mulvaney, P. 1984, 'Compensation issues and the law', paper presented to Repetitive Injuries Seminar, Melbourne, 22 September

Murcott, A. 1977, 'Blind alleys and blinkers, the scope of medical sociology', *Scottish Journal of Sociology*, vol. 1, no. 2, pp. 155–71

National Health and Medical Research Council, 1982, Screening Equipment for Susceptibility to Repetitive Strain Injuries, October Guidelines, AGPS, Canberra

National Occupational Health and Safety Commission (NOHSC), 1985, *Interim Report of the RSI Committee*, AGPS, Canberra

Navarro, V. 1976, *Medicine Under Capitalism*, Croom Helm, London

New South Wales Parliamentary Papers, 1937–38, Report by Special

Medical Committee on Results obtained from the Treatment of Paralysis at Elizabeth Kenny Clinic, Royal North Shore Hospital, vol. III

New Zealand Commission of Inquiry, 1979, *Chiropractic in New Zealand*, Govt Printer, Wellington.

Newburger, J. W., Rosenthal, A., Williams, R. G., Fellows, K. and Miettinen, O. S. 1983, 'Non-invasive tests in the initial evaluation of heart murmurs in children', *New England Journal of Medicine*, vol. 308, pp. 61–4

Niki, R. 1985, 'The wide distribution of CT scanners in Japan', *Social Science and Medicine*, vol. 21, no. 10, pp. 1131–7

NOHSC, 1985 *See under* National Occupational Health and Safety Commission

Padian, N., Marquis, L., Francis, D., Anderson, R., Rutherford, G., O'Malley, P. and Winkelstein, W. 1987, 'Male-to-female transmission of human immunodeficiency virus', *Journal of the American Medical Association*, vol. 258, no. 6, 14 August, pp. 788–90

Parisot, J. 1987, *Johnny come lately: a short history of the condom*, Journeyman, London

Parker, G. and Tupling, H. 1978, 'The chiropractic patient: psychological aspects', *Medical Journal of Australia*, 4 September, pp. 373–6

Parmeggiani, L. 1982, 'State of the art: recent legislation on worker health and safety', *International Labour Review*, no. 121, pp. 271–85

Parsons, T. 1964, 'Definitions of health and illness in the light of American values and social structure', *Social Structure and Personality*, Free Press, London

——1968, 'Professions', *International Encyclopaedia of Social Sciences*, pp. 534–46

Pensabene, T. 1978, 'The supply of general practitioners in Victoria 1870–1930', unpublished paper, Dept of Economic History, Monash University

Pillemer, R. 1979, (Letter to the editor) 'Tenosynovitis', *AMA Gazette*, 2 August, p. 4

Quinlan, M. 1986, 'Occupational illness, industrial conflict and state regulation: establishing some linkages', unpublished paper presented to the Workshop on Social Science Research on Occupational Health and Safety, La Trobe University, Melbourne

——1988, 'Psychological and sociological approaches to the study of occupational illness: a critical review', *Australian and New Zealand Journal of Sociology*, vol. 24, no. 2, pp. 189–207

Radford, E. P. 1981, 'Cancer risks from ionizing radiation', *Technology Review*, Nov/Dec, pp. 74–5

Reed, R. 1988, 'From hot metal to cold type printing technology', *Technology and the Labour Process: Australian Case Studies*, ed. E. Willis, Allen & Unwin, Sydney

Reilly, D., McSharry, C., Taylor. M. and Aitchison, T. 1986, 'Is homeopathy a placebo response: controlled trial of homeopathic potency, with pollen in hayfever as model', *The Lancet*, 18 October, pp. 881–5

Reiser, S. J. 1978, *Medicine and the Reign of Technology*, Cambridge University Press, Cambridge

Richardson, D. 1987, *Women and AIDS*, Pandora, London

Richardson, J. 1987, 'Technology assessment in medicine: an Australian proposal', *Technologies in Health Care: Policies and Politics*, eds J. Daly, K. Green & E. Willis, AGPS, Canberra

Robens Report 1972, *Report of the Committee on Safety and Health at Work 1970–1972*, HMSO, London

Rodberg, L. and Stevenson, A. 1977, 'The Health Care Industry in Advanced Capitalism', *Review of Radical Political Economy*, vol. 9, no. 1, pp. 104–15

Rosen, G. 1944, *The Specialization of Medicine with particular reference to Ophthalmology*, Froben, New York

Salmon, W. ed, 1984, *Alternative medicine: Popular and policy perspectives*, Tavistock, New York, pp. 1–29

Schudson, M. 1980, 'Review of Larson's "Rise of Professionalism" ', *Theory and Society*, vol. 9, pp. 215–29

Scull, A. 1975, 'From madness to mental illness: medical men as moral entrepreneurs', *European Journal of Sociology*, vol. 16, no. 2, pp. 218–61

Segall, M. 1977, 'The political economy of doctors' social practice', unpublished paper, quoted in Robson, J., 'Quality, inequality and health care', *Medicine in Society*, April, p. 19

Shanks, S. C. 1950, 'Fifty years of radiology', *British Medical Journal*, 7 January pp. 44–8

Shekelle, P., Adams, A., Chassm, M., Hurwitz, E. and Brook, R. 1992, 'Spinal manipulation for low back pain', *Annals of Internal Medicine*, vol. 118, no. 7, pp. 599–8

Short, C. 1986, 'Equal pay: what happened', *Journal of Industrial Relations*, vol. 28, no. 3, pp. 315–35

Short, S., and Sharman, S. 1989, 'The nursing struggle in Australia', *Sociology of Health and Illness: Australian Readings*, eds G. Lupton & J. Najman, Macmillan, Melbourne

Smith, P. G. and Doll, R. 1981, 'Mortality from cancer and all causes among British radiologists', *British Journal of Radiology*, vol. 54, pp. 187–94

Smith-Rosenberg C. 1972, 'The hysterical woman: sex roles and role conflict in 19th century America', *Social Research*, vol. 39, pp. 652–78

Social Development Committee of the Victorian Parliament (VSDC), Chairperson Judith Dixon MLC, 1986, *Inquiry into Alternative Medicine and the Health Food Industry*, vols 1, 2, Victorian Govt Printer, Melbourne

Sontag, S. 1978, 'Illness as metaphor', *New York Review of Books*, 26 January, 9 February, 23 February

Stacey, M. 1978, 'The sociology of health and illness: its present state, future prospects and potential for health research', *Sociology*, vol. 12, no. 2, pp. 281–307

Stagoll B. 1981, 'On the social construction of disease: the body as embodiment of social relations', unpublished paper, Melbourne

Stark, D. 1980, 'Class struggle and the transformation of the labour process', *Theory and Society*, vol. 9, no. 1, pp. 89–130

Stone, W. 1984, 'Occupational repetitive strain injuries', *Australian Family Physician* vol. 13, pp. 681–4

Task Force Report, 1985, *Repetition Strain Injury in the Australian Public Service*, AGPS, Canberra

Taylor, R. and Pitcher M. 1984, 'Medical and ergonomic aspects of an industrial dispute concerning occupational-related conditions in data process operators', *Community Health Studies*, vol. 8, pp. 172–80

Templeton, J. 1969, *Prince Henry's: The Evolution of a Melbourne Hospital 1869–1969*, Oxford University Press, Melbourne

Thame, C. 1974, 'Health and the State: The development of collective responsibility for health care in Australia in first half of the twentieth century', unpublished Ph.D. thesis, Dept History, The Australian National University

Turner, B. 1987, *Medical Power and Social Knowledge*, Sage, London

Turtle, A., Ford, B., Habgood, R., Grant, M., Bekiaris, J., Constantinou, C., Macek, M. and Polyzoidis, H. 1989, 'AIDS-related beliefs and behaviours of Australian university students', *The Medical Journal of Australia*, vol. 150, 3 April, pp. 371–6

Versluysen, M. 1981, 'Midwives, medical men and "poor women labouring of child": lying-in hospitals in eighteenth century London', *Women, Health and Reproduction*, ed. J. Roberts, Routledge, London

VSDC, 1986 *See under* Social Development Committee of the Victorian Parliament

Walker, J. 1979, 'Tenosynovitis: a crippling epidemic in industry', *New Doctor*, no. 13, pp. 19–21

Ward, J. 1979, 'Symposium on the sociology of medicine—introductory remarks', *Australian and New Zealand Journal of Sociology*, vol. 15, no. 3, pp. 18–19

Webb Report, 1977, *Report of the Committee of Inquiry into Chiropractic, Osteopathy, Homeopathy and Naturopathy*, AGPS, Canberra

Weber, M. 1968 edn, *Economy and Society*, vol. 3, Bedminster Press, New York

Williams, T. 1985, 'Visual display technology, worker disablement, and work organisation', *Human Relations*, vol. 38, no. 11, pp. 1065–84

Willis, E. 1976, 'The consequences of bureaucratisation: a study of the work settings of the general medical practice profession', unpublished MA thesis, Dept Sociology, Victoria University of Wellington

——1980, 'Health training and class background', unpublished paper, Medical Sociology Research Group, Monash University, Melbourne

——1982, 'Research and teaching in the sociology of health and illness in Australia and New Zealand', *Community Health Studies*, vol. 6, no. 2, pp. 144–53

——1984, 'The role of alternative health care in Australia', *Perspectives on Health Policy*, ed. M. Tatchell, Australian National University, Canberra

——1985, 'Trade union reaction to technological change: the introduction of the chain system of slaughtering in the meat export industry', *Prometheus*, vol. 3, no. 1, pp. 51–70

——1988, *Technology and the Labour Process: Australasian Case Studies*, Allen & Unwin, Sydney

——1989a, *Medical Dominance: The Division of Labour in Australian Health Care*, rev. edn, Allen & Unwin, Sydney

——1989b, 'Doctoring in Australia: a view at the bicentennary', *Millibank Fund Quarterly: Health and Society*, vol. 66, no. 1, pp. 167–81

——1990, 'The sociology of health and illness in Australia: the 1980s and beyond', *Annual Review of the Sociology of Health and Illness*, eds J. Daly & A. Kellehear, La Trobe University, Melbourne, pp. 46–53

——1993, *The sociological quest: an introduction to the study of social life*, Allen & Unwin, Sydney

Wilson, F. 1984, (Letter to the editor) 'Repetitive Strain Injuries' *Medical Journal of Australia*, 13 March, p. 18

Wochos, J. F., Detorie, N. A. and Cameron, J. R. 1979, 'Patient exposure from diagnostic x-rays—an analysis of 1972–1975 NEXT data', *Health Physics*, no. 36, pp. 127–34

Workers' Health Centre, 1979, 'Tenosynovitis/carpal tunnel syndrome survey', Mimeo, Lidcombe, New South Wales

World Health Organization, 1980, *Workers Health Programmes: Progress Report of the Director General 1980*, (WHO document WHO A33/12)

——1982, *Evaluation of Occupational Health and Industrial Hygiene Services*, WHO Regional Office for Europe, (EURO Reports and Studies No. 56)

Wright Mills, C. 1959, *The Sociological Imagination*, Oxford University Press, Oxford

Index

acupuncture, 60, 63–4, 66
AIDS, 3, 114–15, 120 *passim*
alienation, 10
Arbitration Commission, 47
asbestos, 157
Australian Dental Association, 173
Australian Medical Association,
   48, 74, 82, 171–2
authority, 12–13
autonomy, 12

Babbage principle, 184
birth control pill, 118
Brandt, A., 120–1
Braverman, 77, 78, 141, 153

childbirth, 182–3
chiropractic, 16, 58–9, 63, 66–8,
   179–80
class, 22, 79, 146
commensurability, 62, 64
Committee for the study of
   professional issues in nursing
   (SPIN report), 47, 49, 52
compensation, 155
Cooper, Susan, 148–9
CT scanners, 92, 94

division of labour, technical,

10–11; social, 10–11, 12, 15
   passim, 180–1

empowerment, 166

Figlio, K., 135–6, 146, 152
Foucault, M., 3, 4
Freidson, E., 27–8, 38–9, 50–1,
   79–80

Habermas, J., 3, 55, 80
homeopathy, 29, 60

Illich, I., 35–6
insurance examinations, 112

Johnson, T., 40

legitimacy, 55, 64, 71, 73
Larkin, G., 87–9

McKinlay, J., 5, 39, 176–7
managerial prerogative, 163–4
medical sovereignty, 13, 83
midwives, 49
miners nystagmus, 135–6
moral panic, 134

natural therapies, 59–60
Navarro, V., 36, 39

nursing, 17–18, 26 *passim*

osteopathy, 29, 59

Parsons, T., 2, 54
'pass-the-task', 14
physiotherapy, 16
placebo effect, 32, 146
pre-employment screening, 104,
    112, 152
professionalism, 17–18, 36–8

radiography, 22–3, 90–1
radiology, 22–3, 88, 90–4, 101
relative autonomy, 165
resistance, 162–3
Robens model, 164

sexually transmitted disease, 117
skill, 44 *passim*
social shaping of technology, 154
sociological imagination, 2, 4, 5

spinal manipulation, 175
State, 6; defined, 15–16, 25,
    38–9, 70–2, 83–4, 156
subprofessional dominance, 81

technological determinism, 3,
    18–19, 35–6
technological innovation, 159–60,
    162–3
technology assessment, 99–100
Thame, C., 34–5
trade unions, 142
traditional Chinese medicine, 60–1
Turner, B., 4

X-rays, 12, 19–23, 77–8, 84–94,
    97–8

Victorian social development
    committee, 62, 65

Wright Mills, C., 1, 134